DURKHEIM'S
SUICIDE

DURKHEIM'S
SUICIDE

A CLASSIC
ANALYZED

Whitney Pope

THE UNIVERSITY OF CHICAGO PRESS
CHICAGO AND LONDON

WHITNEY POPE received his Ph.D. from the
University of California at Berkeley and is now
associate professor of sociology at Indiana
University.

The University of Chicago Press, Chicago 60637
The University of Chicago Press, Ltd., London

Printed in the United States of America
80 79 78 77 76   987654321

Library of Congress Cataloging in Publication Data

Pope, Whitney.
    Durkheim's Suicide.

    Bibliography: p.
    Includes index.
    1. Durkheim, Émile, 1858–1917. Le suicide.
I. Title.
HV6545.D84P66   362.2'04'22   75-27890
ISBN 0-226-67538-6

To Clifford Hillhouse Pope

CONTENTS

ACKNOWLEDGMENTS

I owe Barclay Johnson my greatest intellectual debt in the preparation of this book. Originally planning to coauthor a book on *Suicide,* we spent one summer discussing it, focusing particularly on Durkheim's theory of suicide. Subsequently, Barclay experienced career demands that conflicted with pursuit of our joint endeavor; these demands, coupled with our differing interpretations of important points in Durkheim's theory, led to termination of the collaboration. Nevertheless, some of the interpretations stated in this book had their beginning in stimulating exchanges with Barclay.

I am grateful to Neil Smelser and Reinhard Bendix, both of whom reacted to an earlier statement of many ideas in this book. Beyond that, I want to thank them for general intellectual stimulation and guidance. The following commented on drafts of portions of this book: Nick Danigelis, Dain Oliver, Hallowell Pope, and Ruth Wallace. Peter Burke, Elton Jackson, and Karl Schuessler offered advice on data analysis. Numerous assistants provided help; I wish to single out Martha McMurry, Meade Grigg, Vickie Renfrow, and, most particularly, Lucille Hake. Carolyn Mullins provided encouragement and editorial assistance. This work was supported by United States Public Health Service grant number RR 7031, administered through the Biomedical Sciences Support Committee of Indiana University; by United States Public Health Service grant number MH 20100-01; and by National Science Foundation grant number GS 30953. My wife supported me throughout, offering advice on writing style and further helping by doing more than her share of everyday household and child-rearing chores; her assistance was not without cost to her own academic career. Lucetta, Delanie, Whitney, and Braxton Pope have all helped just by being themselves. My thanks go to all of these persons and agencies.

The dedication reflects a debt that can only be acknowledged, never repaid.

1   INTRODUCTION

Emile Durkheim is an important progenitor of contemporary sociology; and *Suicide* (1951; originally published in 1897) is one of his seminal works. Given the attention such an important figure rightfully commands, many facets of Durkheim's work have been extensively analyzed. *Suicide* itself has frequently been examined. Nonetheless, there is ample reason for yet another commentary. First, the many articles, limited by space, have not been comprehensive. Books exist, but they frequently cover so much of Durkheim that *Suicide* has received relatively little sustained attention. Space limitations sometimes have prevented even the most perceptive authors of books (e.g., Gibbs and Martin 1964: 5-13) from full development of their insights. In contrast, my analysis is neither brief nor cursory.

Second, my theoretical interpretation differs from those in prior commentaries. For example, it rejects Parsons's (1949:324-38) interpretation, hitherto sociology's most influential statement on Durkheim. Also rejected is Douglas's (1967:13-76) attempt to portray social meanings as Durkheim's key explanatory variable. Third, many prior analyses have concentrated almost exclusively on conceptual analysis. Such analysis is necessary, but this study subordinates it to the larger goal of identifying and then assessing the explanatory adequacy of Durkheim's theory. Fourth, reflecting the pervasive bifurcation between theory and empirical research in sociology, most commentaries have focused on *either* Durkheim's theory *or* his methods and data—an ironic situation since many of their authors consider *Suicide* to be the classic example of a successful *marriage* of theory and data. Because Durkheim manipulated theory and data so as to effect the closest possible alignment, it is difficult to understand the theory without analyzing its relationship to the data. Fifth, central to *Suicide* is its case for social realism. The theoretical adequacy of this argument has received some attention. However, as with the data offered to support his

1

theory of suicide, the empirical adequacy of Durkheim's case for social realism has not been systematically assessed. I assess both the theoretical and the empirical adequacy of Durkheim's arguments in favor of social realism. Altogether my analysis leads to conclusions different from those of prior authors, conclusions that raise important questions regarding the contemporary understanding and evaluation of *Suicide*.

DO THE DATA SUSTAIN THE THEORY?

A central question implied by my intent to assess the theory-data relationship is: Do the data in *Suicide* support its theory? Many commentators (including some of the most eminent sociologists) assert, but do not show, that the theory is convincingly sustained by the evidence cited. Parsons (1949:329n) spoke of the basic "fit" between theory and data. Noting the paucity in sociology of scientific laws, Merton (1967:150) identified Durkheim's generalization that Catholics have a lower suicide rate than Protestants as an approximation to such a law. Nisbet (1970:8; see also 1974:229) noted Durkheim's "demonstration of the unvarying correlation between high incidence of suicide and social and moral disorganization," while Bierstedt (1974:297) felt that Durkheim proved "that the incidence of suicide is highest in those whose primary-group ties are weakest." In perhaps the most forceful formulation, Inkeles (1959: 252; see also 1963:322) argued that "Durkheim found that the rate of suicide, particularly egoistic suicide, was determined by the degree of integration of particular social structures—whether church, family, political party, or national state. Even those who are most skeptical of Durkheim's analysis cannot deny the fact that he has exposed the main pattern of correlation."

Others have disagreed. Halbwachs (1971:28) observed that sometimes "it is the argument rather than the facts" that convinces the reader. Gibbs and Martin (1964:8) argued that *Suicide*'s most important proposition—suicide varies inversely with the degree of social integration—"is supported, not by its predictive power, but by his forceful argumentation." Maris (1969:18) was unequivocal: Durkheim's "generalizations do not account for his data."

Though disagreement clearly exists, the weight of opinion has been that Durkheim's data support his theory. Furthermore, all commentators share a common approach in having stated an opinion without providing the analysis to sustain it. Consequently, one man's opinion appears as good as another's, and the disagreement perpetuates itself.

Suicide AS A RESEARCH CLASSIC

Certainly the disagreement has not threatened *Suicide*'s status as a research classic. Writing more than forty years ago, Sorokin (1928: 463-64, 467) was impressed with the soundness of Durkheim's method. More recently, sociologists have vied with one another in commending it as a model (see, e.g., Inkeles 1959:252; Gibbs and Martin 1964:v; and Nisbet 1970:8, 33). Douglas (1967:13), albeit with sarcastic overtones, characterized sociology's reaction: "Durkheim's *Suicide* seems to have been an unfailing source of wonder to most sociologists. It has been seen as a 'model of research methods' and a 'model of the integration of theory and data.'" In the context of so many laudatory evaluations, it is no surprise that Merton (1967:63) nominated *Suicide* as perhaps the greatest piece of sociological research ever done. Even commentators otherwise critical of (if not hostile to) major aspects of Durkheim's work have acknowledged this basic strength in *Suicide*. Zeitlin (1968:271), in a commentary stressing shortcomings in Durkheim's major writings, began his analysis of *Suicide* as follows: "Durkheim's use of socio-cultural variables to explain an ostensibly idiosyncratic phenomenon such as suicide must be regarded as ingenious and brilliant." In short, virtually all commentators, even those who question whether *Suicide*'s evidence sustains its theory, view it as a model of sociological research.

The numerous authors just noted typically spoke in general terms about those aspects of *Suicide* upon which they based their evaluations, and undoubtedly different authors have had different aspects in mind. Clearly, however, a major factor in such evaluations has been *Suicide*'s methodology. The best known, most instructive commentary on that aspect has been Selvin (1965:113-36); his evaluation (1965:113) has been, if anything, even more laudatory than those noted above: "Emile Durkheim's *Suicide* is still a model of social research. Few, if any, later works can match the clarity and power with which Durkheim marshaled his facts to test and refine his theory." He (136) concluded: "The empirical analysis in *Suicide* is as vital today as it was in 1897—perhaps more so."

Like other analyses of *Suicide*'s methodology (e.g., Hyman 1955; Riley 1963; Rosenberg 1968), Selvin's called attention to Durkheim's skillful handling of different problems and thereby heightened appreciation of his approach, which, though pioneering, was often highly sophisticated. Although the authors of these discussions were aware of limitations in Durkheim's approach, their primary focus on aspects to be emulated nevertheless has given readers a one-sided picture. And if only because they discuss methodology separately from a systematic consideration of the theory that Durkheim's analysis was designed to validate (and that ultimately makes both the data and the methodology theoretically meaningful), such discussions have not indicated whether the data as analyzed by Durkheim support the theory.

Suicide AND THE CONTEMPORARY STUDY OF SUICIDE

The substantive field upon which Durkheim's study has had the greatest impact is, of course, the study of suicide. An act capable of arousing intense reaction, suicide has long been a major interest of social scientists. Dahlgren (1945:1) estimated that there were at least four thousand works on the subject, and many more have been published since 1945.

As numerous commentators have observed, *Suicide* has dominated the sociological study of suicide. Many studies open by acknowledging Durkheim's influence and presenting a brief analysis of *Suicide*. The attention given to other works is generally brief compared with that accorded *Suicide*. Such analyses of Durkheim are not ends in themselves but rather necessary—sometimes ritualistically performed—preludes. Consequently, it is understandable that no researcher has presented a definitive evaluation of *Suicide*. The result is that each subsequent author has felt obligated to offer his own interpretation, ad infinitum. New perspectives have been suggested (e.g., Henry and Short 1964), and numerous works have attempted to extend those originally developed by Durkheim. Some recent authors have argued that contemporary suicidology has long since superseded Durkheim. Nevertheless, current research exists in largely isolated "appendages" (Douglas 1967:79) with no cumulative theoretical development to integrate it. In Giddens's (1971a:46) words, "advance in theory since Durkheim published *Le Suicide* has been limited indeed."

The first step toward such cumulative development is a systematic analysis of *Suicide*. That analysis would rescue future researchers from the necessity of explicating *Suicide* themselves. More important, such an analysis should reveal important aspects of *Suicide* that have thus far gone unnoticed. Although no work can be expected to produce agreement on all important points, careful analysis can identify the relevant problems and, in many cases, provide an adequate basis for either agreement or, at the very least, counterstatements on the road toward further assessment. Only in this way can the common core of what investigators have in mind as they employ *Suicide* be enlarged. Like a magnet, *Suicide*'s irresistible attraction draws sociologists ever back to the same starting point, which they seem destined to be unable either to ignore or to employ as the basis for the cumulative development of a theory of suicide. The time for systematic assessment of the work, which would turn it from a magnet into a launching pad, is past due.

The lack of adequate analysis of *Suicide* has not stopped sociologists from either offering sweeping conclusions about various aspects of the work or holding the book up to students as perhaps the discipline's most compelling example of the union of theory and data, of the unsatisfactory nature of nonsociological explanations of suicide (and, in contrast, the superiority of the sociological), of the continuing relevance of the classics, and so forth. Yet, to the extent that this proceeds without the analysis that could justify it, sociologists argue from authority alone, believe things because they are widely accepted within the discipline, and remain content to express assertions that do not reflect the critical approach that should be applied to all scientific works, even the most highly respected.

Johnson (1965:875) has noted that "although Durkheim's *Suicide* is among the most widely read classics in our field, sociologists rarely seek to clarify the theory it contains." Douglas (1967:13) observed that "it is strange that no sociologist has undertaken to publish a thorough investigation of *Suicide*, either a careful, interpretive analysis of the work itself or a careful consideration of the validity of the theory." My research fills this lacuna. Its purpose is to generate a more thorough understanding of *Suicide* as well as more complete agreement on its strengths and weaknesses. In addition, *Suicide* was a cumulative work with respect to the research of the moral statisticians that preceded it (Douglas 1967:7–22; Giddens 1971a:36–38); careful analysis now should prepare the ground for emulating *Suicide* in this respect by making it a stepping-stone in the development of ever more adequate theories of suicide, deviance, social integration, and society.

The remainder of this book follows a simple outline. My analysis focuses upon the three central aspects of *Suicide*: the theory (Part I), the relationship between theory and data (Part II), and Durkheim's argument for social realism (Part III). The final chapter assesses Durkheim's accomplishments.

I   THE THEORY

2   SUICIDE AND ITS TYPES

In *Suicide* Durkheim attempted to derive a sociological explanation of variation in social suicide rates. Long an area of great interest, suicide was a topic well suited to capture the attention of a wide audience. Furthermore, Durkheim benefited from the voluminous literature on this topic, which enabled him to build upon well-established empirical and conceptual foundations (Douglas 1967:7-22; Giddens 1971a:36-38), argue forcefully for the superiority of his own explanation (by pitting it against earlier attempts), and stress the limitations presumably inherent in all nonsociological explanations of suicide. Furthermore, this subject area was particularly well suited for demonstrating the superiority of sociological explanation to that which Durkheim considered its severest competitor, namely, individual or psychological explanation. He was able to meet psychologists on their own ground by arguing that even such a seemingly individual act as suicide was *socially* caused. This argument in turn provided him with one of his best opportunities to argue in favor of social realism.

The existence of quantities of official suicide statistics permitted Durkheim to present an alternative to the intuitive, overly general, philosophical works that he (1951:35)[1] felt had too long prevented sociology from developing as a genuinely scientific discipline. Using these data allowed him to illustrate the positive fruits attainable by working in accordance with the prescriptions he had set forth two years earlier in *The Rules of Sociological Method* (1950). In short, sociology could be as rigorous and "scientific" as the natural sciences.

Durkheim (37, 50, 203, 367-69, 391) considered suicide rates a measure of the health of the social body and felt that the high suicide rates prevailing in Western Europe reflected the social malaise so characteristic of those societies. By studying suicide, scientists could hope to achieve a better understanding of the causes and consequences of the underlying malaise and ultimately, like

9

Durkheim (378–92; 1960:1–31) himself, suggest appropriate remedies (Marks 1974:329–63).

DEFINITION AND DIFFICULTIES

Brilliant though it was, Durkheim's decision to study suicide had problematic aspects. He defined suicide as death resulting from behavior that the individual knows will lead to his own demise. Whether death is desired is immaterial; only the individual's awareness of the consequences of his behavior is relevant. The suicidal act may be positive (entailing some expenditure of energy) or negative (entailing the conscious refusal to take action necessary for survival): *"Suicide is applied to all cases of death resulting directly or indirectly from a positive or negative act of the victim himself, which he knows will produce this result"* (44). Durkheim (42) wanted a definition that permitted ready identification of all suicides using easily recognizable, objective qualities. He therefore ruled out use of intent and motive as too subjective. In contrast, acts in which the "victim knows the certain result of his conduct" are readily identifiable because it is possible to determine whether the victim knew in advance the consequences of his action (44). However, despite his vigorous argument to the contrary, by referring to the victim's knowledge Durkheim appealed to a phenomenon just as subjective as the motive and intent that he excluded initially.

Durkheim felt that his definition approximated the everyday definition of suicide. Consequently, substituion of his for the everyday definition would have little impact upon official suicide statistics. To the contrary, however, a nonswimmer who jumps into deep water to save his child, only to drown himself, does not appear in official statistics as a suicide. Anticipating Durkheim's analysis of altruistic suicide, in general only those soldiers whose deaths were the *intended* goal of their behavior had been classified as suicides; the records had excluded wartime deaths of those who, in the line of duty, consciously exposed themselves to situations which they *knew* might well result in their own deaths. Thus, suicide has generally been understood as "the *intentional* taking of one's own life [italics added]" (Random House *Dictionary of the English Language, 1967 edition.*)

The dilemma now becomes clear. Insofar as intent is eliminated from the definition, it will not correspond to that commonly employed. Insofar as intent is employed, though, it will, in Durkheim's estimation, lack the objectivity that is the sine qua non for

scientific definitions. Furthermore, even had his definition successfully eliminated reference to any subjective elements, it still would
have had no impact upon the definitions used by those responsible
for identifying suicide. Durkheim, anxious to rid his own definition
of any source of unreliability, apparently never considered the
implications for his research of the definitions used by those from
whom he obtained his data.

Formal definitions aside, other factors affect suicide statistics. If
these could be expected to operate randomly, balancing out in the
long run, perhaps there would be no cause for concern. More likely,
however, systematic biases are present. For example, Douglas
(1967:193-94) cited figures indicating that the number of deaths
recorded as suicides in various European states jumped markedly
when secular officials replaced religious functionaires as those
responsible for recording cause of death.[2] Thus it may be hypothesized that the likelihood of a given death's being recorded as suicide varies inversely with the stigma attached to suicide. Assuming
the existence of such a stigma, the ability of the deceased's family to
have a suicide classified in some less opprobrious way no doubt
varies with their socioeconomic status. The de facto definitions of
suicide employed by officials depend on factors other than their
understanding of the definition per se, and these factors affect
classification procedures differently, depending upon the group,
locality, and nation involved. Unfortunately, Durkheim considered
none of these possibilities and thus failed to demonstrate the fundamental reliability and validity of his primary data.

Types of Suicide

Durkheim investigated not suicides per se but social suicide rates.
Rates may be for a group (e.g., Catholics, soldiers, Germans) or for
some social category (e.g., very young husbands, divorced persons).
Typically, *Suicide* focuses on comparisons; hence, the problem is to
explain why the rate is higher for one group than another, or varies
for the same group over time. Above all, Durkheim wanted to
generate a strictly sociological explanation.

This interest in sociological explanation is nowhere more manifest
than in the derivation of the typology of suicide. Since the explanation was to be sociological, so must the presumed causes. And it was
in terms of these causes that the types of suicide were classified.
Each type—egoistic, altruistic, anomic, and fatalistic—characterized a social state that leads to the type of suicide named for it.

Durkheim used these causes to explain variation in social suicide rates. When discussing the suicide of a given individual, Durkheim perceived that death as having been determined by the nature of his social existence. For example, if John Doe had been an egoistic suicide, to attribute his suicide to his egoistic qualities would constitute, according to Durkheim, an appeal to a secondary, derived phenomenon. Rather, the explanation must identify the reason for his personal egoism, namely, the egoistic social state of the group or condition in which he lived. Egoism, altruism, anomie, and fatalism identify states of groups or social conditions causing people to kill themselves.

The first of Durkheim's two major explanatory variables was integration. Two types of suicide represent opposite ends of the integration continuum. One type is egoistic. Rates of interaction in egoistic groups are low; beliefs, values, traditions, and sentiments are not common to all members. Consequently, they reciprocally enfeeble one another as they come into conflict. Collective life diminishes, and individual interests assert themselves. As the individual increasingly frees himself from the social control of the group, he (1) removes himself from its prophylactic influence and (2) finds little meaning in life, which comes to appear as an intolerable burden. As a result, suicide rates rise when groups become more egoistic and less integrated.

Just as weak integration leads to high suicide rates, so also does strong integration. With the individual completely absorbed into and controlled by the group his individuality, so slightly developed, cannot be highly valued. Society does not hesitate to bid the individual to end his life, nor does he resist society's command to end that upon which he himself places little value. Under these conditions the slightest pretext becomes sufficient cause for suicide. Durkheim identified this as altruistic suicide.

Durkheim introduced a second variable, regulation, and named low regulation "anomie." Anomie is the consequence of social change resulting in a diminution of social regulation. Sometimes anomie entails a sudden change, throwing people into new circumstances so that the moral rules formerly guiding their behavior are no longer applicable. Freed of social control, passions and appetites are subject to no restraint, since only the collective moral authority of a group can perform this function. People's desires quickly outstrip their means. The result is frustration, exasperation, and weariness leading to high suicide rates.

Durkheim recognized that just as egoism and altruism represent opposite ends of a single continuum, so logically there should be an opposite of anomie on the regulation continuum. This end is identified as fatalism, the explicit discussion of which is confined to one footnote (276n) because it is of little contemporary importance. Only the logic of his theory, and not fatalism's empirical importance, led him to mention it. Fatalistic suicide is described as "the suicide deriving from excessive regulation, that of persons with futures pitilessly blocked and passions violently choked by oppressive discipline." It is named fatalistic "to bring out the ineluctable and inflexible nature of a rule against which there is no appeal." Egoism, altruism, anomie, and fatalism identify both types of suicide and the causes that Durkheim perceived as explaining variation in social suicide rates.

3   THE THEORY: OVERVIEW

Implicit in the derivation of Durkheim's typology of suicide is the underlying logical structure of the theory. Durkheim postulated identical relations between each of two independent variables—integration and regulation—and suicide. When either is high or low, the suicide rate is high; when either is moderate, the rate is low. Changes in rates are proportional to changes in the strength of these two variables. The low and high points of each are named—egoism and altruism (integration) and anomie and fatalism (regulation)— and identified as the causes of suicide. Fatalism is not on a par with the others but rather remains an empirically underdeveloped and theoretically residual category. Durkheim (299, 321) himself typically ignored it, as when he spoke of suicide as a function of the "currents of egoism, altruism or anomy running through the society under consideration." The theory, then, postulates that suicide rates are low at some point along the integration and regulation continua, increasing in proportion to the distance from those points.

Suicide conveys the impression that Durkheim was only vaguely and intermittently conscious of the underlying logical structure of his theory. Only twice did he (236-37, 378) note that when either integration or regulation is moderate, suicide rates are low. The above statement, then, makes explicit what is left implicit in *Suicide* itself. The following sections detail this structure.

INTEGRATION
Egoism

In attempting to demonstrate that egoism and suicide vary proportionately, Durkheim successively examined religious, familial, and political society.

Religious society. Durkheim's analysis of religious society (152-70) centered on the strength of collective beliefs relative to that of free inquiry. Collective beliefs are variously referred to as fixed or

14

established beliefs, instinctive or common sentiments, collective prejudices, public opinion, traditional beliefs or sentiments, faith, ancient or established beliefs, or accepted opinions. Durkheim used these terms to identify beliefs common to some group; these beliefs, having originated in the past, are accepted and handed down from generation to generation. The tendency toward free inquiry manifests itself in various ways, including the desire or taste for learning, knowledge, self-instruction, education, free thought, reflection, and the intellectual life. At the scholarly level it is manifested in the development of philosophy first, followed later by science (162). Regarding the circumstances that cause the initial weakening of collective beliefs, Durkheim said little.

Durkheim treated free inquiry in its various manifestations both as an outgrowth of the weakening of common beliefs and as an indicator of the extent to which such weakening has occurred. *Suicide* (158–59, 162) is emphatic about the causal relationship between the strength of collective beliefs and the development of free inquiry: with one exception, free inquiry develops only to fill the vacuum created by a prior weakening of collective beliefs. Free inquiry is the effect; weakening of collective beliefs, the cause. Thus free inquiry does not normally develop in the face of strong collective beliefs. However, once developed, free inquiry may battle in its own right, reacting upon collective beliefs to weaken them still further (169, 159).

In the case of Jews, the development of free inquiry has another origin. The Jew "seeks to learn, not in order to replace his collective prejudices by reflective thought, but merely to be better armed for the struggle. For him it is a means of offsetting the unfavorable position imposed on him by opinion and sometimes by law" (168). In this case the development of free inquiry does not react upon collective thought to weaken it still further. Jewish society remains strong because "knowledge by itself has no influence upon a tradition in full vigor." Thus the Jew represents an exception to the usual relationship between weakened collective beliefs and development of free inquiry.

Durkheim clearly emphasized ideas and beliefs. Although contemporary sociologists have carefully distinguished between beliefs and behavior, Durkheim often failed to draw any sharp distinction. Hence, as in the present case, while focusing upon beliefs he (159–61, 170) also occasionally included behavior almost as an afterthought. Beliefs and actions are mutually reinforcing; common behavior leads to common beliefs just as common beliefs lead to common behavior. More important, he saw behavior as flowing from beliefs, which explains why he focused upon the strength of collective relative to individual beliefs.

The strength of collective beliefs varies inversely with free inquiry. Strength of collective beliefs is the independent variable, and each diminution in its strength results in a concomitant increase in free inquiry and individuality. But to speak of the strength of collective beliefs is really to speak of the vitality, cohesion, or integration of society itself. The more integrated a society is, the more it controls the behavior of its members, protecting them from suicide. Inversely, the less integrated the society, the more the individual is the author of his own beliefs and behavior, the less society is able to protect him from suicide, and the higher the suicide rate. Durkheim's explanation emphasizes that the strength of collective beliefs and, hence, the level of integration in a society determines, and varies inversely with, the strength of free inquiry (moral individualism or, simply, individuality).

Familial society. The level of familial integration is ultimately a function of family size: the larger the number of people, the higher that level (201–2). Two overlapping causal chains can be abstracted from Durkheim's analysis. One links number of people to amount of interaction, and that amount to social integration: the larger the number, the greater the total amount of interaction and, consequently, the higher the level of integration. Durkheim (202n) noted that a distinction normally is made between absolute numbers of people (referred to as volume) and "the number of individuals actually in reciprocal relationship in one and the same social volume." In the instance of the family, however, such a distinction is of "no interest, since, due to the smallness of the group, all associated persons are in actual relationship." Consequently, sheer number of people determines the amount of interaction which, in turn, determines the level of integration. Second, Durkheim also focused on the strength of collective sentiments: the number of people determines the number of consciousnesses (consciences), which determines the number of consciousnesses reacting in common and sharing collective sentiments, which determines the strength of collective sentiments, which determines the degree of social integration.

Stated differently, Durkheim focused (1) on people and the rate at which they interact and (2) on ideas-beliefs (specifically, collective sentiments). This second level explains why the relationships identified in the first should, in fact, hold. The two strands can be integrated as follows: the number of people determines the amount of interaction, which determines the number of reacting consciousnesses, which determines the number of consciousnesses reacting in common and sharing collective sentiments, which determines the strength of collective sentiments, which determines the degree of social integration. It is people, of course, who are integrated, but collective sentiments constitute the integrating force.

Political society. Durkheim's theoretical account of varying levels of integration in political society made no sharp distinction between common activities and common sentiments (208). Recognizing the possibility of identifying more than one causal chain, I infer the following (consistent with Durkheim's statement): the struggle occasioned by the necessity to confront the common danger causes individuals to think less of themselves and more of the common danger, which arouses collective sentiments, which in turn leads to greater social integration. Once again Durkheim explained level of social integration in terms of the strength of collective sentiments.

Egoism and suicide. Having identified the causes of varying levels of integration in three different types of society, Durkheim (208-16) concluded with a general statement explaining why suicide and integration are inversely related. As the level of integration decreases, the individual detaches himself from social life, and his personal goals supersede those of the social community. Depending less on the group and more on himself, he increasingly acknowledges only rules of conduct based on his private interests (209). Egoism, then, is a social condition in which society is weak, while personality and individuality are highly developed and individual interests are expressed at the expense of social interests.

Durkheim (209) developed several interrelated themes that link egoism to suicide. For its part, a strongly constituted society does not permit individuals to evade social responsibilities by taking their own lives. For their part, individuals can more readily endure life's sufferings when they cling to a group and consequently refuse to betray its interests, which they place before their own. Finally, a strongly constituted society provides a reservoir of energy that individuals can fall back upon in time of need (210). From

Durkheim's perspective, however, this explanation is less than satisfactory; even though the suicide rate is a function of levels of social integration, the suicidal thrust itself is conceptualized as in opposition to social forces and as originating with the individual. It may be stretching the point here to maintain that suicide is socially caused. Thus, it is not surprising to find Durkheim (210) characterizing the above reasons as "purely secondary" before going on to explain that excessive individualism, itself the result of the operation of strictly social factors, creates the inclination to suicide "out of whole cloth."

In socializing man, society creates his need to find meaning in life through serving some end beyond himself, and simultaneously fulfills that need by requiring him to fulfill social functions that meet the needs of society itself. As society disintegrates, man becomes increasingly detached from social life, individual interests assert themselves at the expense of social interests, and man no longer finds meaning in life because he is no longer serving some transcendent purpose. Moreover, as society disintegrates, its very reality lessens, causing man to realize that his social life is meaningless because it no longer corresponds to anything real (211-13).

Durkheim did not explicitly entertain the possibility that man might find meaning in serving some transcendent end other than society. Of course, there are individual ends but these are not transcendent; although they satisfy man's individual nature, they are completely incapable of meeting his socially originated need to fulfill transcendent ends. In effect, man's need to serve such ends is equated with the need to serve societal ends. Consequently, to the degree that a society's disintegration means that man is no longer able to satisfy his need for meaning in life, that need remains unfulfilled.

Durkheim concluded this portion of his argument by observing that "no proof is needed" to demonstrate that in the state of confusion produced by the disintegration of society, "the least cause of discouragement may easily give birth to desperate resolutions. If life is not worth the trouble of being lived, everything becomes a pretext to rid ourselves of it" (213).

Suicide provides another reason why suicide and level of social integration should be inversely related. As the parts which together constitute the whole society, individuals are adversely affected by its unhealthy state (213-14). Coupled with this explanation is a more elaborate statement of a related theme: "Society may generalize its own feeling as to itself, its state of health or lack of health" (213). This assessment takes into account society's relationship with the individuals composing it. As it disintegrates, permitting individuals to escape its control, society comes to the realization that their lives are of little value (214). This reality is the basis for society's estimation of the value of human life. "New moralities," i.e., collective opinions in the form of metaphysical and religious systems, "originate which, by elevating facts to ethics, commend suicide" by stressing that human existence is without purpose and human life of no value. Durkheim emphasized that such doctrines are "an effect rather than a cause; they merely symbolize in abstract language and systematic form the physiological distress of the body social." Like all collective sentiments, these doctrines "have, by virtue of their origin, an authority which they impose upon the individual and they drive him more vigorously on the way to which he is already inclined by the state of moral distress directly aroused in him by the disintegration of society." This, then, is Durkheim's account of the relationship between egoism and suicide.

Altruism

Suicide (217–40) identifies two loci of altruistic suicide: primitive society and the modern military. [1]

Primitive society. Just as "excessive individuation leads to suicide, insufficient individuation has the same effects" (217). *Suicide's* account emphasizes many themes that, in terms of Durkheim's framework, mutually imply one another. Though he never explicitly said so, his reference to the compact, continuous nature of the group—coupled with an accompanying reference to his *The Division of Labor in Society* (1960; hereafter cited as *Division*), where the point is stressed—made it clear that primitive societies are characterized by high rates of interaction. Everything being common to all, everyone is like everyone else. Durkheim's conception of the relationship between individual and social factors becomes crucial at this point. Individuality refers to what distinguishes the individual from others; the social component, to what individuals share. By definition they vary inversely. A compact society characterized by high rates of interaction with pervasive commonalities and the lack of individuality mutually imply one another (220–21). The small, compact size of the group makes mutual surveillance intense, precluding the possibility that anyone might successfully develop those differences which mark individuality. Virtually indistinct from his fellows, the individual "is only an inseparable part of the whole without personal value." So little developed and in this sense so lacking in reality, "his person has so little value that attacks upon it"—whether by the individual himself, others, or the society—proceed without the impediment that arises where the individual per se is highly valued (221).

Three types of altruistic suicide are identified: obligatory, optional, and acute. Durkheim distinguished between them on the basis of the specific mechanisms triggering suicide. The functionalist strain in his thought manifests itself in the analysis of obligatory altruistic suicide, a type occurring when the individual is compelled by society to kill himself in the service of social interests (219-20). Individuality is too little developed to be of great moment in the face of social necessities. The individual himself, sharing the values of the group, does not place great value upon his own life, nor does his undeveloped individuality provide him with the wherewithal to oppose society. For these reasons he does not offer strong resistance to societal injunctions dictated by "collective necessities" (221). Obligatory altruistic suicide, then, is a sacrifice "imposed by society for social ends" (220).

Optional altruistic suicide (223) is so similar to obligatory altruistic suicide that the one shades off into the other. If society compels in the one case, it is content to merely counsel in the other (222-23). The slightest offense, a jealous impulse, or the least disappointment is sufficient to invoke the suicidal act. Durkheim (223) distinguished a final type, the acute, in which "the individual kills himself purely for the joy of sacrifice, because, even with no particular reason, renunciation in itself is considered praiseworthy." This is the purest type, an extreme manifestation of the denial of individuality, because social conditions lead directly to the act without the "concurrence of circumstances" required in the other two cases (223).

Collective beliefs play an important role in altruistic suicide. The first two types are associated with beliefs varying only in degree, whereas the acute is associated with a distinctive type of belief system. In obligatory cases suicide is considered a duty under certain circumstances. Compliance yields honor and glory; failure to comply, disgrace. Sometimes these beliefs are supplemented by religious sanctions in the form of beliefs that those who kill themselves will be rewarded in the hereafter, while those who do not will be punished.

Much the same situation prevails in optional altruistic suicide, except that the obligatory suicide acts in part to avoid negative sanctioning, whereas the optional suicide is more oriented toward eliciting approval (222). In acute altruistic suicide the individual is moved by "metaphysical and religious systems" teaching that "what reality there is in the individual is foreign to his nature, that the soul which animates him is not his own, and that consequently he has no personal existence" (226).

For Durkheim these different beliefs arise from the same source as the low valuation placed upon the individual, namely, the underlying social reality (226–27). The specific form of the translation of reality into beliefs varies. In the case of obligatory or optional suicide, social necessities are translated as duties or options for the individual in the form of beliefs about duty, honor, and religious sanctioning in the afterlife. In the case of acute suicide the relevant belief is that the principle of action is external to the individual. These somewhat different beliefs reflect the same reality, the crucial aspect of which is that the society directs the individual. Although such beliefs help to bring about suicide and as such constitute a proximate cause, they are but a translation of the real cause, which must be sought in the underlying social reality.

Military society. The second locus of altruistic suicide is the modern army (228–39). Consistent with the observation that suicide in the military "is the suicide of lower societies, in survival among us" (238), Durkheim's theoretical analysis (234) highlighted the similarities between the modern army and primitive society. Durkheim emphasized two sides of the same theoretical coin. The soldier is imbued with the spirit of renunciation and abnegation. He manifests passive obedience and absolute submission, obeying without question. He is weakly tied to his own individuality, which has little value for him. Thus, on the one hand, there is lack of individuality, impersonality, and low valuation of human life; on the other, the characteristics of group life, including its compact nature, rigid military discipline, and high levels of social control, make individual divergences impossible. Because the principle of action resides in a strongly constituted society, it is understandable that as in primitive society, little is required to trigger suicide (238–39). Durkheim's theoretical account added a few indicators of "impersonalism" (238), but the basic explanatory structure is the same as that employed in connection with primitive society.

The Theory of Social Integration: A Synthesis

There are four statements of the theory of egoism alone (those in the sections on religious, political, and familial society, plus that contained at the end of the two chapters on egoism). To these must be added the two statements (one on primitive society and one on the modern army), of the theory of altruism. Thus *Suicide* contains no less that six more or less complete statements employing the theory of integration. What is missing is Durkheim's own synthesis. While there is much overlap, at some points the different statements employ both different concepts and different causal relationships. Thus a synthesis is not readily apparent.

Further complicating matters is a reference (221) to *Division*. Durkheim never stated what he saw as the exact relationship of the theory developed there to that presented in *Suicide*. Insofar as *Division* amplifies his view, though, it constitutes an additional statement to be considered in identifying Durkheim's theory.

The task is hampered by difficulties, not the least of which is *Suicide*'s propensity to work with a changing number of abstract but poorly defined concepts whose mutual relations are less than adequately specified. Yet an attempt may be made to identify the theory of egoism and the theory of altruism, and then to synthesize the two. As in *Division*, the number of people represents a starting point. In determining the rate of interaction, not only sheer number but spatial relationships are crucial. However, for the kinds of group comparisons that he made, Durkheim implicitly assumed that total area and spatial distributions remain relatively constant; consequently, they do not appear as variables in his causal chain, nor, for that matter, do various possible social impediments to interaction (e.g., conflicting values, linguistic differences). Rather, the assumption is that the rate of interaction is proportional to the number of people.

Rate of interaction is central because it determines the number of consciousnesses acting and reacting in common to each other and to collective sentiments, which in turn determines the strength of the latter. The strength of the collective factor—here collective sentiments—and that of the individual factor vary inversely. Thus, to speak of the strength of the former is also to speak of the relative strength of the latter (variously identified as individuation, individuality, individual differences, individual interests, personality, or egoism). The strength of collective sentiments determines the degree of social integration.

To turn this into a theory of suicide requires adding the following linkages: the strength of social integration determines the extent to which individuals act in service of social interests, which determines the degree to which they find meaning in life, which in turn determines the social suicide rate. In sum, the theory of egoism as a theory of suicide holds that the higher the rate of social interaction, the stronger collective sentiments; the stronger collective sentiments, the stronger social integration; the stronger social integration, the more individuals act in service of social interests; the more individuals act in service of social interests, the more meaning they find in life and the lower the social suicide rate. Alternatively, the lower the rate of social interaction, the weaker collective sentiments; the weaker collective sentiments, the weaker social integration; the weaker social integration, the less individuals act in service of social interests; the less individuals act in service of social interests, the less meaning they find in life and the higher the social suicide rate.

To turn to the theory of altruism: the small, compact, continuous nature of the group insures mutual accessibility of individuals through close physical proximity, thereby leading to high rates of social interaction.[2] High rates of interaction, in turn, lead to a highly developed common group life with extensive likenesses, minimal differences, and undeveloped individuality. Undeveloped individuality and extensive commonalities imply high levels of social integration.

Durkheim employed more than one line of reasoning in explaining why this should be so. High levels of social integration imply a configuration including the following elements: (1) society is powerful, the individual weak; (2) social interests prevail over individual interests; (3) low valuation is placed upon human life. One important theme is that given the low valuation of human life, the slightest pretext is sufficient to trigger suicide. Another is that the individual attaches greater meaning to life in a world beyond this one; thus he readily sacrifices himself in the interest of achieving union with his real goal. Finally, the altruistic suicide may kill himself because social interests are more meaningful to him than his own individually defined interests. Perhaps it is not stretching matters to hold that meaning is important in each case, with the individual attaching so little meaning to his own continued existence that he is willing to forego it in favor of other, more meaningful, values and goals. High levels of social integration lead to lack of meaning in individual existence, which in turn leads to high suicide rates.

Given that egoism refers to low, and altruism to high, levels of integration, it should be possible to integrate the two theoretical statements. Both treat rate of interaction as causally linked to level of social integration. However, the linkages are somewhat different. The theory of egoism speaks of the number of consciousnesses reacting in common as a determinant of the strength of collective sentiments. In contrast, the theory of altruism states that high rates of interaction enable strict social control, thereby insuring highly developed common group life and minimum individual divergences. Again, the theory of egoism speaks of collective sentiments while that of altruism speaks more of similarities, likenesses, and common group life. Clearly, though, not only are collective sentiments one (if not the primary) phenomenon subsumed under commonalities; in addition, they represent the key force controlling the individual and inhibiting the development of individual differences. Commonalities and collective sentiments vary proportionately; in fact, they represent alternative ways of referring to the collective factor. The difference between them is more terminological than substantive. Hence it becomes possible to integrate the theory of altruism and that of egoism. The rate of interaction determines the strength of collective sentiments or, in different terms, the extensiveness of common life. The strength of collective sentiments, in turn, determines the strength of social integration. The similarities underlying certain differences in terminology and causal linkages are such that the theories of egoism and altruism may be synthesized into a single theory of integration.

The egoist commits suicide because his existence fails to fulfill his need to find meaning in life; the altruist, because he attaches little meaning to his continued physical existence. Lack of meaning is decisive in both cases. In egoistic suicide it is a failure to satisfy a highly developed need to find meaning in life; in altruistic suicide, it is the lack of meaning attached to continued physical existence, either because the low value placed on human life deprives it of meaning in itself, or because the meaning in life is located in a world beyond this one.

Emphasizing dominant themes and recognizing that any such attempt inevitably entails selectivity, I now identify the key causal relationships in Durkheim's theory of integration as a theory of suicide. Number of people determines the rate of social interaction, which in turn determines the strength of collective sentiments (alternatively, the extensiveness of common life or degree of individuality). The strength of collective sentiments determines the degree of social integration, which in turn determines the degree to which the individual finds meaning in this life, which determines the social suicide rate. More simply, the rate of interaction determines the strength of collective sentiments which, in turn, determines the degree of social integration. Degree of social integration determines the degree to which the individual finds meaning in this life, which determines the social suicide rate. This, then, is Durkheim's theory insofar as suicide is explained in terms of level of social integration.

REGULATION

Regulation is Durkheim's other major independent variable.

Anomie

Durkheim (241–76) discussed two forms of economic anomie, acute and chronic, and then analyzed chronic domestic anomie.

Acute economic. Durkheim wanted to explain why economic crises cause an increase in social suicide rates. Central to the explanation is the means-needs balance. The crucial consideration is whether man's means are adequate for the fulfillment of his needs. Where means are proportional to needs, Durkheim (246–54) said that they exist in a state of equilibrium; where the former are inadequate to fulfill the latter, they exist in a state of disequilibrium. These needs are not given by man's biological, psychological, or individual nature. Rather, they are social products that vary from one social context to the next. Particular goals, desires, passions, or appetites for comfort, well-being, luxury, and so on may become translated into needs. Durkheim used needs in a very broad sense to include all of these things, and he spoke of needs, ends, and goals, or the passions, appetites, and desires that can turn a want into a need.

Human wants are boundless and insatiable; consequently, unless restrained they represent a constant threat to individual happiness (246–48). Far from serving to satiate the individual, satisfaction of needs serves only to stimulate further needs (248). Thus, the sine qua non for equilibrium between means and needs is some force that limits man's desires. Man cannot do this himself; external restraint is required. Since the needs in question are moral in nature, society alone can provide the required restraint, because it is the only superior moral power whose authority the individual accepts (248–49). Restrained by this societal pressure, each individual "in his sphere" accepts the "limit set to his ambitions and aspires to nothing beyond" (250).

Such is the way in which equilibrium is maintained under normal conditions. During periods of crisis marked by relatively sudden changes in economic conditions, society becomes incapable of exercising its usual moderating influence. In the case of depression, individuals are thrown into a new, lower state (252). This requires a commensurate scaling down of goals. However, although the old rules are no longer applicable to an individual's new situation, new ones appropriate to that situation cannot be immediately established. As a result, individuals are not adjusted to the situation in which they find themselves, and their consequent suffering "detaches them from a reduced existence even before they have made trial of it" (252). For analogous reasons, economic booms also create a disjunction between means and needs; indeed, this disjunction is particularly severe because "the richer prize offered" appetites stimulates them, making them even less amenable to restraint (253).

Durkheim (253–54) closed by noting that his explanation is validated by the remarkably low suicide rates of poor countries. "Actual possessions are partly the criterion of those aspired to," so that the more an individual has, the more he wants (254). Having little, the poor aspire to little; thus their means tend to be adequate for their needs. In contrast, wealth "by the power it bestows, deceives us into believing that we depend on ourselves only," thereby encouraging resistance to collective discipline and suggesting the possibility of unlimited success against the resistance "we encounter from objects." Ironically, by virtue of having more, the wealthy experience greater means-needs imbalance than the poor.

Durkheim's explanation is based on three assumptions. First, the happiness of men is to be explained not as a function of poverty or wealth but rather of the degree to which their means are proportional to their needs. Second, the needs of man are not subject to any inherent limitation. Finally, society is the only power that can restrain these otherwise boundless goals and thereby create the equilibrium between means and needs upon which man's happiness depends. Durkheim related sudden change in economic conditions to society's ability to moderate aspirations. During times of crisis, society's regulatory impact is lessened. Individuals find themselves in new circumstances to which the old rules are inapplicable. Consequently, they are freed from social restraint, needs increasingly outstrip means, and the resulting disequilibrium creates more unhappiness, which manifests itself in higher suicide rates.

Chronic economic. Durkheim's analysis of chronic economic anomie (254-58) focused not on the consequences of sudden change but rather on those of the gradual diminution of social regulation. The restraint over economic, particularly industrial, relations exercised by religion, civil authority, and occupational groups had suffered erosion for a century; thus, far from being regarded as a means to some higher end, industry has come to be viewed as an end in itself. Consequently, in the industrial context the individual is freed from social restraint.

The degree of restraint that the individual can tolerate is proportional to the amount he experiences. Thus, not only does the very weakening of restraint make remaining restraint appear increasingly intolerable, but also the well situated are more adversely affected by anomie than are the more humbly placed (256-58). Observing, characteristically, that belief systems reflect an underlying social reality, Durkheim (257) also noted that in modern society the anarchic state is elevated to a virtue: "The longing for infinity is daily represented as a mark of moral distinction, whereas it can only appear within unregulated consciences which elevate to a rule the lack of rule from which they suffer."

Chronic domestic anomie. Though he (259) cited widowhood as an empirical example of acute domestic anomie, Durkheim passed quickly to chronic domestic anomie, analyzing the way in which marital regulation affects the means-needs balance in men and women. In defining marriage, Durkheim (270) characterized it is as "a regulation of sexual relations, including not merely the physical instincts which this intercourse involves but the feelings of every sort gradually engrafted by civilization on the foundation of physical desire." Men and women have a differential need for the regulation embodied in marriage. Woman's needs are more closely tied to, and are therefore more adequately restrained by, her instinctive, organic nature. With less highly developed needs, she requires less restraint to achieve a means-needs balance.

Durkheim (270) contrasted the situation of married and single persons. The married man is duty bound not to stray outside his marriage to satisfy his appetites. Bachelors, however, experience limitless horizons, which lead to unrestrained passions that create a disjunction between means and needs (271). But what of women? Should not the same contrast between married and single apply to them as well? Durkheim's answer is no. Though useful, the regulation in marriage is also inconvenient (272). Seen in this light, the question is whether the benefits outweigh the inconveniences. Compared with women, men gain more on two counts. Most important, they require greater restraint to bring needs into line with means. In addition, custom grants them privileges that reduce the strictness of the marital regime, privileges that are denied to women, for whom monogamy is strictly obligatory.[3] The benefit-cost relationship is such that men benefit from increases, and women from decreases, in social regulation.

Durkheim's treatment of anomie is tied together by a few recurring themes. A means-needs disjunction creates an unhappiness conducive to suicide. Man's appetites are insatiable, and his goals inherently expansive; thus, unless restrained, needs outstrip means. The only power that can limit man's passions and needs is society itself, but society's ability to perform this function varies. Society normally makes a rough determination of how much the individual may legitimately aspire to—a determination that not only effects a proportionality between means and needs (by scaling down the latter) but is also accepted as just. However, during times of sudden change people find themselves thrown into new situations to which prevailing rules are no longer applicable. Since new rules cannot immediately be established, the individual is temporarily unadapted to his situation. During depressions the individual's means are no longer adequate to his needs, while in times of prosperity the lack of guiding rules permits expanding needs to surpass means, thus creating the means-needs disjunction marking anomie. In contrast to acute anomie, chronic anomie denotes situations in which the gradual erosion of social control permits needs to expand and outstrip means.

In examining the impact of regulation it is necessary to consider whether the inconvenience outweighs the benefits. Heightened levels of regulation are beneficial for men. In contrast, women require minimal social limitation on needs (which are largely curbed by instinct) and therefore find the cost outweighing the benefits; hence, additional regulation elevates rather than lowers their suicide rates. In sum, suicide is a function of means-needs proportionality which, in turn, is a function of society's ability to restrain needs. With the exception of the regulation women experience in marriage, in modern society the greater the social regulation, the more nearly means are proportional to needs and, consequently, the lower the social suicide rate (see figure 3.1).

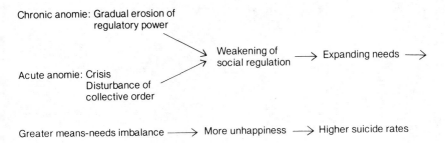

Fig. 3.1. The theory of anomie as a theory of suicide

Fatalism

The frustrating aspect of Durkheim's explicit treatment of fatalism —an eight-sentence footnote (276n) concluding the chapter on anomie—is its brevity. Three empirical examples are cited: very young husbands, childless married women, and slaves. The extreme degree of social regulation is stressed, and the account is wholly negative in tone, seeming to rule out the existence of any beneficial effects that might counterbalance the evils cited.[4] Durkheim may have depicted fatalism in terms of its extreme value in the interest of providing a sharply etched description or lending added plausibility to the contention that fatalism causes suicide. In any case, apart from the definition of fatalism as "excessive regulation," it is impossible to glean a full account of this underdeveloped concept.

Earlier in this chapter I showed how the theories of egoism and altruism could be synthesized. The next step is to integrate this synthesis with the theory of regulation. Because Durkheim said so little about fatalism, this step is tantamount to integrating the theory of regulation (as represented by Durkheim's theory of anomie) with that of integration. Before doing so, however, it is necessary to consider the relationship between integration and regulation.

4 INTEGRATION AND REGULATION: DIFFERENT OR IDENTICAL?

Given the logical structure of Durkheim's theory, the relationship between integration and regulation is crucial. Yet commentators have not agreed on what, if anything, distinguishes them. Parsons (1949:327-38) maintained that integration refers to value content; regulation, to the strength of social control. Nisbet (1966:94; see also 1974:233) suggested that anomie is a breakdown of moral community; egoism, of social community. Coser (1971:134-35) defined the difference in terms of structural integration versus normative regulation. Agreeing with Coser on the meaning of regulation, Wallwork (1972:48-53) saw integration as a matter of attachment to group morals. Giddens (1971b:84-85) has argued that Durkheim linked egoism with moral individualism, whereas anomie referred to a lack of moral regulation. Finally, although Lukes (1967: 139n) initially denied the existence of any difference, he (1972:206) later concluded that integration referred to the social bonds tying the individual to socially-given ideals and purposes; regulation, to those that regulate the individual's desires.

Others, however, noting the overlap between integration and regulation, have stressed the difficulty of identifying any sociological distinction (Sainsbury 1955:22; Gibbs and Martin 1964:6-7; Smelser 1971:18-19; Poggi 1972:200). Some have implicitly acknowledged the overlap by coupling egoism and anomie or by attributing to one concept characteristics that Durkheim linked with the other (Homans 1950:336-37). Wolin (1960:399) characterized anomie as a "riot of egoism," and LaCapra (1972:145) referred to an "anomic absence of meaning in experience." Many other authors have ignored the problem altogether, simply restated the distinctions Durkheim enumerated, or otherwise failed to clarify a viable difference (i.e., Alpert 1961; Hendin 1964:8-9; Henry and Short 1964:132-33; Aron 1967:30-33; Douglas 1967:3-76).

In short, if a difference exists, writers disagree on what it is. Furthermore, the distinctions they draw are not those identified by

Durkheim himself in his own attempts at clarification. Finally, those writers who have argued that there is no distinction have generally failed to indicate *why* Durkheim supplemented his theory of integration with a theory of regulation. This chapter rejects past attempts to identify a sociological distinction, subsequently argues that none exists, and then examines the place of the theory of regulation in Durkheim's explanatory structure.

DIFFERENCES?

I examine Durkheim's attempts to distinguish between integration and regulation before considering those of his commentators.

Durkheim's Distinctions

Figure 4.1 places the differences between integration and regulation delineated by Durkheim into a causal nexus. Because he never explicitly worked with the total configuration (*Suicide* identifies only one or two steps at a time), the figure entails some reconstruction. Nonetheless, each step identifies a contrast explicitly developed in *Suicide*.

Although Durkheim's initial attempts (241, 258) at a distinction do little more than refer to societal attachment and attraction as integration and to societal control as regulation, elsewhere he identified some clear differences. The cause producing anomie and egoism has "different effects, depending on its point of incidence and whether it influences active and practical functions, or functions that are representative" (382; step 2 in fig. 4.1). Though both entail the absence of society in the individual, the sphere of this absence differs. "In egoistic suicide it is deficient in truly collective activity, thus depriving the latter of object and meaning. In anomic suicide, society's influence is lacking in the basically individual passions, thus leaving them without a check-rein" (258, see also 287). The contrast between the meaninglessness resulting from lack of integration and the uncontrolled passions resulting from lack of regulation is clear.

Step 4 (fig. 4.1) identifies the characteristic emotional states associated with suicide. The egoistic suicide experiences depression, melancholy, or sheer apathy, while his anomic counterpart suffers from irritation, disgust, or anger. Furthermore, whereas egoistic suicide is prevalent "among intellectual careers, the world of thought," anomic suicide prevails in "the industrial or commercial

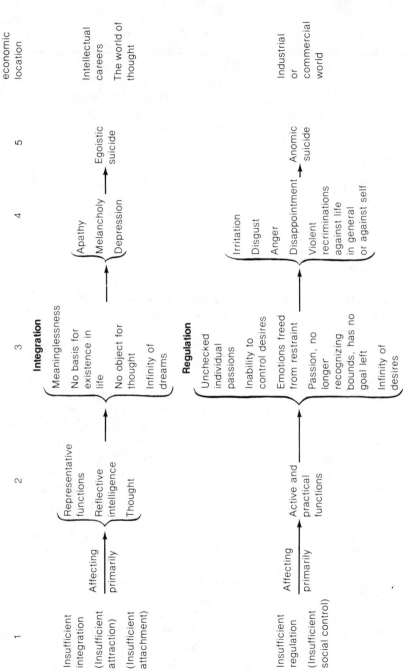

	1	2	3	4	5	Social and economic location

Integration

Insufficient integration (Insufficient attraction) (Insufficient attachment) → Affecting primarily → Representative functions / Reflective intelligence / Thought → Meaninglessness / No basis for existence in life / No object for thought / Infinity of dreams → Apathy / Melancholy / Depression → Egoistic suicide — Intellectual careers / The world of thought

Regulation

Insufficient regulation (Insufficient social control) → Affecting primarily → Active and practical functions → Unchecked individual passions / Inability to control desires / Emotions freed from restraint / Passion, no longer recognizing bounds, has no goal left / Infinity of desires → Irritation / Disgust / Anger / Disappointment / Violent recriminations against life in general or against self → Anomic suicide — Industrial or commercial world

Fig. 4.1. The distinction between egoism and anomie

world" (258). Egoism is associated with thinking; anomie, with feeling and, secondarily, acting.

Durkheim focused primarily on the difference between egoism and anomie, although altruism also received attention. He (258) noted that in contrast to egoistic suicide, which occurs when man no longer finds any basis for existence (step 3), altruistic suicide occurs when "this basis for existence appears to man situated beyond life itself." Egoism and altruism are similar in one important respect: each involves the question of the meaningfulness of the individual's life on earth. Altruistic suicide contrasts with egoistic in being more active and passionate, and with anomic in that the source of the "inspiring passion" is external, coming from society (283–84). When related to the earlier distinctions between egoism and anomie, these contrasts raise questions. Curiously, Durkheim attributed to altruistic suicide two characteristics—activity and strong emotions—that had previously been reserved for anomic (as opposed to egoistic) suicide. This attribution shows why the distinction between egoism and anomie cannot be equated with that between integration and regulation generally.

Suicide successfully identifies several differences between anomie and egoism. The difficulty is that the sociological difference between them as causes of suicide is never elucidated. In terms of key variables, Durkheim drew his distinctions at the level of intervening, rather than independent, variables. Given his tendency to link the sociological with the objective (versus the individual, psychological, and subjective), most of his distinctions are at the individual, subjective level, not at the sociological. But he (287) noted that the former "are like prolongations ... inside of individuals" of the "social causes on which they rest." It is the specific sociological distinction between integration and regulation that Durkheim never identified. *Suicide*'s failure in this regard is one indication that the distinction between the two basic independent variables in his theory, and hence between egoism and anomie, is uncertain at best.

Structural Integration vs. Normative Regulation

Some commentators distinguish between egoism and anomie by holding that the former refers to a structural, and the latter to a normative, dimension. For instance, Coser (1971:134) argued that egoistic suicide occurs when the social bonds tying men to each other and to society are weak; in contrast, anomic suicide results from a weakening of social norms. Though more than one author has claimed to find such a distinction in *Suicide*, no one has systematically analyzed *Suicide* to demonstrate the point. If this is what Durkheim had in mind, it is strange that he failed to mention it in any of his attempts to differentiate integration from regulation. Nor did the discussion of altruism focus on the structural dimension to the exclusion of the normative. Finally, greatly concerned over the social malaise affecting modern society, Durkheim (378–84) suggested the establishment of occupational groups as a practical remedy. He even proposed to overcome the anomie that is especially rampant in the more modern economic sectors of society through such groups (i.e., he proposed to overcome insufficient regulation through an infusion of integration). However, the link between structural integration and normative regulation in his discussion of altruism and in the proposal to overcome anomie is not accidental; given Durkheim's basic theoretical perspective, to be integrated into a group is to be subjected to the moral authority of its rules. Structural integration and normative regulation simply represent different conceptualizations of the same social reality.

Parsons and Value Content

Perhaps the most ambitious attempt to define a difference between integration and regulation was developed by Parsons (1949:327–38). Neither Parsons's discussion nor the structure of his argument stands in close correspondence to that of Durkheim. Furthermore, he often failed to cite the specific passages in the original on which he based his interpretation. Consequently, it is not easy to sort out the relations between these two inherently complex presentations.

Parsons argued that integration refers to the *content* of the collective conscience; regulation, to its strength. Since his understanding of regulation is adequate, the following discussion is largely of his interpretation of integration. To Parsons, altruism stressed the importance of the group's claims relative to those of the individual; egoism, the individual's claims relative to those of the group.

Altruism. Parsons and Durkheim agreed that in the case of altruism, the individual is subordinate to the group. According to Parsons, though, the important factor is not strength of integration but rather the content of values. In fact, this is not the case, as Durkheim (220–21) himself made clear. Parsons simply ignored a pervasive theme in Durkheim (220–21, 226-27, 387): the content of belief and value systems is a derived phenomenon in that it reflects the underlying social reality. The low valuation placed upon things individual (individuality, individual interests, even continued existence), in Durkheim's view, is an inevitable reflection of this social reality in which the group is all, the individual little. High levels of integration cause "this feeble individuation" (220). Subtracting what is central for Durkheim (strong integration) and omitting reference to low valuation of individuality (as reflecting the existing social reality) leaves Parsons with value content. Parsons maintained that value content is crucial, even though Durkheim made it clear that the value content upon which Parsons focused—low valuation of the individual—is caused by the very factor, high levels of integration, whose importance Parsons denied!

Parsons (1949:330) especially wanted to show that Durkheim's position in *Suicide* differed from that earlier adhered to in *Division*. In the latter, Durkheim (1960:129, 79-81, 105, 130) held that personality or individuality refers to "how much of our own individual qualities we have, what distinguishes us from others," while the collective conscience designates "the totality of social similitudes" or "social likenesses" and comprises all the sentiments "common to average citizens of the same society." By definition the individual and the collective factors are mutually exclusive: one consists of what differentiates individuals; the other, of what they share. The collective conscience and individuality vary inversely with each other. The strength of the collective conscience is itself the measure, if not the cause, of the strength of social integration. Given these relationships, commonalities vary proportionately, and individuality inversely, with strength of social integration. Consequently, when he spoke of commonalities and individuality Durkheim was, in effect, also speaking of the strength of integration.

However, Parsons argued that *strength* is not what Durkheim had in mind when he discussed integration generally or altruism in particular. Hence, Parsons denied that commonalities and individuality are decisive components in integration or, if still decisive, that they are indicators of integration. Specifically, he argued that each is capable of varying *independently* of the strength of integration, which, in turn, creates the possibility that something else has replaced strength as the crucial variable aspect of integration. This "something else" is value content. Since Parsons's case is tenable only because he denied that both commonalities and individuality are decisive vis-à-vis integration, it is necessary to consider the place of these variables in Durkheim's theory of integration.

Acknowledging the importance of similarity as a determinant of strength of social integration in primitive or altruistic society, as described in *Division*, Parsons (1949:330) argued that by the time *Suicide* was written, similarity "is no longer ... the central point." Durkheim (202; see also 170, 302), however, held otherwise: "For a group to be said to have less common life than another means that it is less powerfully integrated; for the state of integration of a social aggregate can only reflect the intensity of the collective life circulating in it." Commonality remained central for him, and, equally important, he continued to maintain that the extent of commonality is proportional to the strength of social integration.[1]

Individuality vs. the group. Parsons (1949:330) was also concerned with the existence of individuality and, assuming its existence, its suppression by the group. He felt that whereas *Division* denied the existence of individuality in the primitive or altruistic setting, *Suicide* asserted its existence. Durkheim's position in *Division* (1960:194) is clear: "In lower societies ... individual personality ... *did not exist";* furthermore, he continued to hold this position in *Suicide* (220, 223, 336). Parsons spoke of the suppression of individuality; in contrast, Durkheim explicitly rejected the contention that individuality is "restrained or artificially suppressed" (1960:194) and referred rather to the lack of individuality concomitant with high levels of integration.

Parsons (1949:330) attempted to buttress his case by referring to altruistic suicide in the army: "It is not because the army is an undifferentiated group that it has a high suicide rate, not that there is no difference between officers and men or artillery and infantry." However, the example actually undermined his case. Durkheim's treatment of the military emphasized its strict social control, lack of individuality, and commonalities. Thus Durkheim (238, 234) referred to the "impersonalism" of the military and an "intellectual abnegation hardly consistent with individualism." He ended by noting: "Of all elements constituting our modern societies, the army, indeed, most recalls the structure of lower societies. It, too, consists of a massive, compact group providing a rigid setting for the individual and preventing any independent movement." Durkheim's characterization of the military stressed what it *shares* with primitive societies. Since he called military suicide altruistic, this characterization is indeed understandable. Altruistic societies are distinguished by commonalities, lack of individuality, and high levels of integration—points that Parsons should have observed.

As Parsons noted, Durkheim did not treat the military as one undifferentiated mass. In analyzing military suicide rates, he compared rates among different groups within the military. These groups are identified by attributes shared by all group members (e.g., enlisted men, officers, troops stationed in France, the artillery) and then compared in terms of prevailing levels of integration. If Durkheim's position from *Division* to *Suicide* had shifted in the direction indicated by Parsons, it seems reasonable to expect that (employing ideas developed in *Division*) he would have referred to complementary differences, the division of labor, and functional interdependence. In fact, *Suicide* never mentions integrative mechanisms specific to or contingent upon differentiation. That Durkheim specifically refrained from mentioning such factors is significant, since it reflects his shift away from *Division*'s two types of solidarity model (mechanical and organic) and toward increasingly exclusive reliance upon the mechanical model (which, in *Suicide*, is applied not only to primitive but also to modern societies).

Thus, egoistic and anomic suicide do *not* result from lack of organic solidarity but precisely from lack of mechanical solidarity. Durkheim's famous proposal to heighten levels of solidarity in modern society spoke not of developing individuality, heightening complementary differences, encouraging functional interdependence, or grouping individuals according to differences, but rather of integration produced through commonalities. The lack of solidarity in modern society is to be rectified through massive infusions of mechanical (not organic) solidarity! In referring to the development of individuality and differentiation, even in the mechanical-altruistic setting, Parsons read elements of *Division*'s organic model into mechanical solidarity. Altogether, Parsons reversed the shift in emphasis revealed in comparing *Division* with *Suicide*.

Parsons wanted to show that in the altruistic setting, individuality and differences can coexist with high levels of integration. However, central to Durkheim's theoretical structure is the notion that the social factor (whether identified in terms of extent of commonalities, strength of the collective conscience, or strength of social integration), varies *inversely* with individuality. Thus, Parsons's failure to cite any passages supporting his interpretation is not surprising, for it runs counter to much that is basic to Durkheim's theoretical perspective.

Since Parsons's discussion centered on the change in Durkheim's position, it is instructive to note a passage in *Suicide* (221) that refers to *Division*. In it Durkheim stressed the importance of commonalities and noted the lack of individuality. His reference to "massive cohesion" is a forceful reminder that strong integration is a central attribute of mechanical society. Furthermore, the key characteristic of the collective conscience in the altruistic setting is *not* its content but its strength; that characteristic accounts for the lack of individuality and, simultaneously, for the low valuation placed upon the individual.

Egoism. Egoism is the second point at which Parsons attempted to discern value content as the decisive variable. One comparison important to both Parsons and Durkheim is that between Protestants and Catholics. Protestants, Durkheim claimed, display the higher suicide rates; thus the question of the relevance of different religious values naturally arises. The difference between Protestants and Catholics, Parsons (1949:333) concluded, "lies in the different *content* of the different value systems.... In so far as the high Protestant suicide rate is due to egoism it is a result of the hold over the individual of a *conscience collective*, a system of beliefs and sentiments common to Protestants, which are not shared by Catholics." However, Durkheim's explanation was quite different. "The only essential difference between Catholicism and Protestantism is that the second permits free inquiry to a far greater degree than the first" (157). But "free inquiry itself is only the effect of another cause," namely, "the overthrow of traditional beliefs" (158). The overthrow of traditional beliefs denotes a weakening of the collective conscience, and free inquiry develops to fill the void thereby created. In contrast to Parsons, who held that the spirit of free inquiry represents a shared sentiment—an element of the collective conscience—Durkheim specifically stated that it arises as a consequence of a *breakdown* of traditional beliefs, i.e., a weakening of the collective conscience.

Parsons's interpretive procedure is similar to that employed earlier with regard to altruism. There he subtracted high levels of social integration (central to Durkheim) in order to identify values as crucial. Here he subtracted lowered levels of integration (marked by the breakdown of the traditional, shared beliefs comprising the collective conscience) in order to identify different attitudes as decisive. Parsons's reinterpretation may be contrasted with *Suicide*'s conclusion (159) that "the superiority of Protestantism with respect to suicide results from its being a less strongly integrated church than the Catholic church."

Durkheim could scarcely have been expected to identify, only to deny, the importance of all beliefs that such commentators as Parsons might see as differentiating Protestant and Catholic value systems. However, he recognized the existence of such differences, and insofar as he explicitly considered them, he denied that they cause variation in suicide rates. Whereas Parsons (1949:331-33) focused on attitudes concerning religious freedom and individual responsibility, Durkheim obviously felt that the attitude which, a priori, might be considered to have the greatest impact is that concerning suicide itself. Denying the importance of different attitudes, he (157) noted that both Protestantism and Catholicism "prohibit suicide with equal emphasis." Hence, he concluded, their differential impact on suicide rates results from another characteristic distinguishing them, namely, differing levels of social integration. Later, clinching the argument, he (170) stated that "the religion with least inclination to suicide, Judaism, is the very one not formally proscribing it." Durkheim ruled out the content of religious beliefs generally. "The beneficent influence of religion is therefore not due to the special nature of religious conceptions." In further rejecting such differences as crucial, he once again identified integration as decisive. "The details of dogmas and rites are secondary. The essential thing is that they be capable of supporting a sufficiently intense collective life" (170).

Durkheim's analysis did not end with religious society. To validate his hypothesis relating integration and suicide, he (152-208) attempted to demonstrate that it applies equally to religious, domestic, and political society. Having done so, he (208) concluded that the moderating influence of these societies cannot be due "to special characteristics of each but to a characteristic common to all." In contrast, Parsons focused upon Protestant-Catholic comparisons, thus completely ignoring the rationale underlying Durkheim's approach. Even if Parsons's account of Protestant-Catholic differences were acceptable, his identification of value content as the key factor in egoism is not. It would still remain to be shown that this same factor also explains differences in suicide rates in domestic and political society (not to mention the additional comparisons involving Jews and the nonreligious that Durkheim treated in connection with religious society). Notwithstanding his thesis concerning value content, Parsons did not try to demonstrate its importance to Durkheim's analysis of domestic society; rather, he (1949:331) noted that here "egoism seems to exist as a factor in suicide so far as people are freed from . . . group control." Devoting only one paragraph to domestic society, he then ignored political society completely.

Cult of man. Parsons (1949:333) also referred to "the more general phenomenon of which the Protestant version of religious freedom and responsibility is a special case," namely, "the view that the leading common moral sentiment of our society is an ethical valuation of individual personality as such." He (1949:333n) included only a single reference to Durkheim (1930; chapter I of Book III), and even that reference does not discuss the ideas in question. Parsons's discussion does bring to mind an interesting theoretical paradox. *Division* (1960: 172, 400, 407) and *Suicide* (240, 337, 364) referred to the cult or religion of: personality, personal or individual dignity, the individual, individual personality, or simply man (see also Durkheim 1973; Parsons 1975; Pope 1975b). Durkheim's general position was that the strength of the collective conscience and of individuality vary inversely. But what is the relationship when the collective conscience stresses the value, dignity, and importance of man generally and the individual in particular? The stronger such shared sentiments, the stronger the collective conscience; but also, presumably, the greater the development of individuality.

Durkheim (1960:171–72) first struggled with this dilemma in *Division*. He acknowledged that the cult of dignity, basically a shared belief in the value and dignity of man and his individuality, is growing stronger, not weaker. To accept this as an increasingly important source of social solidarity is inconsistent with his (1960: 173) conclusion that "all social links which result from likeness progressively slacken" as mechanical solidarity is increasingly undercut and replaced by organic solidarity during the course of social evolution. Durkheim (1960:171–72) resolved the dilemma by denying that this shared belief represents a bond of social solidarity. Since a basic premise of his theory asserts that shared beliefs constitute bonds of social solidarity, it is hard to avoid concluding that this represents an ad hoc assertion designed to resolve an otherwise intractable theoretical dilemma. At the same time, insofar as he (1960:172) explained the "completely exceptional place in the collective conscience" of this cult, he did so by appealing to the content of this shared belief, which turns the will toward individual rather than social ends. However, since Durkheim did not elsewhere treat the content of beliefs as relevant to their solidarity-producing qualities, this appeal must, as before, be judged to be ad hoc.

In *Suicide* Durkheim continued to struggle with the problems posed by the cult of man. In particular, he evidenced uncertainty as to whether the cult of man leads to egoistic suicide through its stress on individualism. At one point he (336) denied that the cult is associated with egoistic suicide, thus reasserting his premise that shared sentiments constitute a fundamental bond of solidarity. Of course, this disagrees with his earlier formulation in *Division* (according to which the cult of man does *not* represent a social bond). Elsewhere in *Suicide* he (363-64) came to a different conclusion, more in keeping with the passage from *Division* quoted above. As in *Division* (but contrary to his own formulation earlier in *Suicide*), Durkheim held that a shared sentiment, presumably because its content stresses the value and dignity of the individual, does not represent a social bond but, on the contrary, encourages individualism and egoistic suicide.

The underlying theoretical paradox takes somewhat different forms in its different contexts. In *Division* the question is whether an increasingly important component of the collective conscience can be seen as an increasingly important element of solidarity in modern, organic society. In *Suicide* the problem is whether a shared belief which emphasizes the importance of the individual leads to individuality and egoistic suicide. The underlying dilemma, however, is the same in both cases: Does a shared belief that stresses the value of the individual strenghthen social solidarity (as do other shared beliefs), or does it, because of its emphasis on the individual, actually weaken social solidarity?

Granting the existence of the dilemma and recognizing that at one point in *Suicide* Durkheim denied that a shared sentiment represents a social bond (thereby implicitly acknowledging the importance of value content), one must also acknowledge that this statement appears late in his book, long after his primary development of the contrast between egoism and anomie. Furthermore, the point is unrelated to any of the distinctions he drew between integration and regulation, and is never directly employed to explain variation in social suicide rates. Clearly this reference cannot be read back into Durkheim's systematic contrasts between more and less integrated groups in religious, domestic, and political societies; it is thus an unconvincing foundation upon which to reinterpret integration in terms of value content. Indeed, overall Parsons's attempt to distinguish between regulation and integration is based on such an array of pervasive misrepresentations that it may be unhesitatingly rejected.

To summarize, several attempts to distinguish between integration and regulation have been considered. Taken individually, none are successful. Taken collectively, they show widely varying distinctions, none of which are compatible with those originally proposed by Durkheim himself. The numerous failures and their mutual incompatibility suggest that, whatever the distinctions, they are sufficiently obscure as to be nonexistent.

INTEGRATION AND REGULATION: AN IDENTITY
Similarity of Empirical Examples

The empirical phenomena analyzed by Durkheim as he developed the theory of egoism closely parallel, and sometimes overlap, those analyzed in connection with the theory of anomie. The first chapter on egoism (152–70) focused on Protestant-Catholic-Jewish comparisons. Protestantism is more representative of the weakened state of social institutions in modern society, while Catholicism and especially Judaism retain more of the vigor that characterized earlier religions. There is a marked similarity between this analysis and that of chronic economic anomie (254–58), in which the agricultural context is seen as representing the vigor of the earlier economic social order, in contrast with "industrial and commercial functions" (257) that are all too characteristic of the weakened condition of social institutions in modern society. In terms of Durkheim's evolutionary perspectives, the two non-Protestant religions and agriculture represent earlier stages in the development of religious and economic institutions, respectively, in contrast with Protestantism and industrial and commercial functions. The salient consideration is that both of the latter represent states characterized by the relative erosion of institutional vigor. Seen in this context, there is no necessary reason why they should originally have been subsumed under different theoretical concepts.

In his analysis of domestic society, having once made the analytic distinction between marital and familial society, Durkheim (198) stated his intent to explain familial suicide rates using the theory of egoism, while reserving marital society for the theory of anomie, which had been coupled with an assumption regarding the different needs for social control of men versus women (an assumption foreign to the theory of egoism). To this degree, then, there is a difference in the basic assumptions of the two theories. However, this assumption remains foreign to the main thrust of Durkheim's overall theory; its introduction appears to have been necessitated by the very same factor that first caused him to refer data on marital society to the theory of anomie, namely, negative evidence on the suicide rates of married women, particularly those without children. In his treatment of domestic anomie, Durkheim (266) quite explicitly employed his *empirical* results to ground his argument that the theory of anomie applies to marital but not familial society; he failed, however, to provide any analytic reasons for not applying the theory of egoism to marital society, and the theory of anomie to familial society. Hence, the lack of complete overlap between the empirical configurations designated anomic and those designated egoistic is ultimately traceable to the results shown by the data rather than to any analytic distinctions between integration and regulation.

Durkheim originally explained the suicide rates of widows using the theory of egoism. Later, in the chapter on anomie, he (259) referred to this earlier explanation: "The suicides occurring at the crisis of widowhood, of which we have already spoken, are really due to domestic anomy resulting from the death of husband or wife." This willingness to explain a configuration in terms of egoism, only to claim subsequently that it is really due to anomie, further undermines any sense of a distinction between egoism and anomie.

There are two further instances in which Durkheim first examined a social condition in connection with domestic egoism but later decided that it would be more properly analyzed in terms of strength of regulation. Very young husbands and childless married women were first considered in the analysis of egoistic suicide, thus suggesting the relevance of this theory; indeed, at no point did Durkheim make any suggestion to the contrary. The difficulty with these two social conditions is that their suicide rates run counter to theoretical expectations. Durkheim's search for a way to eliminate the inconsistency between his theory and the data is therefore understandable. Long after his initial discussion (in the chapter on egoism), such an opportunity presented itself (at the very end of the chapter on anomie), as he sought examples of fatalistic suicide. By identifying these cases as examples of fatalism, he transformed them from examples counter to his theoretical expectations (concerning egoistic suicide rates) into examples that were congruent with theoretical expectations concerning fatalistic rates. This shift clearly suggests that the examples' eventual placement was dictated more by considerations of fit between theory and data than by virtue of any conceptual distinction between egoism and anomie. Furthermore, such shifting is possible only because of the conceptual overlap between integration and regulation. Finally, Durkheim's discussion of egoism and political crisis (see below) parallels his discussion of acute anomie and economic crisis.

In short, Durkheim's empirical examples of egoism and anomie are parallel when they are not identical. These parallel, identical, or shifting examples need not necessarily pose a problem. Even though they identify an overlap, this does not preclude the possibility that other examples could identify some divergence. When the conceptual difference has not been clearly identified, however, a treatment like this one reinforces the assumption that the major variables in question—in this instance integration and regulation—lack a viable theoretical distinction.

Failure to Control Independent Variables

In order to examine the relationship between either major independent variable and suicide, it is necessary to control for the other. Durkheim, of course, pioneered both in developing the logic underlying controls and in using them in empirical research. Clearly, then, for him use of controls was far from automatic. Nonetheless, as his analysis of religious (152-70, especially 152-56) and familial societies (171-202, especially 171-75) forcefully demonstrates, he understood the necessity of attempting to neutralize the effects of contaminating influences on the relationship between independent and dependent variables. It is curious, then, that he never controlled for either integration or regulation in determining the relationship between one of them and suicide rates. Occasionally he (243-45) referred to the influence of integration on rates being explained in terms of anomie, but such references stop short of a systematic attempt at control and seem to be primarily aimed at explaining why the figures do not conform more precisely to expectations.

If it could be assumed that his two independent variables fluctuate independently of each other, the failure to control might not be so serious. However, Durkheim was fully aware that they show a pronounced tendency to vary proportionately. Thus his failure to exercise controls becomes even more noticeable; but it is now impossible to determine the cause of this failure. Perhaps he never consciously realized the necessity of exercising these controls. Without denying this possibility, another may be suggested: Durkheim found it impossible to apply controls to one variable while examining the relationship between the other and suicide. For instance, how would one exercise a control for regulation when examining the relationship between religious affiliation and suicide? In assessing the relationship between integration and suicide, is it possible to compare Catholics and Protestants at identical levels of regulation? Do integration and regulation vary independently enough that a control is possible? And what indicators could be employed?

The social scientist wishing to apply Durkheim's theory confronts a dilemma. If there is a difference between integration and regulation, controls are necessary, and these require empirical indicators. However, those employed in *Suicide* vary proportionately with both independent variables, and to date no more satisfactory ones have been developed. Until they are, it is impossible to operationalize the integration-regulation distinction, which is thereby eliminated in empirical applications of Durkheim's theory.

Durkheim's Identification of Egoism with Anomie

In light of the preceding, it is not surprising that Durkheim sometimes called egoism and anomie—and, by implication, integration and regulation—the same thing. Noting their "peculiar affinity," he (288) observed that egoism and anomie "are usually merely two different aspects of one social state." Again, he (382) referred to the "identical cause" producing them. His typology of suicide is etiological; the different types are named after the social conditions giving rise to them. If egoism and anomie have the same cause, if they are aspects of the same social state, then by definition they are identical. Consistent with the theme that they are caused by the same social state, Durkheim (323) referred to "the hypercivilization which breeds the anomic tendency and the egoistic tendency." Following through, he (382) indicated that the remedy is "the same," namely, the establishment of occupational groups. *Suicide* (288) even indicates *why* the egoist is likely to be anomic and vice versa: "It is, indeed, almost inevitable that the egoist should have some tendency to non-regulation; for, since he is detached from society, it has not sufficient hold upon him to regulate him. . . . Inversely, an unregulated temperament does not lack a spark of egoism; for if one were highly socialized one would not rebel at every social restraint." Produced by the same cause, aspects of one social state, displaying a "peculiar affinity for one another," related so that the egoist is anomic and vice versa, subject to the same sociological remedy, altogether *Suicide* makes a strong case for the identity of egoism and anomie. Indeed, pitted against Durkheim's explicit attempts to distinguish between them, *Suicide* is far more precise about the sociological identity of egoism and anomie than about their difference. Durkheim's independent variable, then, may be called integration, regulation, integration-regulation, or (to use a phrase capturing the essence of Durkheim's meaning) group control over the individual.

One Cause of Suicide?

In the most theoretically "radical" (Martin 1968:79) interpretation of *Suicide*, Johnson (1965) argued that Durkheim's theory is best formulated so as to postulate but one cause of suicide, a reduction effected in two steps. He (1965:879–81) argued first that altruism and fatalism do not belong in the theory; next (1965:882–86), that egoism and anomie (and, hence, integration and regulation) are identical.[2] The theory is thereby left with but one cause of suicide, which may be identified as egoism-anomie. Johnson (1965:886) stated his final reformulation as: "The *more* integrated (regulated) a society, group, or social condition is, the *lower* its suicide rate." The net result of this reformulation is to leave the theory as Durkheim (209) himself stated it in concluding the second of his two chapters on egoism: "Suicide varies inversely with the degree of integration of the social groups of which the individual forms a part." I accept Johnson's equation of integration with regulation but reject the rationale underlying the elimination of altruism (and fatalism).[3]

Briefly, Johnson (1965:880) eliminated altruism because, except in the instance of the modern army, the necessary data were not available to Durkheim. Consequently, according to Durkheim's own standards, "he *cannot legitimately study*" (Johnson 1965:879; emphasis added) altruistic groups. Durkheim's own resolution of the problem—theorizing even in the face of questionable data—is preferable to Johnson's. Indeed, Johnson's principle of denying theoretical license when data are unavailable has never been part of good social science research (fortunately, as its application would deprive any science of numerous theoretical advances). Even if it were, Johnson has, in effect, proposed two reformulations: a one-cause (egoism-anomie) formulation appropriate before the availability of data on altruism, and a two-cause (egoism-anomie and altruism) formulation thereafter. To the degree that data on suicide in primitive society are now available, Johnson's rationale for eliminating altruism is itself eliminated. He would have done better to employ theoretical rather than empirical grounds in dismissing altruism, for once the validity of empirical evidence is considered relevant, it becomes mandatory to assess it systematically. Otherwise, judgments on when to employ data as a relevant criterion appear arbitrary, and assertions about the quality of the data will be unfounded at best, erroneous at worst.

Problems of just this kind emerge in Johnson's treatment. Although he (1965:886) asserted that "once altruism and fatalism are eliminated, the single case in *Suicide* that clearly contradicts the theory is the army," the relationship between theory and data proves otherwise. Contrary to Johnson, Durkheim's examples of egoism and anomie do not support the theory (see Part II below). Johnson's one-cause reformulation eliminates Durkheim's hypothesis of a positive relationship between altruism and suicide that—at least in the instance of primitive society—is by virtue of the very inadequacy of the data *not* subjected to empirical test. Ironically, he at the same time accepts Durkheim's hypothesis of an inverse relationship between suicide and egoism, a hypothesis not sustained by the data in *Suicide*.

Durkheim's purpose was to validate a sociological theory empirically, thereby demonstrating its superiority to competing explanations. Because explanation was so important to him, it is difficult to understand his theoretical structure apart from the data it was designed to explain. One consequence of Johnson's failure to assess the theory-data relationship in *Suicide* is that he left the central question unanswered: Why, if they were identical, should Durkheim have introduced two variables and insisted upon their difference? Until this question is answered, one is left with the image of Durkheim as a careless or confused theorist.

Despite the passage of more than a decade, no published interpretations accept the "one-cause" formulation. Many commentaries (LaCapra 1972; Poggi 1972; Wallwork 1972; Nisbet 1974) have ignored Johnson, while others (Giddens 1971b:85; Lukes 1972:213) have only briefly noted one or another aspect of his arguments and then rejected it. This situation is unfortunate because Johnson's equation of egoism and anomie was an important step in the right direction.

Egoism and Anomie: Their Links to Suicide

A final consideration in arguing for the similarity of integration and regulation concerns the links that exist between each and suicide. Durkheim, of course, linked weakened integration to lack of meaning in life (208–16) and weakened regulation to a means-needs (or means-goals) imbalance (245–54, 270–76). The question is whether these links cannot be interpreted in terms of each other. At several points Durkheim (e.g., 248, 256, 287) indicated that the disjunction accompanying anomie leads to meaninglessness. At other points he (211–14) asserted that the loss of meaning caused by egoism leaves the need to find such meaning unfulfilled. Furthermore, the particular links given in *Suicide* appear arbitrary in that the means-needs disjunction could as readily be linked to integration and loss of meaning to regulation. Better yet, both integration and regulation may be linked either to loss of meaning or to a means-needs disequilibrium. Focusing on the links not stated in *Suicide* (see diagonal arrows in fig. 4.2) reveals that weakened regulation increasingly frees the individual from the social control of

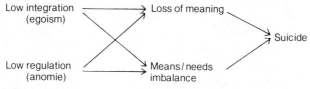

Fig. 4.2. Links: Egoism, anomie, and suicide

the group. Consequently, he acts more in terms of individual interests and less in terms of collective necessities—behavior that Durkheim identified as causing loss of meaning. On the other hand, weakened integration means that the individual is no longer so closely bound to the group, which can no longer exercise restraint on his passions. Consequently, expanding needs create a means-needs disequilibrium.

The unsuccessful nature of existing attempts to distinguish between egoism and anomie, Durkheim's own failure in this regard (especially in contrast with the many indications in *Suicide* that anomie and egoism are essentially the same), the similarity of Durkheim's empirical examples, his failure to control for either in analyzing the relationship between the other and suicide, and the possibility of coupling the links between suicide and either major independent variable with those of the other strongly argue for the essential similarity of integration and regulation. Of course, demonstrating the overlap between integration and regulation does not necessarily rule out the possibility that they are in some measure distinct. However, to be viable, any identification of a distinction between the two must be accompanied by a demonstration that the distinction is comparable in theoretical importance to their overlap, which lies at the very core of Durkheim's theory.

IMPLICATIONS OF IDENTIFYING INTEGRATION WITH REGULATION

Identifying integration with regulation raises several questions. Why did Durkheim use two variables if they prove the same? What is the function of the theory of regulation? Would his theory of suicide be unchanged if the theory of regulation were eliminated? I argue that insofar as the two theories are not interchangeable, that of regulation explains both exceptions to the theory of integration and empirical outcomes opposite to those predicted by that theory. To sustain this interpretation, I shall consider *Suicide's* analysis of male-female differences, single-widowed comparisons, and political and economic crises.

The theory of integration is here considered the basic statement. This procedure is partly a matter of convenience, but it is well justified: this theory is presented first; *Suicide* devotes two chapters to egoism but only one to anomie; altruism takes up an entire chapter, whereas fatalism seems largely an afterthought.

Male-Female Differences

Durkheim felt that the biological and the social define a continuum. Each is a determinant of human behavior; the more operative one is, the less the other. Man is double—social man superimposing himself upon biological man (213; Durkheim 1964). The more man remains a biological creature, the more his needs are determined and fulfilled by his biological nature; the more social, the more developed are his social needs, which can only be fulfilled or restrained by his social existence.

One of Durkheim's most important applications of this perspective occurs in his discussion of the differences between the sexes. He held that women's different biological nature causes them to participate in social life less than men.[4] Women are therefore characterized by less sociability, less complete socialization, less development of mental and intellectual life, and less development of the relatively more complex needs that can only be fulfilled by collective life, particularly in its more complex forms (215–16, 272, 299, 385–86).

Although many of these themes are first mentioned in the second of his two chapters on egoistic suicide, Durkheim treated his views on male-female differences as a part of the theory of anomie. Being "to a far greater extent the product of nature," woman finds her passions and appetites both less fully developed (384-85) and more "naturally" (272) controlled. Durkheim (272) assumed that social regulation, chafing against passions and appetites, causes irritation. This irritation must be weighed against the gain derived. Women, with passions naturally limited, gain less from social regulation and thus experience a given level of regulation as, on balance, less rewarding than do men. Related to social regulation in marriage, "the interests of husband and wife ... are ... opposed," one needing discipline and the other, liberty (384).

Durkheim predicted that the larger the family, the lower the suicide rates. Married persons without children and widowed persons are hypothesized as having lower suicide rates than never-married persons. Childless wives and childless widows constitute striking exceptions to this theory, displaying higher suicide rates than single women. Acknowledging that "in itself conjugal society is harmful to the woman and aggravates her tendency to suicide," Durkheim (189) attributed the "evil effects of marriage" to the adverse impact of social regulation experienced by women in marriage. Never denying that the data contradict his theory of egoism, he indicated his intent to explain them using the theory of anomie.

Given the similarity of the two theoretical statements, though, it is not surprising that referral to the theory of anomie does not resolve the problem. Durkheim's basic hypothesis relating regulation and suicide in modern society held that the two vary inversely. Compared with being single, the married state represents a net increment in social regulation. It is at this point that his views on women become crucial. Because they experience increments in regulation as harmful, childless married women and childless widows have higher suicide rates than single women. Moreover, his explanation has additional implications, which *Suicide* tests against the data. Using divorce as the indicator of social regulation in marriage (the higher the rate, the weaker the regulation), Durkheim argued that, relative to men, women should benefit from a weakening of social regulation in marriage. Indeed, this proved to be the case: *"From the standpoint of suicide, marriage is more favorable to the wife the more widely practiced divorce is; and vice versa"* (269). Empirically, he was interested in how the suicide rate of married men relative to that of single men changes when *compared* with that of married women relative to single women. He found that the situation of married women improves as divorce rates increase, whereas that of married men improves as rates decrease. Women suffer from an increase in social regulation whereas men benefit; likewise, men suffer from a decrease whereas women benefit. On the one hand, data in the chapter on anomie help Durkheim to sustain his argument about the different needs for social regulation of men versus women; on the other, the argument helps explain the data.

Though undeniably useful, then, the argument remains problematic. *Suicide* (185) makes a key distinction between marital (conjugal) and familial society, the former referring to husband and wife or widowed persons without children, the latter to one or two parents with children. Given Durkheim's emphasis on the great difference in their biological-social balance, would not husband and wife have different, even opposed, interests in familial society? If women suffer from greater social restraint, why shouldn't they suffer from such restraint regardless of whether its locus is marriage or the family? Durkheim (269) briefly suggested that as mother and father, they have common interests vis-à-vis the children. But such common interests in no way negate the opposed interests resulting from their different needs for social regulation. Of course, it would be inconvenient for him to argue that men and women have different interests in the family; data in his chapter on egoism show that both are identically affected by familial society (suicide rates decreasing as levels of integration increase). In short, once having developed his argument about male-female differences—and thinking of it in the context of the theory of anomie—Durkheim did not then return to seek out its implications for the theory of egoism. Nor, given the empirical results on family society, is there an empirically derived need to do so. But this leaves him in the incongruous position of having stressed male-female differences in connection with the theory of anomie, while having denied their import for that of egoism. It is, of course, the overlap between integration and regulation that so forcefully calls Durkheim's procedure into question. When these two variables are seen to overlap to the point of merging, the thesis that men and women react similarly to changing levels of integration, but differently to changing levels of regulation, loses all plausibility.

Society, or more specifically, the currents of egoism, anomie, or altruism running through it, causes suicide (299–300). Less extensively exposed to these causes because of their lesser involvement in collective life, women display lower suicide rates than do men (299).

Yet Durkheim also held that in modern, egoistic-anomic society, suicide and integration-regulation vary inversely. Rather than arguing (consistent with the theory of egoism-anomie) that women should have higher suicide rates, Durkheim held just the opposite.

Juxtaposed to his social realism, Durkheim's thesis concerning male-female differences raises two additional difficulties. He emphatically rejected reductionist appeals, biological or otherwise, in explaining suicide. Consistent with this position, he (99, 341) denied that women's lower suicide rates may be attributed to biological differences. Yet the theory of social regulation depends on an appeal to the biological differences between men and women.

Basic to Durkheim is the assumption that society constitutes a sui generis reality. Since married men's suicide rates vary inversely, and married women's proportionately, with regulation, men are anomic and women fatalistic. Though together constituting the same society, the husband is held to be anomic; the wife, fatalistic. Thus a given social reality is both anomic and fatalistic. But this formulation creates a theoretical impasse, because anomie is weak, and fatalism strong, regulation. It is possible to approach this contradiction by appealing to the different biological-social balance in the two sexes. However, such an approach amounts to an admission that, in order to characterize a given social condition, it is necessary to consider it not only as a sui generis reality but also in terms of how a nonsocial factor (sex) influences the way in which individuals experience that social condition. In light of all its problematic aspects, it seems fair to conclude that, though constructed with characteristic ingenuity and skillfully employed, Durkheim's doctrine regarding the differential biological-social balance in the two sexes has all the earmarks of an ad hoc, post-factum doctrine developed to explain theoretically embarrassing empirical configurations.

Single-Widowed Comparisons

The theory of egoism explains suicide rates of married persons as a function of the amount of interaction experienced in the familial context. Having experienced (during marriage) higher levels of such interaction than single persons, widows are hypothesized (193, 263) to have lower suicide rates than single persons because the effects of marriage are felt by the widowed beyond the termination of the marriage itself. However, the theory of acute anomie holds that the shock of widowhood and the change in circumstances elevate suicide rates; unfortunately, though, it does not specify by how much the rates rise. Clearly, rates for the widowed should exceed those for the still married, but whether they should also exceed those for single persons is unclear. Thus, although it does not necessarily lead to such a prediction, the theory of acute anomie could be employed to explain data showing that suicide rates for the widowed exceed those for the single, whereas the theory of egoism could explain data showing that single persons have the higher rates. Once again, after the fact, Durkheim's theory can explain either of two opposite outcomes.

Political and Economic Crisis

There is a third point at which Durkheim's theory predicts different outcomes: the theory of egoism explains a decrease in suicide during periods of political crisis; anomie, an increase during periods of economic crisis. However, unlike the predictions derived from applying Durkheim's theoretical perspectives to domestic society, both theories make the same predictions when applied to the same phenomenon.

To explain falling suicide rates during times of political crisis, *Suicide* (208) argues that collective sentiments are strengthened. Since collective sentiments are the major source of control over individual needs, strengthening such sentiments reduces the means-needs disequilibrium and thus lowers suicide rates. That is, the theory of anomie explains the decrease in suicide rates during times of political upheaval just as well as does that of egoism. *Suicide* (252–53) also argues that during periods of abrupt economic change (whether depression or prosperity), "something like a declassification occurs" in which people become partially freed from collective authority because rules governing their previous situation are no longer applicable and new ones "cannot be immediately improvised." Extending this argument in a way Durkheim did not, I argue that in such situations, people increasingly act more in terms of their own individual interests and less in terms of social dictates. As a consequence, life begins to lose meaning; this situation, in turn, causes higher suicide rates. The specific links between lowered levels of social control and suicide are different in the two theories, as always, yet the theory of egoism explains higher suicide rates during times of economic crisis just as well as does that of anomie.

Given that either theory can be used in conjunction with either type of crisis and that both predict an inverse relationship between level of social control and suicide, how convincing are the links between political crisis and higher levels of social control and between economic crisis and lower levels of social control? During times of prosperity, greater resources could reduce the means-needs disequilibrium, and individuals might find additional meaning in life as these resources are employed to realize their goals. Depressions could give individuals the feeling of "all being in the same boat," and thus they might concentrate "activity toward a single end" (208), namely, ending the depression. *Suicide* (208) acknowledges the existence of crisis during times of great political upheavals. Emphasizing the crisis, an *increase* in suicide would be predicted. Durkheim (203) himself noted "a sudden rush of suicides . . . on the eve of the [French] Revolution."

Commenting on his empirical findings for political society, Durkheim (208) observed "that great social disturbances and great popular wars rouse collective sentiments, stimulate partisan spirit and patriotism, political and national faith, alike, and concentrating activity toward a single end, . . . cause a stronger integration of society." Much of this explanation seems applicable to only one of his empirical examples, great national wars. However, other types of war create a different type of crisis; e.g., the war in Vietnam produced discord in the United States. In stimulating "partisan spirit," a divisive election concentrates activity toward mutually exclusive ends, each party working for the election of its own candidates. While this heightens levels of intraparty integration, it creates conflict at the interparty level. As the Watergate scandal illustrated, during the crisis of an election campaign (or, to cite another of *Suicide*'s examples, during a coup d'etat), it may be that "the limits are unknown between the possible and the impossible, what is just and what is unjust, legitimate claims and hopes and those which are immoderate," which is a state of anomie (253).

Durkheim's procedure of analyzing political crises in terms of egoism, and economic crises in terms of anomie, obscures important facets of his analysis. Since the suicide rates reported in *Suicide* can be explained equally well by either theory, the theory of anomie fails to add explanatory power to that of egoism. In addition, Durkheim's theory can be used to explain either an increase *or* a decrease in suicide. Emphasizing the strengthening of collective sentiments, a decrease is predicted; emphasizing the weakening of collective moral authority, an increase. Under these conditions, deciding which to emphasize is a crucial matter. In explaining different phenomena with different parts of his theory, Durkheim effectively created a link in the reader's mind between political upheaval, higher levels of social control, lower levels of egoism, and lower suicide rates, on the one hand; and economic crisis, lower levels of social control, higher levels of anomie, and higher suicide rates, on the other. But despite the plausibility of his arguments, the links between higher levels of social control and political crisis versus lower levels and economic crisis are more equivocal than acknowledged. To the extent that this is the case, a latent function of the theory of anomie is to provide the theoretical wherewithal to explain outcomes opposite to those predicted employing the theory of egoism.

Falsifiability and the Theory of Anomie

Popper (1961:40-42, 78-92) emphasized that a scientist's willingness to accept a theory increases in proportion to its success in resisting falsification. Durkheim found that childless wives and childless widows have higher suicide rates than single women, and he interpreted this finding as sustaining the theory of domestic anomie. However, the only reason the data were referred to that theory in the first place was that they contradicted the theory of egoism; had single women displayed the higher suicide rates, this finding would surely have been interpreted as sustaining the theory of egoism. Although Durkheim did not apply it to familial society, the theory of anomie can be employed to predict an inverse relationship between levels of regulation and suicide for women in familial society. Systematic application of Durkheim's perspectives makes it possible to explain either *a positive or a negative* relationship between levels of social control and suicide for women in *either* marital or familial society. His perspectives also generate opposite predictions with respect to single-widowed comparisons. Finally, his theory can be used to explain either rising or falling suicide rates during crises.

Both the theory of anomie and that of egoism predict an inverse relationship between level of social control and suicide. Though the links between each and suicide differ, it is possible to interpret their respective links in terms of each other. As employed in *Suicide,* the two theories differ at more than one point. The theory of anomie is supplemented by a problematic doctrine concerning women as well as by a chronic-acute distinction, both absent from the theory of egoism. The two theories are linked to different empirical configurations. Most important, (1) Durkheim linked the theory of egoism to political, and that of anomie to economic, crisis; and (2) the theory of egoism is linked to familial, and that of anomie to marital, society. However, since the theory of social regulation does not differ from that of social integration in basic sociological content and since, therefore, the theory of anomie does not add to the explanatory power of the theory of egoism, the real function of the theory of anomie is to protect the overall theoretical statement from falsification.

5   DURKHEIM'S THEORY
RESTATED

If the distinction between integration and regulation is eliminated, the relationship between varying levels of integration-regulation and suicide may be represented as a V- or U-shaped continuum (fig. 5.1). Egoism-anomie is the left-hand portion of the continuum, on which integration-regulation and suicide are inversely

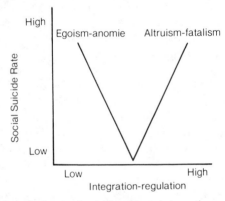

Fig. 5.1. Durkheim's theory of suicide with no integration-regulation distinction.

related; altruism-fatalism (or simply altruism) is the right-hand portion, on which the relationship is proportional.

One difference in *Suicide*'s development of the theories of integration and regulation is Durkheim's use of several variables to explain varying levels of integration. In contrast, he assumed varying levels of regulation (chronic anomie), or he simply identified the conditions under which society's ability to control the individual decreased (acute anomie) but treated the changes themselves as given (he did not explain them in terms of variation in his independent variables). Consequently, in seeking the starting points of his causal chain, my obvious choice is to focus primarily on the theory of integration. Even here, matters are not as clear as they might be, because Durkheim often identified indicators of varying levels of integration without saying much about causes. Insofar as they are mentioned, sundry causes are sometimes identified in the analysis of different types of society (e.g., political, familial, and religious), while still others are identified in the more general accounts of the development of modern society.

Rate of interaction occupies a central place in Durkheim's causal chain. This factor is given implicit emphasis throughout *Suicide;* the emphasis becomes explicit in the analyses of familial society (198–202, especially 201–2) and (at one point) religious society (160). It is also evident in the analysis of altruistic society, which includes a reference (221) to *Division;* there, as throughout his works generally, rate of interaction is repeatedly treated as a key causal variable. This rate, in turn, is determined by the number of mutually accessible people in a given group or area which, in turn, is a function of society's morphological structure. The rate determines the strength of collective sentiments,[1] which determines the degree of integration-regulation (fig. 5.2, part A).

To turn this statement into a theory of suicide requires including links between the level of integration-regulation and social suicide rates. The stronger collective sentiments are, the higher the degree of restraint exercised by the group over individual needs and the more nearly means are proportional to needs (theory of anomie), or, alternatively, the greater the meaning in life (theory of egoism) and the lower the suicide rate. This, then, is Durkheim's theory of egoism-anomie as a theory of suicide (fig. 5.2, part B).

In contrast to this theory, which postulates an inverse correlation between level of social control and suicide, that of altruism postulates a positive relationship. Otherwise the variables and their mutual relations are the same, with one exception—the variable linking degree of social control to suicide. In the case of egoism-anomie, means-needs equilibrium and meaning in life can be seen as alternative links between level of social control and suicide, while in the case of altruism the former is ruled out. Clearly, the high level of social control in altruism insures the restrained individual passions and modest needs that preclude the development of a means-needs disequilibrium. Here it is a matter of the relative lack of meaning in continued physical existence per se, because meaning resides either in adhering to social dictates or in achieving union with some goal beyond this life (219–28). When "meaning in life" is defined as including these possibilities, it constitutes the link

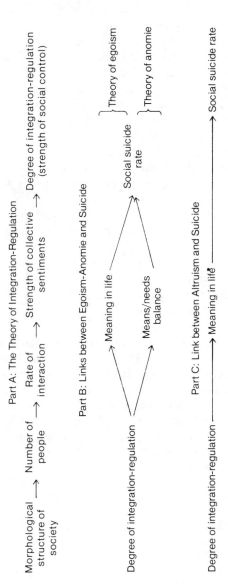

Fig. 5.2. Durkheim's theory of suicide. Combining parts A and B gives the theory of egoism-anomie as a theory of suicide; combining parts A and C gives the theory of altruism as a theory of suicide.

between degree of social control and the social suicide rate. Through degree of social control, the relationships between variables are the same as for the theory of egoism-anomie.

The final relationships are as follows: the higher the degree of social control, the less meaning is attached to continued life per se, and the higher the social suicide rate. Alternatively, the lower the degree of social control, the more meaning is attached to continued life per se, the less willing the individual is to part with it, and the lower the social suicide rate (fig. 5.2, part C).

The complete theory of suicide is produced by joining the theory of egoism-anomie with that of altruism:

(1) The morphological structure of society determines

(2) number of people in a given group or area, which determines

(3) rate of social interaction, which determines

(4) strength of collective sentiments, which determines

(5) level of integration-regulation (social control), which determines

(6) means-needs proportionality (meaning in life) ⎫
    (theory of egoism-anomie),   ⎬ which determines
    meaning attached to continued existence ⎭ the
    (theory of altruism),

(7) social suicide rate.

The theories of egoism-anomie and altruism are identical except for two importance differences. To link social control and suicide (step 6), the former employs means-needs proportionality or meaning in life; the latter, meaning attached to continued physical existence. Most important, the former postulates an inverse, and the latter a positive, relationship between social control and suicide. These differences notwithstanding, there is clearly a unified theoretical structure underlying the various elements that together constitute Durkheim's theory of suicide.

II THE RELATIONSHIP BETWEEN THEORY AND DATA

6   EGOISTIC SUICIDE

Part II assesses the degree to which Durkheim's theory is sustained by the data in *Suicide*. I have made every reasonable attempt to use analytic techniques similar to, if not identical with, those in *Suicide*. One exception: the ecological fallacy has been defined as the assumption "that associations computed from group means or group proportions are valid estimates of the associations that would be obtained from individual data" (Selvin 1965:125; see also 125–29 for discussion of *Suicide* and the ecological fallacy). Although instances of this fallacy are noted below, it has become commonly known throughout sociology only since Robinson (1950), and the reader should not infer that Durkheim is to be faulted for not having recognized it. To check both Durkheim's assessments and those developed below, I use the product moment correlation coefficient (r). The purpose of this analysis is to determine what conclusions Durkheim could have sustained with a systematic application of his own methods.

If we omit his brief reference (276n) to fatalism, Durkheim (276, 299–300, 321) identified egoism, altruism, and anomie as the causes of suicide. In analyzing egoistic suicide, he treated religious society, familial society, and political society in successive attempts to prove that suicide and integration vary inversely.

RELIGIOUS SOCIETY

Arguing that Protestants are less integrated than Catholics, who, in turn, are less integrated than Jews, Durkheim tried to show that their social suicide rates vary accordingly.

Protestant-Catholic Comparisons

Durkheim (152) began by listing the suicide rates (per million) for Protestant states as 190, mixed states, 96, Catholic states, 58, and Greek-Catholic states, 40. These figures (hereafter identified as the Durkheim-Morselli averages) were described (152) only as "averages compiled by Morselli." Since Morselli's original table (IV, 1882:30)[1] does not show religious affiliation, it is impossible to determine how Durkheim classified the countries listed therein. Morselli (1882:128) defined countries as "Protestant" or "Catholic" if 90 percent or more of their populations fell into one or the other category; all others were defined as "mixed religious." Applying this definition to the information in Morselli's tables, I derived table 6.1; in it

TABLE 6.1 MORSELLI'S SUICIDE RATES (PER MILLION) BY RELIGION AND STATE

Country	Suicide Rate
Protestant	
England-Wales[a]	66
Norway	75
Sweden	81
Mecklenburg	167
Schleswig-Holstein	240
Denmark	258
Hamburg	301
Kingdom of Saxony	311
Average	187.4
Catholic	
Spain	17
Kingdom of Italy	37
Belgium	69
France	150
Bohemia	160
Average	86.6

SOURCE: Morselli (1882:30).

[a]Percentage Protestant for England taken from Morselli (1882: 128-29).

the Protestant average of 187.4 is close to the 190 cited by Durkheim, but the Catholic average is half again as high (86.6, in contrast to 58).

These figures may be checked against the national rates given in *Suicide* (table 6.2). Though Durkheim often classified countries as either Protestant or Catholic, in most cases he failed to give figures on religious affiliation; furthermore, he never stated his guideline for classifying countries. Therefore, I constructed table 6.2 using (1) Morselli's 90 percent criterion and (2) data on religious affiliation from various sources (including Morselli). Half of all Protestant entries in table 6.1 (from Morselli) are in Germany, thereby raising an issue not explicitly addressed in *Suicide:* What

TABLE 6.2   DURKHEIM'S SUICIDE RATES (PER MILLION) BY RELIGION
AND COUNTRY

Country	Years	Suicide Rate
Protestant[a]		
Finland	n.d.	30.8
Scotland	1856–60	34
England	1874–78	69
Norway	1874–78	71
Sweden	1874–78	91
Denmark	1874–78	255
Saxony	1874–78	334
Average		126.4
Average excluding Saxony		91.8
Average excluding Saxony and Denmark		59.2
Catholic[a]		
Spain	n.d.	17
Italy	1874–78	38
Belgium	1874–78	78
Austria	1874–78	130
France	1874–78	160
Average		84.6

SOURCES: Dates and rates from <u>Suicide</u> (50, 74, 259, 351). Where
more than one rate was available, those closest to the period
1874–78 were chosen. Data on religious affiliation from Morselli
(1882:122, table XVII: 128–29) except for Scotland (Mulhall
1892:513) and Finland (Miesmaa 1952:24).

[a]Defined as "Protestant" or "Catholic" according to Morselli (see
discussion in text).

criteria determine which areas constitute separate instances? Durkheim compared nation-states. However, even as late as the mid-
nineteenth century, the area of Germany, while having the size and
homogeneity typically associated with a nation, was split into many
partly autonomous states. Even after unification in 1871, suicide
statistics continued to be compiled by individual states, thereby
encouraging treatment of each state as a separate instance.

It can be argued that lack of political unification is an insufficient
basis for counting the German states as separate instances. Treating
Germany as a single instance puts it into the mixed category: though
predominantly Protestant, it had a substantial Catholic minority (36
percent in 1871; computed from Mulhall 1892:446, 514). However,
excluding Germany (and therefore Saxony) has serious consequences for Durkheim's analysis. In that case (table 6.2), *five of six*

Protestant nations have rates less than half the 190 Durkheim-Morselli average for Protestant countries. Furthermore, removing the one non-German Protestant nation (Denmark) with an exceptionally high rate results in a Protestant average of 59.2—30 percent *lower* than the Catholic average of 84.6. For ten of eleven countries, then, *Protestant nations display a lower average suicide rate than do Catholic nations.*[2]

Accepting Morselli's averages, Durkheim never specified the countries he had in mind when referring to Protestant countries with high suicide rates. Prussia, Saxony, and Denmark are mentioned (152) but presumably do not exhaust the list. Furthermore, his reference undoubtedly changed, depending upon the context. Germany, though, was clearly his primary referent. Among its five "great states" (153), Bavaria was 28 percent Protestant; Baden, 34; Prussia, 66; Württemberg, 69; and Saxony, 98 (Morselli 1882: 128-29). The first four are not Protestant by Morselli's definition, but Saxony perfectly fits Durkheim's characterization of an advanced Protestant state with high suicide rates. In a sense, then, a single German state, populated by fewer than three million persons (Martin 1880:146), constituted the empirical basis on which Durkheim associated Protestantism with high suicide rates.

In addition, noting (367) that suicide has been called the ransom money of civilization, Durkheim repeatedly emphasized that suicide and civilization show an unfortunate tendency to develop together, thereby suggesting the need to control for the effect of civilization. Moving beyond the analysis in *Suicide* itself, I therefore used three controls: urbanization, railroad mileage, and labor force composition. *Suicide* (70, 75, 353) indicates that rates are higher for urban than for rural populations. Railroad mileage is employed as an indicator of economic development. Finally, in analyzing anomie, Durkheim (257) observed that the old regulatory forces are most powerful in agriculture. Labor force composition, then, functions as a control on anomie.

The control for urbanization divides countries into high and low categories according to the percentage of the total population living in cities of 100,000 or more (table 6.3). In urbanized countries the average Protestant suicide rate exceeds the Catholic; for the relatively rural, rates are nearly equal. With regard to the next indicator (miles of railroad per 1,000 square miles), Protestants display the higher suicide rates in both categories. For the final indicator, the high category indicates that a relatively large proportion of the labor force was not in agricultural occupations; the low indicates the reverse. For both high and low categories, Protestant suicide rates exceed Catholic rates, marginally in the high category, greatly in the low. Though differing only slightly in two instances (the low category on urbanization and the high on labor force composition), Protestant rates in all cases exceed the Catholic. However, a different pattern emerges in the averages weighted by population size. In the high category, Catholic countries have the higher average suicide rate; for the low, the Protestant average is higher.

This analysis has limitations. Using different indicators or different cutting points would produce different results. With so few countries in each group, a single extreme rate has a great impact upon the averages derived. Weighted averages mitigate this problem somewhat in the case of Protestant countries because both Saxony and Denmark are small. Finally, definitions and classifications used in compiling the data are not always the same from one country to another.

Weighted and unweighted averages display different patterns. The former produce results less favorable to Durkheim's hypothesis; for countries high on civilization, it is invariably the Catholic that have the higher average suicide rates. If the high and the low categories represent equally valid tests of the hypothesis that the social suicide rate is higher for Protestants than for Catholics, there can be no doubt that Durkheim's main interest centered on countries with highly developed civilizations, particularly France and Germany. He felt that these countries, being more advanced, indicated the direction of evolutionary development. The weighted-average pattern suggests that his concern regarding the relationship between Protestantism and suicide in relatively advanced countries is poorly founded empirically; even the higher, unweighted, average suicide rates for Protestants result from Saxony's inclusion. Excluding Saxony from unweighted Protestant-Catholic averages gives equal averages for urbanization. For the other two indicators, the Protestant average is either just over (railroads) or just under (labor force) *half* the corresponding Catholic average. Even here, too, Durkheim's case ultimately rests on the exceptionally high suicide rates of one Protestant area with less than three million persons.

Durkheim considered the possibility that the Protestant-Catholic difference in the Durkheim-Morselli averages might have resulted from influences other than religion; in effect, however, he (152) argued that the exercise of controls is relevant to determining only the *magnitude* of this difference, and not its *existence*. This

TABLE 6.3 AVERAGE NATIONAL PROTESTANT AND CATHOLIC SUICIDE RATES (PER MILLION) BY THREE INDICATORS FOR LEVEL OF CIVILIZATION

Country	Rate	High-Low Urb.	High-Low RR	High-Low LF	Urb. H	Urb. L	RR H	RR L	LF H	LF L
					Average Rates (weighted averages in parentheses)					
Protestant					*Protestant*					
Denmark	255	H	L	L	173.0	64.3	145.7	112.0	127.0	125.7
					(101)	(72)	(89)	(107)	(88)	(114)
England	69	H ·	H	H						
Finland	31	L	L	L						
Norway	71	L	L	H						
Saxony	334	H	H	H						
Scotland	34	H	H	H						
Sweden	91	L	L	L						
Catholic					*Catholic*					
Austria	130	L	L	L	119.0	61.7	92.0	73.5	119.0	61.7
					(149)	(63)	(106)	(81)	(149)	(63)
Belgium	78	H	H	H						
France	160	H	H	H						
Italy	38	L	H	L						
Spain	17	L	L	L						

SOURCES: Suicide rates from table 6.2. Most are for 1874-78. Data on Urb. (urbanization) taken from Banks (1971: 55-98) except: Finland (Keltie 1890:891); Saxony (Martin 1879:146); Scotland (Martin 1872:247, 249); and Austria (Keltie 1885:22, 25). Data on RR (railroad mileage) taken from Martin (1872:xxvii-xxviii) except: Finland (Keltie 1890:846, 886); and Saxony (Keltie 1890: 610, 614). Data on LF (labor force composition) taken from Clark (1940: 200-203) except: Denmark (Howard 1935:50); England (Booth 1886:324); Finland (Pipping and Barlund 1965:30); Saxony (Keltie 1886:116); Scotland (Booth 1886:337); Austria (Keltie 1885:462); Sweden (Keltie 1885:22, 24); and France (Tracy 1964:80).

NOTE: Categories defined as follows: Urb.: 7 percent or less of population in cities of 100,000 or more is low, over 7 percent is high; RR: 32 miles or less of railroad per 1,000 square miles is low, over 32 is high; LF: 50 percent or more of labor force in agriculture is low, less than 50 percent is high.

Dates for indicators are as follows: Urb.: all countries 1870 except Saxony, 1875; Austria, 1869; Finland, 1887; and Scotland, 1871. RR: all countries 1870 or 1871 except Austria, 1869; Finland, 1887 and 1888; and Saxony, 1889. LF: Austria, 1890; Belgium, Denmark, and Finland, 1880; England, France, Italy, and Scotland, 1881; Norway, 1891; Spain, 1887; Saxony, 1882; and Sweden, 1870.

The population figures used to compute weighted average suicide rates are for 1876. All figures are taken from Banks (1971:6-44) except: Austria (Martin 1880:20); England, Saxony, and Scotland (Keltie 1885:151-262); and Finland (Keltie 1890:891).

assumption would better have been demonstrated empirically since, having exercised no controls, he failed to rule out the possibility that the difference may indeed result from the influence of variables other than religion (e.g., level of civilization).

Durkheim presented several replications that had the effect of controlling for some of these variables. He (153) first analyzed inconclusive data for each of the five great German states. Then he analyzed data for the Prussian and the Bavarian provinces. Unfortunately, these analyses suffer from the ecological fallacy. This fallacy aside, though, they fail to show any exact relationship between Protestantism and suicide, and breakdowns finer than those used by Durkheim sustain further reservations about his conclusions. *Suicide* (157) lists the specific percentage Catholic for three Bavarian provinces. Coupling these with the rates in *Suicide* shows that the Upper Palatinate, with 92 percent Catholic, has a suicide rate (per million) of 64; Upper Bavaria, with 96, has 114; Lower Bavaria, with 99, has 19. These results make it impossible to grant Durkheim's assertion (153) that "if one compares the different provinces of Bavaria, suicides are found to be in direct proportion to the number of Protestants and in inverse proportion to that of Catholics."

Durkheim (154) next examined figures for Switzerland: given the presence of both French and German populations, "the influence of the confession is observable separately on each race." Although Durkheim's conclusion—that regardless of nationality, "Catholic cantons show four and five times fewer suicides than Protestant"— is overstated (the ratio in German cantons is 3.4:1), the data nevertheless support his hypothesis.

Table xviii (154), "Suicides in Different Countries per Million Persons of Each Confession," constitutes Durkheim's final direct attempt to ground his hypothesis empirically. Here he did not commit the ecological fallacy, and this is the only table that shows time trends. However, generalization is severely limited because the table pertains only to Germany and Austria. The Protestant-Catholic suicide ratios by region range from 3.2:1 to 1.2:1, a variation of which *Suicide* takes no note. These reservations aside, however, the table permits Catholic-Protestant comparisons for twelve areas (eleven German, plus Austria), and all comparisons support Durkheim's hypothesis.

Following this table, Durkheim (154, see also 73) noted that "everywhere without exception, Protestants show far more suicides than the followers of other confessions." Some of the figures in his table are from one of Morselli's (1882:122), which also includes the following figures for the years 1852-54 and 1858-59: for Galicia (Austria), the suicide rate (per million) for Catholics is 45, and for Protestants 16; for Military Frontiers (Austria), the parallel figures are 28 and 25; for Transylvania, 113 and 74. Without any indication that he had done so, Durkheim omitted these counter instances.

Following these analyses, Durkheim (156) noted that the minority status of Jews (everywhere) and Catholics (frequently) might explain their relatively low suicide rates. He cited data (for Prussia, Bavaria, and Austria) showing that as Catholics move from minority to majority status, the size of the Protestant-Catholic suicide ratio diminishes. Equally important, even when Catholics are a majority (as in both Bavaria and Austria), they still commit suicide less frequently than members of the Protestant minority. Data for three Bavarian provinces show that as the percentage Catholic per province goes from 92 percent (Upper Palatinate) to 99 percent (Lower Bavaria), the Protestant-Catholic suicide ratio actually increases. Though Durkheim's attempt to ground his case empirically was only a minimal effort, he nevertheless identified instances in which the Catholics' lower suicide rates cannot be attributed to their minority status.

The Durkheim-Morselli averages presented here are central to Durkheim's case because they alone permit a Protestant-Catholic comparison based on a large number of European countries. The logic of his analysis requires demonstrating that the hypothesized relationship is not eliminated when controls for nationality and region are exercised; hence, the foregoing demonstration—that Protestantism and suicide are *not* correlated for Europe generally—undercuts his presentation at its core. Furthermore, as noted, the additional tables presented in *Suicide* are quite limited, pertaining only to a particular cultural and geographical area (Germany, Austria and Switzerland). In addition, these areas are characterized by mixed religious affiliations. Since the relationship between religion and suicide may differ between mixed and nonmixed areas, results from such areas should not be generalized to Europe, nor do they negate the relationship revealed in figures for nonmixed areas.

By comparing "the two religions ... in the heart of a single society," Durkheim (153) controlled for nationality and region. However, he failed to control for other relevant variables. My exercise of controls for level of civilization (table 6.3) reduced the magnitude, and even reversed the direction, of Protestant-Catholic suicide differentials. Again, Durkheim's data suggest that suicide differentials are far smaller where Protestants and Catholics presumably live in close proximity to one another (Germany and Austria) than where they live in different areas (Switzerland). Finally, Durkheim never asserted that Catholic and Protestant residents of the same countries are alike in all relevant respects except religion. To suggest only one possibility, those familiar with Weber (1958:35) might suspect that Protestants are more involved than Catholics in modern business, particularly at its higher levels; Durkheim (257) himself suggested, in his well-known analysis of chronic economic anomie, that such involvement leads to higher suicide rates. On the basis of his analysis Durkheim (154) concluded that Protestants "show far more suicides than" Catholics. Reanalysis reveals, however, that his data are incapable of sustaining this generalization.

Jewish Suicide Rates

Basic data. Having concluded that Catholics have lower suicide rates than Protestants, Durkheim attempted to show that Jewish rates are lower still than the comparatively low Catholic rates. Table XVIII (154) contains the data for *Suicide*'s analysis of Jewish suicide rates. Durkheim (155) noted that "the aptitude of Jews for suicide is ... in a very general way ... lower than that of Catholics." If "occasionally however, the ... relation is reversed ... especially in recent times," Jews nonetheless "still very rarely greatly exceed the rate for Catholics." "Occasionally" and "greatly exceed" hardly describe the situation: Jewish rates exceed those for Catholics in six of twelve cases cited; in the most recent figures for each country (omitting those for Austria, which refer only to an earlier period, 1859) the Jews *always* show the higher rate. The most recent data for Prussia and Bavaria indicate that Jews kill themselves about *twice* as often as Catholics. Finally, contrary to the expectation created by Durkheim's argument that Jews in general kill themselves less frequently than do Catholics, the average rate for Catholics is 96; that for Jews, 111.

The striking aspect of the Jewish-Catholic comparison is change over time: in the middle of the century, Catholic rates generally (but not always) exceeded Jewish rates; by about 1880 the Jewish rates *invariably* surpassed the Catholic rates. Although Durkheim (155) briefly mentioned this phenomenon, he offered no explanation. Instead, he (72, 157, 160, 170, 376, 401) repeatedly insisted that the

Jewish social suicide rate is lowest of all. For Durkheim, exceptionally low rates, and *not* change in rates over time, was the theoretically relevant configuration.

One of Durkheim's sources (Morselli 1882:122) for table xviii shows figures permitting twenty-five Catholic-Jewish comparisons for the same area and period, but Durkheim's table xviii showed only two of the thirteen instances in which Jewish rates exceed Catholic rates. Once again, Durkheim buttressed his case through selective presentation of data.

Protestant-Jewish differences: Large or small? As prototypes of egoistic and nonegoistic religious society, Protestants and Jews fall at opposite ends of the egoistic continuum. Calculations based upon table xviii can be used to determine the amount of lag between the time when Protestant suicide rates for a particular region attain a given level and the time when Jewish rates reach the same level. For the earliest time periods included in Durkheim's table xviii, this lag ranged from 35 years (Prussia) to 13 years (Bavaria); for the latest, from 24 (Prussia) to 13 (Bavaria). Computing the average for the earliest and latest periods for all states gives an average time lag of 21 years.

These results raise a serious question regarding the correspondence between theory and data. If 21 years is sufficient to transform nonegoistic Jews into egoistic ones, and egoistic Protestants into nonegoistic ones, then what does it mean to call Protestants egoistic and Jews nonegoistic? Relative to one another, Jews may be nonegoistic and Protestants egoistic, but to simply designate Protestants as egoistic and Jews as nonegoistic is misleading. The differences that Durkheim portrayed as theoretically large are small when measured in terms of the "time lag" criterion. Since Durkheim's theory explains only small suicide differences, it is necessary to alter either the theory or his portrayal of Protestants and Jews or, barring these possibilities, to turn elsewhere for an explanation of the major variation in suicide rates.

Use and meaning of controls. A second issue concerns Durkheim's use of controls; particularly important is the theoretical status of various controls as applied to the Jews. Durkheim (155–56; see also 160) was well aware of the relevance of controls: "Jews live more exclusively than other confessional groups in cities and are in intellectual occupations. On this account they are more inclined to suicide than the members of other confessions, for reasons other than religion. If, therefore, the rate for Judaism is so low, in spite of this aggravating circumstance, it may be assumed that other things being equal, their religion has the fewest suicides of all." He offered no data to show that Jews *are* urban or are employed in intellectual occupations. Moreover, *Suicide*'s treatment of the relationship between urbanization and suicide shows more complexities than is implied in this passage. Data on Jewish suicide rates are limited to four German states and Austria (table xviii). No data on urban-rural differences in suicide are provided for either these countries or for European countries generally. Aside from a few scattered references, the only such data pertain to France; they show (208) that the suicide rate for the urban population exceeded that of the rural population by 94 percent in 1866-69 and by 46 percent in 1870-72. However, Durkheim (135) also showed that comparing city rates with those for their respective surrounding regions reveals *no* tendency for urban rates to exceed rural ones; furthermore, there is no correlation between the size of a town and its suicide rate (136-37). Finally, Durkheim (137n) denied that the social environment of the city itself is an important cause of higher rates. Seen in the larger context of *Suicide*, then, arguing that the Jews' greater degree of urbanization inclines them, more than Protestants or Catholics, to suicide is unconvincing.

Suicide (165-66) offers little evidence on the relationship between intellectual occupations and suicide rates; the available data refer to different years and groups for each country. In addition, comparing this evidence with that in Durkheim's table xxiv (258) reveals inconsistencies; the former clearly shows that liberal occupations have the highest rates of any occupational group, while the latter is less reassuring. Overall, Durkheim's data are inadequate to support his conclusion. More generally, since he refers to the impact of nonreligious factors that might *raise* suicide rates, presentation of a balanced picture requires him also to consider nonreligious factors that might lower Jewish suicide rates. This he failed to do.

In speaking of the Jews, Durkheim (160) was more inclusive than he was with comparable references to Catholics or Protestants: "Each [Jewish] community became a small, compact and coherent society with a strong feeling of self-consciousness and unity. Everyone thought and lived alike; individual divergences were made almost impossible by the community of existence and the close and constant surveillance of all over each." But if Judaism governs *"all* the details of life" (160; emphasis added), where does religion end? Where do the nonreligious aspects of life begin? Clearly Durkheim has shifted his unit of analysis, a shift obscured by his references to Protestant, Catholic, and Jewish religious "societies" without specification of their boundaries. Judaism is simply a convenient label for a distinctive social environment in which the strictly religious component, while important, is nonetheless just one element in a larger configuration. This situation makes it impossible to determine whether Jewish suicide rates result from the effects of Jewish religious society per se (implied by the logic of Durkheim's analysis insofar as he explicitly refers to religious society and Protestant-Catholic-Jewish differences therein) or, rather, from the entire Jewish social existence (implied by Durkheim's characterization of Jews).

These considerations force the researcher to question whether certain controls have the same theoretical status in relation to Jews as to Protestants and Catholics. Durkheim maintained that living in cities should elevate Jewish suicide rates. However, if they live in small, compact, self-conscious, self-contained units with high rates of interaction and the "constant surveillance of all over each," should it make any difference whether those communities are urban or rural? Similarly, does employment "in intellectual occupations" (155) mean the same thing for Jews as for Protestants and Catholics? Durkheim (158) held that "free inquiry" develops to replace the gap created by "the overthrow of traditional beliefs." Using educational attainment as his indicator of free inquiry, he (163–67) argued that the former should vary proportionately with suicide. Because educational attainment is highest among Jews, application of these perspectives might predict that Jews would have *higher* suicide rates than do Catholics and Protestants. But, he (168) argued, such a conclusion is unwarranted because the Jew "seeks to learn, not in order to replace his collective prejudices by reflective thought, but merely to be better armed for the struggle." Furthermore, "since knowledge by itself has no influence upon a tradition in full vigor, he superimposes this intellectual life upon his habitual routine with no effect of the former upon the latter." Educational attainment thus has a different theoretical meaning for Jews.

However, should not the same considerations apply to high suicide rates among individuals in intellectual occupations? The postulated reason for high rates in such groups is the weakening of traditional beliefs normally associated with the development of free inquiry. When the development of knowledge does *not* reflect a weakening of traditional beliefs (and, therefore, lower levels of integration), there is no basis for arguing that this development leads to high suicide rates. To paraphrase Durkheim (168), "since knowledge by itself has no influence upon a tradition in full vigor," Jews superimpose employment in intellectual occupations upon their "habitual routine with no effect of the former upon the latter."

The different theoretical meaning of variables as applied to Jews also raises a question concerning the impact of minority status. Though Durkheim (157) denied that the "great difference" between Catholic and Protestant suicide rates can be attributed to the minority status of Catholics, he did acknowledge that this variable might be a "partial cause" of the difference. If the minority status of Catholics lowers their suicide rates, could this factor not also explain the Jews' lower suicide rates? In the areas Durkheim (156–57) considered, Catholics constitute at least one-third of the population, Jews a far smaller minority. If the impact upon rates is proportional to the relative size of a minority group, the Jews' minority status, and not strictly religious phenomena, may well account for their low rates. Durkheim (168) himself acknowledged the relevance of the Jews' minority status. The Jew "seeks to learn ... to be better armed for the struggle. For him it is a means of offsetting the unfavorable position imposed on him by opinion and sometimes by law." Minority status is relevant because in setting Jews apart, it ultimately leads to higher levels of integration, which, in turn, help to account for the Jews' low suicide rates. In comparing Catholics and Protestants, then, Durkheim implicitly invoked an "all other things being equal" qualifier. However, for comparisons involving Jews, he made no such assumption, although many aspects of Jewish social existence obviously set them apart. It is the sum total of these differences, including but in no way limited to strictly religious differences, that accounts for the Jews' relatively low suicide rates.

In his first chapter on egoistic suicide Durkheim tried to show that suicide rates are higher for Protestants than for Catholics and higher for Catholics than for Jews. If some results suggest that Catholics have higher suicide rates, and others that Protestants have higher rates, then taken together the results provide no warrant for asserting that either group has the higher rates. The contention that Jews have lower suicide rates than Catholics is also unconvincing. Indeed, in regions for which relatively recent data were available,

Jews invariably had the higher rates. Even Protestant-Jewish comparisons reveal that only an average time lag of twenty-one years separates their suicide rates. Modern sociology has long believed that the social suicide rate is higher for Protestants than for Catholics and higher for Catholics than for Jews. Insofar as this idea derives from *Suicide,* it is not empirically well founded.

FAMILIAL SOCIETY

Durkheim's analysis of familial society (171–202) includes numerous generalizations, some inconsistent either with each other or with the data or both. In addition, much of the presentation is more concerned with laying the empirical groundwork for themes later amplified in the treatment of anomie than with developing those more germane to egoism. Frequently the analysis is sidetracked on points only marginally relevant to the development of main propositions. Finally, Durkheim often failed to specify the exact relationship between a given empirical configuration and his theory.

Not until the end of his analysis does his purpose become clear. At that point the central empirical generalization which emerges is simple enough: rate of interaction is proportional to numbers, integration is proportional to rate of interaction, and suicide rates are inversely related to integration. The empirical generalization to be established is: Suicide rates of adults vary inversely with the rate of interaction in their families. More simply, suicide varies inversely with family size (198–202).

Simplifying assumptions permit linking marital status to family size. Living outside the familial context, unmarried adults live alone and are literally "single" persons (171).[3] Married persons without children live in two-person families. A married couple with children constitutes a family of three or more. Widowed persons without children, like unmarried adults, live alone; those with children live in a family of two or more. Durkheim (199, 201) recognized that married or unmarried adults may live with their parents, that children may not reside with their parents, and that family size may be increased by the presence of individuals who are not members of the nuclear family. Through no fault of his, most of his data do not reflect these possibilities; however, his final set of data gives the number of people per family household (199).

Durkheim's analysis employed a *"coefficient of preservation"* (177), which may be defined as the ratio of the suicide rates of two groups of the same age and sex.[4] Since unmarried persons are typically used for comparison, in practice the coefficient generally turns out to be the ratio of the suicide rate of the unmarried to that of another group of the same age and sex. For example, if the suicide rate of unmarried men were 300 per million and that of married men of the same age only 100, the coefficient of preservation of married with respect to unmarried men (e.g., unmarried/married) would be 3. The *lower* the suicide rate of a group, the *higher* will be its coefficient of preservation. In Durkheim's words, the coefficient is "the number showing how many times *less* frequent suicide is in one group than in another" (177, italics added). The name of the coefficient anticipates the thrust of the argument by implying that the suicide rate of the group in question will be lower than that of the unmarried. For instances where the coefficient falls below unity (indicating that some specified group has a higher suicide rate than the referent group), Durkheim (177) continued to employ the coefficient, sometimes renaming it the "coefficient of aggravation."

The coefficient of preservation can range between 1 and infinity; the coefficient of aggravation, between 1 and zero. This difference in range makes it difficult to compare the relative impact upon suicide rates represented by coefficients of preservation as compared to coefficients of aggravation. It also means that comparing *averages* for series that contain coefficients above and below unity may be misleading. Given these limitations of Durkheim's coefficients of aggravation and preservation, I also make use of a standardized difference defined as $(a-b)/a \times 100$, where a is the rate of the control group (e.g., single men) and b is the rate of a second group (e.g., married men). This figure follows Durkheim in comparing the suicide rate of the group in question to that of a control group. It divides (i.e., measures or standardizes) this difference by the rate of the control group. When the rate of the control group exceeds that of the group in question, the standardized difference will be positive; in the reverse case, negative. Thus positive standardized differences correspond to Durkheim's coefficients of preservation; negative, to his coefficients of aggravation. Where the suicide rate of the control group equals that of the group in question the standardized difference will be zero (in contrast to Durkheim's coefficient which would be 1). Conceptually, the standardized difference follows Durkheim's theoretical interests in measuring the impact on suicide rates associated with the change from one status (e.g., single) to another (e.g., married). The standardized difference avoids using a figure for which one coefficient (preservation) can range from 1 to infinity while the other (aggravation) can range only between 1 and zero. Consequently, comparing averages for series of coefficients will not produce the misleading results which may sometimes derive from comparing averages for Durkheim's coefficients of aggravation and preservation. Finally, both to avoid small ratios and to present results in a form analogous to percentages, the initial ratio $(a-b/a)$ is multiplied by 100.

Following an introductory analysis that shows the need to control for age (171–75), *Suicide* gives suicide rates by age, sex, and marital status for Oldenburg (table xx:177), France (table xxi:178), and France broken down into the Seine and the provinces (table xxii:196). The paucity of cases (and, I might add, the uneven distribution of cases across cells), led Durkheim (175) to observe that little can be concluded from the figures for the small German state of Oldenburg. There were apparently no cases in four cells (see dots).[5] The table is most useful for the general pattern shown across cells representing a reasonable number of cases, and for the check these data provide on findings based on other data. Durkheim used the table both as a check on the data for France and, in conjunction with that data, to generate four "laws" (178–80). The French data cover about twenty-five thousand suicides.[6]

These tables control for age. They show that married people generally have lower suicide rates than do the unmarried. Very young husbands (under twenty) provide the most marked exception (indicated by their extreme coefficients of aggravation in all three tables).

Widowhood. One complicating factor in Durkheim's analysis is his discussion of widowhood. At this point in particular, Durkheim's ultimate concern seems to lie primarily with the theory of anomie so that implications for the theory of egoism are often slighted. The following two paragraphs trace out implications generally left implicit in *Suicide.*

Widowed persons can be compared to both the married and the unmarried in terms of total amount of interaction experienced in the familial context. Before the spouse's death, this amount would equal that of married persons; after the death, it would be reduced. During the period of the marriage the amount of interaction would be greater than that of the unmarried; if children were present, the amount would be greater even during widowhood. These considerations suggest that rates for the widowed should fall between those for the married and those for the unmarried.

Anticipating his treatment of anomie, Durkheim (190, 193, 198) argued that the shock of losing a spouse and the change in marital status were sources of anomie and hence a cause of suicide; he thereby implied an increase in suicide rates for the widowed, though he did not specify how much. This consideration creates a problem for unmarried-widowed comparisons. Both the marital past and possible presence of children should cause rates for the widowed to be lower than those for the unmarried; the shock of widowhood, however, could be the basis for predicting that rates for the widowed would exceed those of the unmarried. Although it is theoretically possible to predict any of several outcomes, the theory of egoism predicts that suicide rates for widowed persons will fall between rates for the married and those for the unmarried.

This interpretation is consistent with one part of Durkheim's analysis (193). "Nothing is more plausible than" the hypothesis "that the habits, tastes, and tendencies formed during marriage do not disappear on its dissolution." The immunity to suicide that marriage confers should persist, albeit in attenuated form, even after the loss of a spouse. This expectation may be tested against data for Oldenburg (177) and that for the Seine and the provinces (196) employing standardized differences for widowed with respect to the unmarried. Figures for widowers in the provinces support the hypothesis; figures for widows in the Seine do not. Four of seven comparisons show coefficients of aggravation; the average standardized difference is -11. The third case, widows in the provinces, runs even more sharply against the hypothesis. Seven of nine cases show a coefficient of aggravation; excluding the extreme figures for the fifteen-to-twenty age group, the standardized difference is still -21. The final instance, men in the Seine, goes most sharply against the hypothesis. Without exception, widowers there kill themselves more frequently than do the unmarried, producing an average standardized difference of -37.

These findings may be compared with those for Oldenburg. Widowers show coefficients of aggravation in four of six instances; the average standardized difference is -57 (or -7, excluding the extreme figures for the twenty-to-thirty age group). In three of the four comparisons, widows show coefficients of preservation; the average standardized difference is 4. Taking France and Oldenburg together, average standardized differences for four of the six groups run counter to the hypothesis; in France, three of four run counter. Rather than falling between rates for the married and unmarried, rates for the widowed are generally higher than those for the unmarried. These results constitute a first suggestion that Durkheim's hypothesis relating family size and suicide is inaccurate.

Marital and familial society. Halfway through his analysis Durkheim (185) introduced an important distinction. The conjugal group, marital society or marriage consists of husband and wife without children whereas the family includes one or two parents with one or more children. Durkheim employed "the family" or "domestic society" as general terms to include both types of society.

Recognizing that his basic tables (xx–xxii) did not permit this distinction between marriage and the family, Durkheim proceeded to make it. In so doing, he raised difficult data-analysis problems and produced highly interesting results. For unstated reasons, Durkheim did not control for presence of children in compiling tables xxi and xxii.[7] Consequently, he was led to employ questionable procedures in his attempt to control for age.

He wanted to compare groups of the same age. In practice this proved to be impossible. In order to control for age, Durkheim was forced to compare the suicide rate of the group in question with the rate for unmarried people of the same average age as that group. For instance, in comparing childless wives with single women, Durkheim compared the suicide rate for *all* childless wives with that of single women of the same age as the *average* age of childless wives. This procedure introduced inaccuracy at two points. (1) The average ages employed are for all married or all widowed by sex; no distinction is made between those with and without children. However, those with children are older than those without. (2) More important, given the strong relationship between age and suicide, no single suicide rate adequately represents the rate for groups that include persons of widely varying ages. Yet, comparing one suicide rate for such a group to one for the unmarried implies the existence of a representative rate.

Durkheim knew that his procedures had limitations. Indeed, most of the section (171–75) leading up to the presentation of his first two tables is devoted to demonstrating the shortcomings of employing average age as the only control for age in comparing suicide rates of different groups. This is precisely why Durkheim compiled tables xxi and xxii, and why he was justified in feeling they represent a significant improvement over otherwise available data. The coefficients of preservation and aggravation in these

TABLE 6.4 Derivation of Coefficients of Preservation (Aggravation) for Married and Widowed Persons, with and without Children

Group (1)	Rate (2)	Age (3)	Group Used to Estimate Ave. Age (4)	Ave. Age, Col. 4 Group (5)	Unmarried Age Group Used for Comparison[a] (6)	Rate, Col. 6 Group (7)	Coef. Ratio Col. 7 to Col. 2 (8)
Men							
Childless husbands	644	?	All married men	46 years 8 1/3 mos.	40-50	975	1.51
Husbands with children	336	?	All married men	46 years 8 1/3 mos.	40-50	975	2.90
Widowers with children	937	?	All widowers	61 years 8 1/3 mos.	50-60, 60-70	1,601[b]	1.71
Childless widowers	1,258	?	All widowers	61 years 8 1/3 mos.	50-60 60-70	1,601[b]	1.27
Women							
Childless wives	221	?	All married women	42-43[c]	42-43	150	0.68
Wives with children	79	?	All married women	42[c]	42-43	150	1.90[d]
Widows with children	186	?	All widows	60	50-60, 60-70	196	1.05
Childless widows	322	?	All widows	60	50-60, 60-70	196	0.61

SOURCE: Suicide (186-90, 198).

NOTE: ? = unknown.

[a]Age group whose suicide rate Durkheim compared to that in (2) to derive the coefficient in (8). Suicide does not show how the (sometimes rather inclusive) age categories in (6) were converted into the rates in (7). Due to recalculation, most coefficients in (8) differ slightly from those shown by Durkheim.

[b]Suicide (187) gives the average age for all widowers as 61 years, 8 and 1/3 months. "The rate of unmarried men of the same age (see Table XXI) is between 1,434 and 1,768, or about 1,504." The first two rates are those for unmarried men 50 to 60 and 60 to 70, respectively. The average rate for these two groups is 1,601. It appears that this is the figure Durkheim meant to derive; the 1,504 apparently resulted from an error in calculation. The average age of widowers is slightly higher than the average age (60) of the two unmarried groups whose suicide rates he averaged. Consequently, he would certainly not want to use a lower suicide rate for the unmarried (to do so would suggest that the average age for widowers was below 60 years). Also, Durkheim felt that widowers with children are older, on the average, than all widowers. Elsewhere, when faced with selecting a suicide rate for the unmarried at an age near the cutting point between two age intervals shown in table XXI, he chose the average age for the two intervals. In short, all indications suggest that Durkheim would not intentionally have chosen 1,504 in preference to 1,601.

[c]Suicide (188) gives the average age for childless women as between 42 and 43. However, the following page showed 42 as the average age for married women with children, thus suggesting that the figures of 42 and 42-43 are for all married women, not those for either childless married women or married women with children.

[d]In the text Durkheim (189) gave this figure as 1.80; his summary table (197-8) gave the figure of 1.89; the rounded figure is 1.90.

tables are sometimes quite consistent across age groups; for others, though, particularly the unmarried-widowed comparisons, they fluctuate greatly.

Durkheim's goal was to determine how much of married persons' immunity to suicide should be attributed to marriage and how much to the family. Basic to this analysis are coefficients derived for married and widowed persons with and without children. Table 6.4 summarizes the derivation of these coefficients. Durkheim identified coefficients that (he felt) under- or overestimated the true coefficients. In terms of average ages, childless husbands are younger, and husbands with children are older, than the average for all married men (186–87). Comparing the suicide rate of 644 for childless husbands not to that for unmarried men of forty-six (the average age of all married men), but rather to that of younger men, who have a lower suicide rate, would, as Durkheim noted, lower his 1.5 coefficient for childless husbands. Similarly, "the age of husbands with children is above that of husbands in general and, consequently, the coefficient of preservation 2.9 should be considered somewhat below reality" (187n). As for widowers, he (187) noted that those "with children are certainly older than widowers in general. . . . Widowers with children should therefore really be compared with unmarried men above 62 years (who, because of their age, have a stronger tendency to suicide)." Such a comparison would produce a higher coefficient of preservation than the 1.71 derived by Durkheim. Although he did not mention it, a parallel argument suggests that childless widowers must be younger. Consequently, childless widowers should be compared with unmarried persons under sixty-one, which would reduce the magnitude of the derived coefficient, 1.27.

For married and widowed men, Durkheim stressed that those without children are younger than those with; however, he did not mention this possibility in discussing women. If the same relationships prevail, then childless wives will be younger than wives with children. Thus, the coefficient of aggravation for childless wives and the coefficient of preservation for wives with children both underestimate the difference between these two groups and unmarried women. Suicide rates for single women fluctuate so as to make it difficult to determine whether distinguishing between the average age of widows with and without children would have appreciable impact upon their coefficients. Table 6.5 lists Durkheim's coefficients, their corresponding standardized differences, and the direction of necessary adjustment.

Results may be ordered by the degree to which they sustain the theory (table 6.6). The top three groups sustain it. The direction of adjustment in the coefficients for childless husbands and childless widowers makes it impossible to ascertain whether the coefficients for these two groups constitute significant support. Particularly given the limits of the procedures used to derive coefficients, the coefficient for widows with children is too close to unity to be interpreted as sustaining the theory, while those for the last two groups undercut it. The results are ambiguous. Six of eight coefficients are in the predicted direction; at the same time, taking into account the adjustment, only three or perhaps four coefficients clearly support the theory. Given the great variablility in suicide rates and the inadequacy of the control for age, the average standardized difference of 12.9 is probably too small to sustain the conviction that Durkheim's theory provides important explanatory power.

TABLE 6.5   Coefficients of Preservation (Aggravation) and Standardized Differences for Married and Widowed Persons, with and without Children

Group	Coefficient	Standardized Difference	Remarks	Notation
Men				
Married				
Childless	1.51	33.8	Coefficient too high; Durkheim's observation	↓
With Children	2.90	65.5	Coefficient too low; Durkheim's observation	↑
Widowed				
Childless	1.27	21.3	Coefficient too high; Pope's observation	↓
With Children	1.71	41.5	Coefficient too low; Durkheim's observation	↑
Women				
Married				
Childless	0.68	-47.0	Coefficient too high; Pope's observation	↓
With Children	1.90	47.4	Coefficient too low; Pope's observation	↑
Widowed				
Childless	0.61	-63.9	· · ·	· · ·
With Children	1.05	4.8	· · ·	· · ·

SOURCE: Table 6.4.

Durkheim introduced his coefficients primarily to distinguish between the effects of conjugal and of familial society. Figures for the family strongly support the theory (table 6.6), but the average standardized difference of -13.9 for marriage undercuts it; unless children are present, married persons have higher suicide rates than do single persons.

TABLE 6.6 COEFFICIENTS OF PRESERVATION (AGGRAVATION) AND STANDARDIZED DIFFERENCES FOR DOMESTIC SOCIETY

Group	Coefficient	Standardized Difference	Notation
Ordered by Degree of Support for Durkheim's Theory			
Husbands with children	2.90	65.5	↑
Wives with children	1.90	47.4	↑
Widowers with children	1.71	41.5	↑
Childless husbands	1.51	33.8	↓
Childless widowers	1.27	21.3	↓
Widows with children	1.05	4.8	. . .
Childless wives	0.68	-47.0	↓
Childless widows	0.61	-63.9	. . .
Average	1.45	12.9	
Averages by Groups			
By Parental Status			
Family	1.89	39.8	
Family, excl. widowed	2.40	56.4	
Married	1.02	-13.9	
Married, excl. widowed	1.10	- 6.6	
By Sex			
Men	1.85	40.5	
Men, excl. widowed	2.20	49.6	
Women	1.06	-14.7	
Women, excl. widowed	1.29	0.2	
By Marital Status			
Married	1.75	24.9	
Widowed	1.16	0.9	

SOURCE: Table 6.5.

Consistent with Durkheim's treatment of widowhood as an extension of marriage and in order to provide as comprehensive a test as possible, figures for the widowed have been combined with those for married persons. In view of his suggestion that the former are subject to anomie, it is instructive to test his hypothesis against results for married persons only. If the widowed are excluded, the average standardized difference for the family increases while that for marriage is cut in half.

The figures by sex show that those for men sustain the theory (table 6.6); for women, however, only one coefficient clearly supports the theory while two clearly contradict it. The average standardized difference of -14.7 for women undercuts the hypothesis. If, as before, the widowed are excluded, the average standardized difference for men sustains the theory, but that for women does not.

Finally, married and widowed persons can be examined separately (table 6.6). Results for married persons support the theory: three of four coefficients in the predicted direction produce an average standardized difference of 24.9. For the widowed, taking into account the adjustment for childless widowers, only one of four groups (widowers with children) clearly provides support. The average standardized difference of 0.9 indicates that overall rates for the widowed are virtually indistinguishable from those of the unmarried. Neither here nor in results derived above from tables for Oldenburg (table XX:177) and France (table XXI:178), which do not control for presence of children, does it appear that the rates for the widowed are lower than those for married persons. In sum, since the theory is sustained for familial but not marital society, for men but not women, and for the married but not the widowed, one can only conclude that the data do not warrant asserting that family size and suicide rates are inversely related.

Durkheim's Interpretations

Frequently, Durkheim's primary interest seemed to lie more in explaining particular results than in systematically tracing out their implications for the theory of egoism. Empirical results (e.g., on widowhood, marriage, and women) are often referred for explanation to the theory of anomie. In the case of widowhood he (193-97) spent considerable time arguing that rates for the widowed could be explained as a function of those for married persons, a theme more germane to anomie than to egoism. He also held that the shock of widowhood explained the relatively high rates for widows.

Durkheim (185-89) argued that marriage per se did little to explain the immunity to suicide enjoyed by married persons. *"In France... married but childless women commit suicide half again as often as unmarried women of the same age"* (188). The coefficient of aggravation he derived for childless widows, with respect to the unmarried, is even more extreme than that for childless wives (table 6.6). For women, then, marriage itself does not produce immunity to suicide. Similarly, Durkheim felt that the figures for childless married and childless widowed men show a limited effect from marriage (see table 6.6). In assessing the comparative importance of marriage and the family to married persons' relative immunity to suicide, Durkheim (198) argued that the family is relatively all-important, while marriage has little importance for men and none for women. Noting his intent to reserve study of this "special effect of marriage" for consideration in the chapter on anomie, Durkheim (198; see also 189) concluded that "the family is the essential factor in the immunity of married persons."

His treatment of women is mixed with that of marriage; the coefficients of aggravation for childless married and childless widowed women run most strongly counter to the hypothesis of an inverse relationship between suicide rates and family size (table 6.6). Durkheim (189) noted that "in itself conjugal society is harmful to the woman and aggravates her tendency to suicide." Consequently, unless children are present to offset its evil influence, married and widowed women suffer, displaying higher suicide rates than their single counterparts. Although he made this observation in the chapter on egoism, not until the chapter on anomie did Durkheim explain why women suffer, and men benefit, from marriage.

All these results that do not support the theory of egoism are referred to the theory of anomie for explanation. This approach is unsatisfactory. The theory of anomie as applied to domestic society has severe limitations, not least of which is its failure to find support in *Suicide*'s data. In addition, Durkheim's procedure undercuts attempts to draw implications for the theory of egoism. His approach constituted a selective test of the theory. Data congruent with the theory of egoism—particularly data on the family—were referred to that theory for explanation. Data inconsistent with it—for women, marriage, and widowhood—were referred to the theory of anomie. This procedure effectively safeguarded the theory from falsification, and, indeed, nowhere in the chapter on egoism did Durkheim acknowledge that the data falsify the theory.

Additional Findings

Durkheim presented additional figures on suicide and family size. In the first set (199), he related suicide rates to the average number in family households. However, the data given pertain to whole departments; to draw inferences about the relationship between family size and the suicide rates of individuals living in those households is to commit the ecological fallacy. Durkheim used no controls. Furthermore, it is not clear whether departments were grouped with suicide rate or with size of family household as the independent variable. Finally, within each of the six groups distinguished in the chart, the relationship between suicide and household size is also unclear. A second set (199–200) of related data follows the first and suffers most of the same limitations.

These two sets of data are introduced at a point (198) when Durkheim has just concluded that (1) the family is the essential factor in the immunity of married or widowed persons, and (2) the "special effect of marriage" will be reserved for study in the chapter on anomie. Clearly the intent is to relate suicide rates to family size. Equally apparent, however, the data pertain only to number of people in the family household. Consequently, Durkheim could make no distinction between marriage and the family, nor did he mention the possibility that household size might be increased by the presence of relatives who do not belong to the immediate family. Although Durkheim (201) talked in terms of the family, he explicitly rejected any notion that children, being of special importance, should be given particular weight in relating family size to suicide rates. Indeed, in referring to the family at this point, Durkheim may have been using it in the sense of domestic society (i.e., to subsume what he elsewhere distinguished as marriage and the family), though his focus upon children and birth rates makes it seem that he was referring to the family in the sense of parents and children. In any case, the particular virtue of this table in Durkheim's eyes (198; see also 199, 266) is that it reveals with special clarity the inverse relationship between family size and suicide rates.

Most of the figures thus far considered pertain to France; the remainder, to Oldenburg. This raises the question of the generalizability of results. At the onset of his chapter, a few relevant figures are given. Durkheim determined the average age of all married persons. He then compared their suicide rate to that of unmarried persons of the same age. Though he (173) recognized the shortcomings of this approach, the limitations of the available data forced him to use it. *Suicide* (173) gives the figures shown in table 6.7. The difference between the suicide rates of married and

TABLE 6.7   Unmarried-Married Suicide Ratios in Selected European States

Country	Years	Suicide Rate (per million) Unmarried	Married	Ratio	Standardized Difference
France	1848-57	112	69	1.6	38
Italy	1873-77	121	75	1.6	38
Württemberg	1846-60	...	...	1.43	30
Prussia	1873-75	...	...	1.11	10

SOURCE: Suicide (173); standardized difference figures added.

unmarried persons varies greatly from country to country; it is almost four times as large in France and Italy as in Prussia. France's relatively high ratio of 1.6:1 may not be truly exceptional (Italy displays an identical ratio), but neither is it typical. It is noteworthy because it suggests that the difference in suicide rates between married and unmarried persons may be greater in France than it is elsewhere. This difference is crucial because, according to Durkheim's hypothesis, each addition to the family should be accompanied by a decrease in the suicide rate. In Prussia the difference between the married and unmarried is so slight that additions to the family group produce only marginal effects. When the unmarried/married ratio is as large as it is in France, the data do not sustain the theory; when the difference is smaller, as in Württemberg and especially Prussia, there is even less reason to suppose that the theory would be sustained by the relevant data.

There are additional clues concerning the generalizability of Durkheim's findings. On the basis of patterns revealed in the tables for Oldenburg and France, Durkheim (178-79) formulated four laws. The third reads: *"The coefficient of preservation of married persons by comparison with unmarried persons varies with the sexes."* He elaborated: "In France it is men who are in the favorable position.... But in Oldenburg the opposite is true.... *The sex enjoying the higher coefficient of preservation in the state of marriage varies from society to society."* The coefficients cited (179) do not control for the presence of children; however, those for

France are congruent with coefficients that do. (The latter show that with or without children, for both married and widowed persons, women invariably have lower coefficients of preservation or aggravation than men[table 6.5].) If the French pattern prevails in Oldenburg, then in each case the women would be better off than the men. If, in addition, as proved to be the case in France, the hypothesis relating family size to suicide rates proved to apply only to the sex with the highest coefficient of preservation for the married, then in Oldenburg the hypothesis would be sustained for women but not for men.

The comparison between France and Oldenburg parallels an internal French comparison. Commenting on the table for the Seine and the provinces Durkheim (194-95) observed: "In the departments the husband has much more immunity than the wife.... In the Seine the reverse is true." Application of the same line of reasoning as in the French-Oldenburg comparison reveals that the hypothesis relating family size to suicide rates may well hold for men, but not women, in the provinces and conversely in the Seine. Following up Durkheim's own argument—that the sex with the highest coefficient of preservation for married persons varies from one country to another, and even by region within a given country—centers attention on aspects of the data that may be interpreted as suggesting that his larger hypothesis (relating family size and suicide rates) may apply to men in one country but not to women (France); to women but not to men in another country (Oldenburg); and, finally, to men in one region of a given country (France) but not to women, and to women in another region of the same country but not to men. Such outcomes pose considerable embarassment for the theory: not only would Durkheim have to explain why it applies to only *one* sex in a given area but also why that sex *varies* from one area to the next.

Summary and Evaluation

I evaluate Durkheim's presentation in terms of its success in demonstrating that the suicide rates of adults vary inversely with the number of people with whom they interact in marital or familial contexts. This evaluation, like the original analysis itself, focuses on the data permitting comparison of suicide rates for the married and the widowed with those for the unmarried. On the one hand, the data which permit comparison of rates for groups at five- and ten-year intervals, thereby adequately controlling for age, do not control for the presence of children. On the other hand, data controlling for presence of children use only average ages which, as demonstrated, do not provide a satisfactory control for age. In terms of adequate controls, the strength of each set is the weakness of the other. Data controlling for presence of children *and* exercising an adequate control for age would permit a far more definitive test of the theory than do *Suicide*'s data.

Durkheim presented one table each for Oldenburg, France, and France divided into the Seine and the provinces. These figures show that married persons generally have lower suicide rates than the unmarried. They exercise no control for presence of children, however; thus, it is not possible to determine whether the lower rates of married persons are to be attributed to marriage or to the family. While ratios vary from Oldenburg to France, and even within France itself, rates for the widowed are generally higher, instead of lower, than those for the married, thereby creating the first major contradiction of Durkheim's hypothesis.

Data that use presence of children as a variable suggest that both childless husbands and childless widowers have lower suicide rates than do the unmarried, while rates for childless married women and childless widows are higher than those for the unmarried. The average standardized difference of −13.9 (table 6.6) for married persons indicates that, on balance, marriage increases rather than depresses suicide rates. In contrast, figures for the family clearly sustain the hypothesis. With regard to sex, the hypothesis is supported by the evidence for men but not for women. Finally, though incomplete, the relevant data suggest that the hypothesis is more congruent with data for France and Italy than with those for Württemberg and Prussia. Other data show mixed results by area and by sex. These findings cast even more doubt on the hypothesis.

The limitations of the data, coupled with the findings contrary to those predicted, sustain a firm conclusion: Durkheim failed to show that suicide rates are inversely related to family size. The data for the family, men, and the married support his hypothesis, while those for marriage, women, and widowhood do not. Weighing these positive and negative results against each other leaves his hypothesis with a net balance of zero. Durkheim did not empirically validate the proposition that "*suicide varies inversely with the degree of integration of domestic society*" (208).

POLITICAL SOCIETY

Durkheim (202-8) concluded his empirical analysis of egoistic suicide by examining data on political society. He used political crisis as an indicator of changing levels of social integration. Treating successively great political upheavals, coups d'etat, election crises, great national wars, and purely dynastic wars, he attempted to demonstrate that the greater the crisis, the greater the decrease in suicide.

The Findings

Great political upheavals. Durkheim (203) began by considering the impact of "great political upheavals." Observing that "all the revolutions which have occurred in France during this [the nineteenth] century reduced the number of suicides at the moment of their occurrence," he cited figures to show that suicide fell 7.8 percent from 1829 to 1830, and 9.5 percent from 1847 to 1848. He then noted that the crisis shaking France in 1848 spread throughout Europe in 1848-49 with an accompanying drop in suicide (table 6.8). The basic difficulty in interpreting the data in table 6.8

TABLE 6.8   SUICIDE AND POLITICAL UPHEAVALS

Country	Suicides per Year (absolute numbers)			Percentage Change[a]		
	1847	1848	1849	1847-48	1848-49	1847-49
Denmark	345	305	337	-11.6	10.5	-2.3
Prussia	1,852	1,649	1,527	-11.0	-7.4	-17.5
Bavaria	217	215	189	-0.9	-12.1	-12.9
Kingdom of Saxony	377[b]	398	328	5.6	-17.6	-13.0
Average				-4.5	-6.7	-11.4
Average excluding Denmark				-2.1	-12.4	-14.5

SOURCE: <u>Suicide</u> (203) unless otherwise indicated. Austria has been dropped because suicide figures for 1847 and 1848 are not given.

[a]Most of these figures (including all averages) added.

[b]Figure added from <u>Suicide</u> (47). Durkheim gave no reason for omitting this rate which, compared with the number of suicides in 1848, produces a percentage change in the direction opposite from that predicted.

lies in the uncertainty concerning which years to compare. Suicide fell an average of 4.5 percent in 1848, and another 6.7 percent in 1849. Comparing 1847 (the last precrisis year) to 1849 (the final year of the crisis) reveals an average drop of 11.4 percent. Durkheim (203) observed that "in Germany public feeling ran much higher than in Denmark and the struggle lasted longer even than in France," an observation that may suggest that suicide in Denmark should not be expected to drop after 1848. Omitting Denmark produces an average decline of 12.4 percent from 1848 to 1849, and 14.5 percent from 1847 to 1849, thereby providing stronger support for Durkheim's hypothesis that political crises are associated with a decrease in suicide. In short, the data sustain Durkheim's hypothesis.

Coups d'etat. Durkheim (204) focused on the coup d'etat by Louis Bonaparte in December 1851. Since the coup occurred so late in the year, there is some question as to when its effect on suicide should become manifest. In 1851 the number of suicides was virtually unchanged from the preceding year; the following year shows a 2 percent increase (computed from table 1:47). These findings are incongruent with Durkheim's hypothesis and, indeed, *Suicide* makes no attempt to relate them to the coup. Though employing national figures up to this point, Durkheim (204) here shifted to figures for a single city, Paris, where there were 483 suicides in 1851, 446 in 1852, and 463 in 1853.[8] No figures for 1850 are provided, making it impossible to determine whether the number of suicides fell in 1851. Durkheim called attention to the 8 percent drop in 1852; however, if it were granted that levels of integration in France generally were higher in 1852 than in 1851, the increase in suicide for France in 1852 runs counter to his hypothesis. Suicide rates for the period surrounding the coup d'etat of Louis Bonaparte do not, on balance, appear to sustain the theory.

Election crises. In analyzing data on election crises Durkheim (204) turned from yearly to monthly comparisons. He (204-5) stated that the parliamentary crisis of 16 May 1877 began at the end of June and lasted through October. Compared with the same month of 1876, the months July through October in 1877 show an average decrease in suicide of 5.9 percent, which may be contrasted with the 3.7 percent rise for the remaining months. "The phenomenon is yet more pronounced" during "the 1889 elections which ended the Boulanger agitation" (204-5). Here the crisis began in the first part of August, lasting until the end of September (205). The average percentage drop for these two months, comparing each with the same month in 1888, is 11.5 percent, which contrasts with the average 1.3 percent drop for the noncrisis months in 1889 included in Durkheim's chart (204). The results support Durkheim's hypothesis.

Great national wars. Identifying two types of wars—"great national" and "purely dynastic"—Durkheim (205-7) treated the former first. Table 6.9 summarizes the data. The results are consistent with

TABLE 6.9 SUICIDE AND GREAT NATIONAL WARS

Country	Suicides per Year (absolute numbers)				Percentage Change from Preceding Year[a]		
	1865	1866	1867			1866	1867
Italy	678	588	657			-13.3	11.7
Austria	1,464	1,265	1,407			-13.6	11.2
Average						-13.4	11.4
	1863	1864	1865			1864	1865
Denmark	...	411[b]	451			....	9.7
Saxony	643	545	619			-15.2	13.6
Average						-15.2	11.6
	1869	1870	1871	1872	1870	1871	1872
Prussia[c]	3,186	2,963	2,723	2,950	-7.0	-8.1	8.3
Saxony	710	657	653	687	-7.5	-0.6	5.2
Bavaria	425	452	.....[d]	412	6.3	....	....
Baden	222	....	244	....	....	....	....
France	5,114	4,157	4.490	5,275	-18.7	8.0	17.5
Average					-6.7	-0.2	10.3

SOURCE: *Suicide* (205, 207).

[a] Most figures added.

[b] Durkheim (205) said that this figure is "the lowest since 1852." Actually, his data (47) show that Denmark had fewer suicides in both 1854 and 1855—363 and 399, respectively.

[c] *Suicide* (47, 205) gives two different sets of Prussian figures for these years. The most significant difference occurs in the percentage change from 1870 to 1871: -8.1 in one set, -4.1 in the other. *Suicide* does not give a source for either set, nor did Durkheim note the discrepancies between them.

[d] Durkheim (207) noted a "slight decrease" in suicides in 1871 compared with 1870.

Durkheim's hypothesis. With one exception (Bavaria), great national wars are associated with a 7 to 19 percent decrease in suicide during the first year of war.

Dynastic wars. The discussion (207) of dynastic wars is brief. Four are mentioned. In each case Durkheim referred to the effects upon only one participant. The only suicide statistics cited are those for France during the Crimean War. Mention is also made of the Italian wars and "the wars of 1864 and 1866" involving Prussia. To the figures cited for the Crimean War, I add those for the other three countries and wars cited (table 6.10). Years are the last prewar and first war years. Durkheim (207) observed that there was a rise in

TABLE 6.10 SUICIDE AND DYNASTIC WARS

	Suicides (absolute numbers)		Percentage Change
	Last Prewar Year	First Year of War	
France			
Crimean War (1853-54)	3,415	3,700	8.3
Italian War (1858-59)	3,903	3,899	-0.1
Prussia			
1863-64	2,374	2,203	-7.2
1865-66	2,361	2,485	5.3
Average			1.6

SOURCE: Suicide (47, 207); percentage change added.

suicide in France in 1854 compared with 1853. He added that the "same fact is observed in Prussia at the time of the wars of 1864 and 1866. The figures are stationary in 1864 and rise slightly in 1866." Actually, suicide fell 7.2 percent in Prussia in 1864, a drop commensurate with the yearly decreases earlier reported for Prussia (in 1870 and 1871) when it was engaged in a great national war (table 6.9). While three of the four wars are associated with a change of 5 percent or more, the average of 1.6 is consistent with Durkheim's assessment (207) that such wars "have had no appreciable effect" on suicide rates.

Analysis

Because a variety of political crises are considered, *Suicide* seems to present a wealth of data. In fact, however, few examples of each type are considered (only four dynastic wars, three great national wars, two elections, and one coup d'etat.) Thus, while the presentation treats many types of political crises, the limited number of examples constitute illustration rather than a systematic test of his generalization.

No explicit mention is made of the criteria governing selection of examples. The first sentence (204) about elections is hardly reassuring: "Mild as they are, mere election crises sometimes have the same result." Since Durkheim obviously felt that the only two elections he mentioned were associated with a decrease in suicide, use of the word "sometimes" suggests that other data reveal no such decrease.

Another problematic aspect of the analysis is Durkheim's failure to demonstrate that magnitude of political upheaval is correlated with impact upon suicide rates. His conclusion (208) that suicide varies inversely with social integration is phrased in terms of variation. However, his analysis focused on a highly limited form of variation because he only attempted to demonstrate that crisis is associated with a decrease in suicide. He could have ordered both types of political disturbance and the specific instances of each type in terms of magnitude of crisis and then determined whether the greater the crisis, the larger the decrease in suicide. *Suicide* does contain some implicit rankings of presumed magnitude of various political crises; election crises are termed "mild" (204), and the distinction between "great national" and "purely dynastic" wars is one of impact on the passions of the masses (206-7). However, Durkheim made no systematic attempt to demonstrate that the magnitude of upheaval in political society is correlated with the amount of decrease in suicide.

Perhaps the most frustrating aspect of the analysis is the loose fit between theory and fact. In citing only the initial year of a given crisis, as he frequently did, Durkheim overlooked many important considerations. Whether a crisis occurred early or late in the year, and how long it lasted, are both crucial. In his treatment both of crises confined to a single year and of those spreading over two or more years, he generally left it to the reader to guess how many months of the years in question were times of crisis. Identifying crisis dates also begs the question of duration of change in levels of integration. Do levels continue to rise throughout the crisis period, or is some peak reached, after which they level off or, perhaps, begin to decrease? Durkheim never explicitly asked whether a crisis extending over two years should cause a decrease in the first year only, or a decrease in suicide for the first year plus an additional decrease during the second year. In fact, however, this question is important to the interpretation of empirical results. In two of the three countries for which figures are given (table 6.9), data for the war of 1870–71 show that in 1871 suicide rates either remain essentially unchanged (Saxony) or rise appreciably (France). [9] If the theory is interpreted as predicting an increase in integration for the second as compared to the first year of the war, these results do not sustain it. In short, using yearly dates frequently permits only a loose test of the theory.

A more serious aspect of the looseness of the theory-data fit is Durkheim's failure to employ quantifiable, objective indicators. Lacking these, his analysis often turns on unsupported assertions that one political event had greater impact upon popular political passions than did another. Indeed, impressionistic characterizations permeate the entire analysis. In discussing the crises of 1848–49, Durkheim (203) asserted that public feeling ran much higher in Germany than in Denmark but gave no supporting evidence. He implied that the distinction between great national and purely dynastic wars is the degree to which popular passions become aroused; yet he made little attempt to validate his placement of wars into one category or the other.

Elsewhere, Durkheim attempted to explain why, in contrast to Prussia and Saxony, suicide in Bavaria actually increased in 1870, the first year of the war of 1870–71 (table 6.9). Part of the commentary (207) consists of a forceful suggestion that the magnitude of the political crisis in Bavaria was equal to that in Prussia. Both took an equally important part in military events, and the resulting administrative disturbance must have been the same for both countries. Yet Durkheim (207) concluded that Bavaria "simply did not take the same moral share in events." In lieu of supporting evidence, this assertion seems inconsistent with the commentary immediately preceding it. Though perhaps in exaggerated form, the last sentence of the paragraph reflects the manner in which Durkheim (207) assessed popular passions: "It required the breath of glory wafted over Germany on the morrow of the victory of 1870 to warm somewhat the hitherto cold and unresponsive land of Bavaria." The failure to employ objective indicators also shows up (204–5) with particular clarity in the discussion of elections in

France, where much of Durkheim's discussion consists of unsupported assertions about the waxing and waning of the political crisis and popular passions.

That Durkheim sometimes assumed that suicide rates themselves measure the magnitude of a crisis and, hence, the changing levels of integration in political society, comes through most clearly at three points. The only evidence (208) offered to support the assertion that the war of 1870–71 produced "its full moral effect only on the urban population" in France are figures on the incidence of suicide.[10] Introducing the discussion of purely dynastic wars, Durkheim (206) declared that "the best proof that we confront a phenomenon of social psychology," in the decrease in suicide associated with great national wars, "is that not all political or national crises have this influence. Only those do which excite the passions." He then idenitified instances in which wars were not accompanied by a decline. Suicide rates are the only evidence cited to show that popular passions were not excited. In assessing the impact of the coup d'etat of Louis Bonaparte upon Paris as compared with the provinces, Durkheim (204) appealed to suicide rates. While this use of suicide to measure levels of integration comes through most clearly in these examples, the loose relationship between theory and the data, coupled with Durkheim's post factum interpretations, suggest that his approach to the data is based on the premise that suicide varies inversely with degree of integration in political society. The data are presented to illustrate rather than to test this claim.

Two additional aspects of the analysis, again reflecting the kinds of problems mentioned, should also be noted. Durkheim's first paragraph (203) on political society concluded as follows: "In France, on the eve of the [French] Revolution, the turmoil which shook society with the disintegration of the older social system took shape in a sudden rush of suicides mentioned by contemporary authors." Yet, he also held that great political upheavals, including specifically the French revolutions of 1830 and 1848, were accompanied by a *decline* in suicide. Why some revolutions should produce an increase and others a decrease was not explicitly considered. Some clues (203) are present, however. The revolution of 1789 marked the disintegration of the old social order. In contrast, "great social disturbances," of which the revolutions of 1830 and 1848 are presumably examples, concentrate "activity toward a single end," thereby causing "a stronger integration of society" (208). It is unfortunate that Durkheim did not identify objective indicators, thus making it possible to ascertain whether given revolutions cause an increase or a decrease in level of integration.

The references to turmoil, disturbance, and crisis that recur throughout the discussion of political society recall the social conditions of acute anomie. Employing the concept of anomie, Durkheim's theory can be used to predict an increase—not a decrease—in suicide. Given the possibility of predicting opposite outcomes, guidelines on how to determine whether there is an increase in anomie or a decrease in egoism are crucial. The "salutary influence" of political disturbance "is due not to the crisis but to the struggles it occasions" (208). Durkheim acknowledged the fact of crisis and thereby the relevance of anomie and the possibility of an increase in suicide.[11] ("Every disturbance of equilibrium ... is an impulse to voluntary death"; 246.) He balanced crisis and anomie against integration and egoism by simply asserting that the struggle —not the crisis—is decisive. Unfortunately, nothing is said about how this determination was made. The possibility remains that the decision to use the theory of egoism to predict a decrease in suicide, rather than the theory of anomie to predict an increase, was made with the help of a look at the suicide statistics themselves.

The data presented to demonstrate that *"suicide varies inversely with the degree of integration of political society"* (208) are suggestive and provide illustrative support for the hypothesis. At the same time, however, they are sketchy. The data in *Suicide* neither sustain nor disprove the hypothesis. An adequate test is still needed.

ALTRUISTIC SUICIDE

Just as low levels of social integration lead to egoistic suicide, high levels lead to altruistic suicide. *Suicide* identifies two loci of altruism, primitive society and the modern army.

PRIMITIVE SOCIETY

Durkheim (217–28) wanted to demonstrate that suicide occurs frequently in primitive society.[1] Since level of integration is not treated as a variable, he eschewed an attempt to show that suicide varies proportionately with degree of social integration.

The diversity of his sources is striking. They include works by travelers, ethnographers, religious functionaries, doctors, essayists, and others on a bewildering variety of peoples (Visigoths, Hindus, Fiji Islanders, Troglodytes, etc.). Certainly Durkheim cannot be faulted for limiting his references to a particular period, place, or sociocultural type. If the result is a conglomeration of disparate works, the majority still fall into one of two groups: those written by nineteenth-century social scientists, and classic works written by Roman and Greek historians, rhetoricians, philosophers, administrators, and so on. The reliability of these sources was never questioned—an anomaly for a scientist who self-consciously evaluated the quality of his other evidence. Perhaps he entertained reservations but felt compelled to employ the data for lack of better evidence.

One consideration in particular raises doubts about Durkheim's handling of his sources. Despite a brief allusion (217) to contrary opinions in the first sentence of his commentary on primitive society, Durkheim never cited an author who felt that suicide was less than frequent in lower societies or explicitly referred to any evidence suggesting that this was the case. However, it is unlikely that there was total agreement among the references consulted, and Durkheim made no such claim.

Durkheim built his case by citing many different social phenomena as evidence of a high incidence of suicide. He mentioned norms, beliefs, attitudes, and sanctions that require or encourage suicide for different categories of people in various circumstances. Missing, however, is evidence of the impact of these phenomena upon behavior. At only one point (219) are figures cited, and they do not indicate exceptionally high suicide rates—the figure (for 1821) for widows in India works out to a rate of 168 per million.[2] Since Durkheim implied that the rate for this group was unusually high, presumably other groups, and India generally, would display a lower rate. The rate of 168 per million may be compared to rates cited in *Suicide* for Europe: Protestant states range from 31 to 334, Catholic from 17 to 160 (see tables 6.1 and 6.2); rates for widows range from 97 in Württemburg to 240 for Saxony (262). Indian rates do not seem particularly high when compared with those in the egoistic Protestant and the nonegoistic Catholic countries of Europe. The one piece of empirical evidence cited scarcely justifies Durkheim's conclusion that suicide rates in altruistic societies are exceptionally high.

Only 231 Hindu widows in a million (see footnote 2) killed themselves; 999,769 did not. That is, only a minute fraction followed the practice of suttee, thereby demonstrating the necessity of distinguishing between the ideal and the practice.

It is safe to assume that suicide rates in primitive societies vary greatly, just as they do in nonaltruistic settings. The question is whether Durkheim's formulation adequately handles such variation. He identified categories of people who are particularly inclined to commit suicide, but to explain varying suicide rates in terms of varying levels of integration would require that he also argue that some individuals or groups in primitive society are more integrated than others. However, this argument would run counter to his stress on the homogeneity of such societies. Because he did not treat level of integration as a variable, he was hardly in a position to explain variation in his dependent variable (suicide) in terms of variation in his independent variable (integration). And, indeed, at no point, either in inter- or intrasocietal comparisons, was it suggested that variation in integration explain variation in suicide. Durkheim indicated the importance of sanctions and beliefs, which do vary, but he treated them not as independent variables, but as reflections of the underlying social reality, which, again, is highly integrated (226–27, 312–13, 387). Durkheim's tendency to treat levels of integration and suicide rates as universally high deflected attention from the need to explain variation in social suicide rates.

Embedded in Durkheim's analysis is the assumption, part and parcel of his evolutionary perspectives, that primitive societies are basically alike; what is true of one is true of all. In terms of this perspective, it made sense to treat evidence about one such society as indicating the situation in all. Paradoxically, though, as he jumped from society to society, Durkheim asserted as true for all something that he never demonstrated to be true for even one. This difficulty is compounded by his indiscriminate identification of such societies. More or less every society outside of modern Europe and its offshoots—anything from preliterate tribes to the great world civilizations of China, Japan, and India—is classified as primitive. Following this logic, then, information on suicide among the Australian aborigines is evidence on suicide in Tokugawa Japan, Vedic India, and China during the T'ang Dynasty.

No empirically based attempt was made to prove that levels of integration in primitive societies are high. For the most part this level of integration was simply assumed. Durkheim described primitive (altruistic) societies in terms that, within the context of his theory, imply high levels of integration. Both in *Suicide* and earlier (at greater length) in *Division*, Durkheim stressed that primitive societies are small, compact, and undifferentiated. In these terms the prototypical primitive society is a small, preliterate tribe. But if small size, compactness, and undifferentiated social structure are hallmarks of primitive society, then China, Japan, and India do not qualify. At minimum, Durkheim's appeal to the high levels of integration that prevail in primitive societies does not sustain a belief that China, Japan, and India are highly integrated and therefore should have high suicide rates. In sum, nothing in *Suicide* demonstrates that in the context of primitive society, high levels of integration prevail together with frequent suicide.

THE MODERN ARMY

Durkheim considered the modern military milieu to be a second locus of altruistic suicide.[3] Since the frequency of such suicide varies proportionately with degree of social integration, the general proposition to be established is that the higher the level of social integration in the army, the higher the social suicide rate. Durkheim developed his case by attempting to establish three generalizations: (1) military rates exceed civilian; (2) rates for different military groups vary proportionately with degree of altruism; and (3) military coefficients of aggravation vary inversely with civilian suicide rates.[4]

Cross-National Military-Civilian Comparisons

Findings. Beginning with his most comprehensive cross-national data (table xxiii:228), Durkheim concluded that "in all European countries . . . the suicidal aptitude of soldiers is much higher than that of the civilian population of the same age." There are grounds for doubting this conclusion, once the impact of two controls, presence of children and age, is considered. Durkheim compared the military rate to that for unmarried civilians of the "same" age as the average age of army personnel.[5] As was noted in the section on familial society, this procedure effects only a crude control. What would be shown by a finer control for age—one permitting comparison of civilian and military rates at each age interval—is uncertain.

The coefficient of preservation for husbands with children compared to single men is 2.90 (table 6.5). According to Durkheim (229), "soldiers who are not officers do not marry"; that is, the army is composed largely of men without children. There are indications both in *Suicide* (275n) and in the French census (France, Ministère du commerce 1894:190) that a significant portion of civilian men in this age category have children; exercise of a control for presence of children should therefore reduce the coefficient of aggravation derived for French army personnel. Similar considerations apply to all the other military coefficients derived by Durkheim.[6]

Durkheim (229) argued that the military coefficients of aggravation (table xxiii:228) should not be ascribed to bachelorhood because highly integrated military society should act to offset the low level of the soldier's familial integration. But this argument *assumed* what he was attempting to demonstrate, namely, the altruistic nature of military society. Thus his rejection of bachelorhood's relevance as a control in civilian-military comparisons is unconvincing, particularly given his own control on bachelorhood in subsequent military-civilian comparisons.

Denmark was not included in Durkheim's table. The suicide rate for Danish army personnel and civilians is about the same, 382 and 388, respectively; however, this military rate does not include officers (228–29). Since officers in other countries have been shown to have higher rates than soldiers, Durkheim's speculation that their inclusion would raise the military rate is reasonable. Yet his assertion that including officers would reverse Denmark's military-civilian balance must be questioned. If soldiers' rates are exceptional, perhaps those for officers are also. Furthermore, Durkheim's argument slights an important consideration: rates for soldiers (who, after all, constitute the bulk of the modern army) are lower than rates for civilians. Again, in another context Durkheim (235) asserted that in Denmark, "soldiers kill themselves ... no more than the other inhabitants." On the basis of the evidence provided, Denmark must stand as an apparent exception to the generalization that military suicide rates exceed civilian rates.

Limitations of the data make it difficult to assess definitively just what the figures in Durkheim's table reveal. The adequate exercise of controls (e.g., age, children) previously identified in *Suicide* as important might diminish to the point of insignificance, or even reverse, the ratios of the two or three countries that show the lowest coefficients of aggravation (including France, on which Durkheim's analysis centers). These three (France, Prussia, and Saxony), plus Denmark, leave five of nine countries with an appreciable excess of military over civilian suicides. Since Durkheim's analysis focused upon Europe, inclusion of the United States was gratuitous. Removing it leaves four of eight countries that forcefully sustain Durkheim's hypothesis. His analysis might better have been directed toward explaining why military suicide rates are often higher than, but sometimes about the same as, civilian rates; certainly it cannot explain the universality of higher military rates.

Interpretation. In his interpretation of table xxiii (228), Durkheim assumed that higher suicide rates demonstrate the altruistic nature of military society. However, even if civilian rates were *higher* than military ones, the latter society could still be altruistic. Discovering that military rates exceed civilian is not essential to Durkheim's case, but such a finding would have considerable importance nonetheless. The argument that military society is more integrated than the civilian is accepted for purposes of this analysis. Durkheim blended this argument with a second, more restrictive argument, namely: civilian suicides are egoistic; military suicides, altruistic. This second argument, far more problematic than the first, turns in part upon the ratio of military to civilian suicides. To understand why requires consideration of two empirical possibilities: (1) civilian rates exceed military; (2) military rates exceed civilian.

The first outcome can be explained in two ways. One is to postulate that, although egoistic, military personnel are simply less so than civilians; the second, that civilian society is more egoistic than military society is altruistic. The difficulty is that both possibilities may be associated with the *same* military rates. The only difference is that military suicides are moved from the egoism to the altruism portion of the integration continuum. Low military rates force the investigator to decide whether they represent low levels of egoism or low levels of altruism—obviously a difficult and perhaps, ultimately, arbitrary decision.

The situation is quite otherwise when military rates exceed civilian. The theory provides two possible explanations. One is that military society is more egoistic than civilian, an explanation ruled out by Durkheim's contention that military society is more integrated. The other possibility is that civilian society is egoistic; military society, altruistic. In sum, it is important to Durkheim's analysis that military suicide rates exceed civilian. As figure 7.1

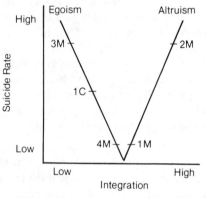

Fig. 7.1. Hypothetical civilian and military suicide rates. M=military; C=civilian; numbers refer to different possibilities noted in text.

shows, it is easier for him to make the case that civilian and military suicides lie at points 1C and 2M, respectively—and not at points 1C and 3M—than it is to argue that military and civilian rates should be at points 1C and 1M, as opposed to points 1C and 4M.

Internal Comparisons

Findings. Durkheim's attempt to demonstrate that civilian suicide rates exceed those for the military overlapped with his attempt to demonstrate that the suicide rates of groups within the military vary proportionately with the levels of integration characterizing those groups. Although he made no attempt in his table (228) to control for the effects of marriage and the family, Durkheim was aware of their relevance and, in the case of France, attempted to show that the military coefficient of aggravation holds even when such controls have been exercised. He did this by comparing in turn soldiers, noncommissioned officers, and officers with their civilian counterparts. Since soldiers are unmarried, Durkheim suggested comparing them to single male civilians of the "same" age, choosing the twenty-to-twenty-five age bracket. Dividing the rate of 380 for soldiers by 237 (the rate for single, unmarried men aged twenty to twenty-five) gave Durkheim a coefficient of aggravation of 1.6 for soldiers "wholly independent of bachelorhood" (229). Since *Suicide* (229n) gives the average age for military men as twenty to thirty, it would appear more reasonable to employ the average suicide rate for civilians twenty to twenty-five, 237, and twenty-five to thirty, 394 (178), which is 315.5. Dividing 380 by 315.5 produces a military coefficient of aggravation of 1.2, a coefficient that reduces by two-thirds the difference found by Durkheim. It would not be surprising if a finer control for age further reduced or eliminated this remaining difference. For France, the only country for which the necessary figures are given, exercising controls on marital status and age leaves only doubtful indications that soldiers, the bulk of the modern army, have higher suicide rates than civilians.

Because his data did not permit comparison of suicide rates for noncommissioned officers and civilians for the same period, Durkheim did not attempt to settle on an exact coefficient for noncommissioned officers. Rather, he (230) derived "a coefficient of aggravation of 1.94 which may be increased almost to 4 without fear of exaggerating the facts." Taking change in rates over time into account, I derive a coefficient of aggravation of 3.0 for noncommissioned officers compared to unmarried male civilians.[7] In the case of officers, Durkheim bent the figures slightly to increase the coefficient.[8] For this analysis, however, his coefficient of aggravation of 2.15 may be accepted.

In addition to comparing soldiers, noncommissioned officers, and officers, *Suicide* (233) also compares volunteers and reenlistees. Durkheim assumed that reenlistees were more integrated into the service than were volunteers (presumably entering service for the first time). One problem here is that he failed to indicate how he determined the probable average ages. *Suicide* (229n) gives the average age for the army as "from 20 to 30" or 25. If reenlisted men are 30, noncommissioned officers, 31 or more, officers, 37.75, and the average army age, 25, then volunteers must have an average age of less than 25. How much less cannot be ascertained from the information provided. Their average age is probably at least three years less than that for the entire army. Using this estimate, one can compare volunteers with unmarried civilians aged 22. Dividing 670 (the suicide rate for volunteers) by 224.6 (that for unmarried civilians) produces a coefficient of aggravation of 3.0. Dividing 1,300 (the suicide rate for reenlisted men) by 471.5 (the rate of unmarried civilians aged 30) produces a coefficient of aggravation of 2.8.[9] Given the data's limitations, there is no reason to believe that the difference is significant; but neither is there reason to believe that, relative to their civilian counterparts, suicide rates for reenlisted men are higher than those for volunteers.[10]

An additional set of figures is introduced with the observation (237) that "in all armies, the coefficient of aggravation is highest among the elite troops." The expectation is that the figures will compare elite and nonelite troops. However, Durkheim's chart includes no such comparisons, nor did his commentary, except for the remark that the veterans' coefficient "is far higher than that of ordinary troops." The coefficients of 2.45 and 2.37 for the special corps of Paris and of veterans, respectively, are much higher than that of 1.25 for the French army but lower than the 3.0 for non-commissioned officers, the 3.0 for volunteers, or the 2.8 derived for reenlisted men. The reader is given no information about the source of these figures, the range of those available, how "real or proba-ble" ages were determined, or the percentage having children. Durkheim (237) went on to note that "in the army of Algeria, considered the school of military virtue, during the period 1872–78 suicide had a mortality double that of the same period for troops stationed in France." He also noted that the least severely affected troops are those with the least pronounced military character, e.g., engineers. No figures are cited, nor is consideration given to the possible impact of controls. Altogether, his analysis, if suggestive, nonetheless cannot sustain the generalization that elite troops display higher suicide rates than other troops, nor is there any indication that the more elite the unit, the higher the suicide rate.

Interpretation. There is one striking anomaly in the findings. Durkheim's initial table (228) gives 1.25 as the coefficient of aggravation for army personnel in France. Dividing the army by rank, he derived the following coefficients of aggravation: soldiers 1.6, noncommissioned officers 1.94–4, and commissioned officers 2.15. However, it is impossible for *all* of these groups to have coefficients higher than that for the whole they compose. Method-ologically, the discrepancy can be approached by noting that the various coefficients refer to different years and are based on an inadequate exercise of controls. The finding that soldiers apparently display little if any coefficient of aggravation reduces the discrepancy. The logical difficulty nevertheless remains: either the 1.25 coefficient for the army as a whole, or one or more of the coefficients derived for the different ranks, is wrong.

Durkheim also wished to demonstrate that the more altruistic the group, the higher its suicide rate. To this end he argued that the ranks should be ordered ascendingly as follows: soldiers, officers, and noncommissioned officers. It is difficult to avoid concluding that this is a post-factum ordering, dictated by their respective coefficients of aggravation. Having noted that soldiers have the lowest coefficient, and implicitly anticipating that noncommissioned officers should have the next highest, Durkheim (234) noted "the strange superiority of non-commissioned officers over officers." He explained it as follows: If noncommissioned officers "commit suicide more frequently, it is because no function requires so much of the habit of passive submission. However disciplined the officer, he must be capable of initiative to a certain extent; he has a wider field of action and, accordingly, a more developed individuality." These variables (habit of passive submission, etc.) may explain why suicide rates for noncommissioned officers exceed those of officers; but, if so, they suggest in equal measure that soldiers should have higher suicide rates than either officers or noncommissioned officers. Surely it is the soldier who is least able to display initiative, has the most restricted field of action, must display most consistently the habit of passive submission, and is least able to express his individuality. This conclusion also follows from another passage (234) in *Suicide* (in which Durkheim used "soldier" to designate all army members): "Discipline requires [the soldier] to obey without question and sometimes even without understanding. For this an intellectual abnegation hardly consistent with individualism is required. He must have but a weak tie binding him to his individuality, to obey external impulsion so docilely. In short, a soldier's principle of action is external to himself." Once again it would appear that soldiers represent the purest embodiment of altruism; thus the coefficient for soldiers should exceed that for noncommissioned officers, whose coefficient should, in turn, exceed that for officers.

I do not mean to imply that no aspect of the theory suggests the ordering identified by Durkheim. Indeed, a major difficulty is that the theory generates different, even conflicting, predictions. For instance, it could be argued that officers represent the purest embodiment of altruism. After all, are they not most imbued with the traditional military values of honor, duty, and country? Are they not also an elite? This line of reasoning leads to the expectation that officers would have the highest coefficients; soldiers, the lowest. Another theme prevalent not only in *Suicide* but throughout Durkheim's work is that the number of people in a given area (volume or material density) determines the rate of interaction (moral or dynamic density), which in turn determines the level of integration. Because they generally live and work under more crowded conditions than officers, soldiers should have higher rates of interaction, be more highly integrated into the military, and, hence, display the highest suicide rates.

One prediction appears consistently: on the relevant variables, noncommissioned officers should tend to fall *between* soldiers and officers. Durkheim, though, found noncommissioned officers at one extreme. Thus, far from validating his proposition that suicide in the military varies proportionately with level of integration, his comparison of coefficients by rank, on balance, undercuts the proposition.[11]

Military Rates as a Function of Civilian Rates

Perhaps the most obvious approach to relating integration and national variation in military suicide rates is to develop indicators for altruism and then use these to predict military suicide rates. Durkheim gave no indication of ever having entertained this possibility. But had he done so, perhaps his initial table (xxiii:228) would have discouraged him. Prussia, with its strong military tradition and authoritarian army, shows a military suicide rate of 607, placing it fourth from the top in a list of nine countries. With a relatively nonauthoritarian army and without a comparable military tradition, the United States displays the second highest rate, 680. England's rate of 209 makes it more similar to Württemberg, 320, than the latter is to either of its fellow German states: Prussia, 607, or Saxony, 640. Austria's rate of 1,253 is almost or more than double that of any other country except America; it remains unclear why its rate should be twice that of Prussia, three times that of Italy, 407, and France, 333, and six times that of England. On the surface, the figures do not support the notion that the more integrated the army, the higher its suicide rate. In any case, it is unfortunate that Durkheim did not directly demonstrate that national military

suicide rates vary with degree of military altruism; such a demonstration would have done much to help validate his theory.

Durkheim's approach. Underlying Durkheim's analysis is the
implicit assumption that, *divorced from external influences,* all
armies would be equally integrated. He treated civilian society as the
sole external influence upon the army and, therefore, the determinant of varying levels of military integration. The value of the
integration level that would prevail if military society were divorced
from civilian society is here identified as the military constant.
Stated as an equation: level of civilian integration plus the military
constant equals level of military integration. Durkheim never specified the value of the military constant nor, given his approach, did
he need to. In a comparison of two or more countries, it cancels out,
leaving varying levels of integration in military society to be
explained as a function of varying levels of integration in civilian
society.

The army is altruistic; civilian society, egoistic. As a country
becomes decreasingly egoistic, it moves in the direction of altruism.
As this happens, the altruism generated by the army encounters less
opposition in the lower levels of egoism in civilian society, more
readily superimposes itself upon those in the military, becomes
excessive, and leads to a high rate of suicide (236–37, 322). Taking
the individual as the unit of analysis, the army man is subject to two
sui generis forces, civilian society and military society. The less
egoistic civilian society is, the more readily the altruistic forces of the
army impose themselves, inclining him toward suicide. Taking the
army as the unit of analysis, the suicide rate of any given army is a
function of the extent to which the altruistic forces it generates are
weakened through conflict with the egoistic environment of civilian
society.

In testing his hypothesis, Durkheim (228) employed the military
coefficient of aggravation, i.e., the ratio of military to civilian
suicide rates. Use of this coefficient, however, is misleading. The
theory makes no predictions about the *ratio* of military to civilian
suicide rates; rather, it holds that military rates are a function of the
level of integration in civilian society. Consequently, military suicide
rates, *not* military coefficients of aggravation, should be employed
as the dependent variable, as may be seen in table 7.1. Part B
represents diagrammatically the hypothetical results given in Part A.
Military suicide rates are equal to civilian rates plus the "military

TABLE 7.1   SUICIDE **R**ATES VS. **C**OEFFICIENTS AS A **T**EST OF **D**URKHEIM'S
THEORY

			Part A	
Country	Military Rate	Civilian Rate	Military/Civilian Rate Difference[a] (Military Constant)	Military Coefficient of Aggravation
A	50	10	60	5
B	40	20	60	2
C	30	30	60	1

[a]Computed as the sum of the military and civilian rates.

Part B

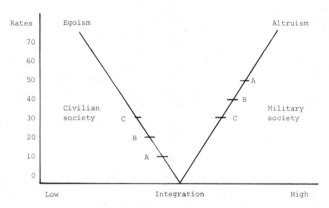

constant" (in this case, 60); the rates are those predicted by the
theory. Use of the coefficients of aggravation, however, conceals the
fact that the theory has been confirmed. It would be possible to
present a second example to demonstrate that even in instances in
which coefficients vary as Durkheim said they should (coefficients
rising as civilian suicide rates fall), direct comparison of military
and civilian rates would reveal that the theory has not been
confirmed. Rather than following Durkheim in using these misleading coefficients, I directly compare civilian and military suicide rates
to determine whether variation in the latter can be explained by
variation in the former.

Findings. "From Table XXIII it appears that the military coefficient
of aggravation is higher the less tendency the civilian population has

to suicide and vice versa" (234-35). However, direct comparison of military and civilian suicide rates produces altogether different results; there is negligible correlation ($r = .06$) between civilian and military suicide rates (table 7.2). Durkheim (235n) questioned the

TABLE 7.2   MALE CIVILIAN AND MILITARY SUICIDE RATES (PER MILLION) IN SELECTED EUROPEAN COUNTRIES AND THE UNITED STATES

Country	Years	Civilian Rate (Males Same Age as Soldiers)	Military Rate	Military Constant[a]	Rank Order Civ. Rate	Rank Order Mil. Rate (Inverse)
Italy	1876-90	77	407	484	1	5
England	1876-90	79	209	288	2	9
U.S.	1870-84	80	680	760	3	2
Austria	1876-90	122	1,253	1,375	4	1
Württemberg	1846-58	170	320	490	5	8
France	1876-90	265	333	598	6	7
Saxony	1847-58	369	640	1,009	7	3
Denmark	1845-56	388	382[b]	770	8	6
Prussia	1876-90	394	607	1,001	9	4

SOURCE: *Suicide* (228); last three columns added.

[a]Computed as the sum of civilian and military rates.

[b]Rate does not include officers and noncommissioned officers.

validity of Austrian data. Excluding Austria, the countries with lower civilian suicide rates also have lower military suicide rates ($r = .31$), contrary to theoretical expectations.

The military suicide rates in table 7.2 were compared to those for civilians of the same sex and average age, a procedure that treats the individual as the unit of analysis. So understood, the theory explains variation in suicide rates as a function of the relative strength of civilian and military forces as they impinge upon military personnel.[12] Durkheim's perspective emphasized the sui generis reality of society. With society as the unit of analysis, civilian society is the environment of military society. Here Durkheim's hypothesis relates civilian and military societies, making it appropriate to use the overall civilian suicide rate as the indicator of integration in civilian society. Table 7.3 relates national civilian and military suicide rates. The product moment correlation coefficient between military and civilian rates for all countries is .21, or .66 excluding Austria. Countries with higher civilian rates also display higher military rates. If anything, then, military and civilian suicide may be a function of somewhat similar, and not "opposite" (238), causes.[13]

Durkheim generally employed the civilian suicide rate as his indicator of integration in civilian society. However, at one point he (236) eschewed the use of objective indicators, simply asserting that "traditionalism, the chief opponent of the spirit of individualism, is far more developed in Italy, Austria and even in England than in Saxony, Prussia and France."[14] Table 7.4 employs these impressionistic assessments of relative levels of egoism.[15] The data show little relationship between egoism levels and military suicide rates. Countries low on egoism rank one, four, and six on military suicide. Thus, even employing Durkheim's own impressionistic assessments of egoism levels in civilian society does not sustain a conclusion that military suicide rates are higher in the less egoistic nations.[16]

SUMMARY AND CONCLUSION

Proceeding on the assumption that higher military rates indicate their altruistic character, Durkheim first attempted to demonstrate

TABLE 7.3   CIVILIAN AND MILITARY SUICIDE RATES (PER MILLION) IN SELECTED EUROPEAN COUNTRIES

Country	National Rate	Years	Military Rate	Years	Difference (Military Constant)	Rank Order Civ. Rate	Rank Order Mil. Rate (Inverse)
Italy	38	1874-78	407	1876-90	445	1	4
England	69	1874-78	209	1876-90	278	2	9
Belgium	78	1874-78	391	1885	469	3	5
Württemberg	108	1846-56	320	1846-58	428	4	8
Austria	130	1874-78	1,253	1876-90	1,383	5	1
France	160	1882-88	333	1876-90	493	6	7
Saxony	245	1856-60	640	1847-58	885	7	2
Denmark	258	1846-50	382[a]	1845-56	640	8	6
Prussia	260	1882-88	607	1876-90	867	9	3

SOURCE: Military rates from Suicide (table XXIII:228). Belgium added (238). For civilian suicide rates, see Suicide (50, 74, 351). Civilian rates chosen to refer, as nearly as possible, to same periods as military rates.

[a]Rate excludes officers and noncommissioned officers.

TABLE 7.4   LEVELS OF EGOISM IN CIVILIAN SOCIETY AND MILITARY SUI-
CIDE RATES

Country	Level of Egoism	Military Suicide Rate	Years	Rank Order Suicide Rates
Austria	Low	1,253	1876-90	1
Saxony	High	640	1847-58	2
Prussia	High	607	1876-90	3
Italy	Low	407	1876-90	4
France	High	333	1876-90	5
England	Low	209	1876-90	6

SOURCE: Suicide (228; also 236).

that military suicide rates exceed civilian rates. In fact, however,
military rates may be altruistic regardless of whether they are higher
than civilian rates. This situation places an additional burden of
proof on attempts to account for variation in military suicide rates.
The theory does not lead to one determinant prediction of the
comparative size of coefficients of aggravation for soldiers, noncommissioned officers, and officers, nor does the particular order
stated by Durkheim himself appear to be consistent with theoretically based expectations. Additional attempts to demonstrate that
suicide rates vary with degree of altruism in various parts of the
army meet with mixed results. Durkheim's final crucial thrust—the
attempt to explain military suicide rates as a function of the level of
integration in civilian society—produces more negative than positive
results. If different attempts at validation inevitably find varying
mixtures of confirmation or refutation in the data, which itself is of
mixed quality, more often than not results turn out to be either
neutral or negative. Neither in the analysis of primitive society nor in
that of the modern army does *Suicide* establish that suicide varies
proportionately with degree of social integration.

Anomie is the state of low social regulation. As with egoism, Durkheim hypothesized that suicide varies proportionately with anomie. He distinguished between acute anomie (caused by sudden change) and chronic (associated with more gradual, long-term change). *Suicide* treats both economic and domestic anomie.

ECONOMIC ANOMIE

Durkheim's analysis of economic anomie considered first the acute, and subsequently the chronic, cases.

Acute Economic

Crashes. Employing economic crisis as the indicator of anomie, Durkheim (241–42) cited data for Vienna, Frankfort on the Main, and France showing that various financial crises (crashes) were accompanied by an increase in suicide ranging from 7 to 70 percent (table 8.1). Crisis severity (242) was measured by number of bankruptcies. Figures on the percentage increase in bankruptcies and suicide are, respectively: 1861, 20 and 9; 1847, 26 and 17; 1854, 37 and 8. There is a negative correlation ($r = -.27$) between increase in bankruptcies and suicide. For the one point at which Durkheim employed an empirical indicator of crisis severity, his data fail to reflect the hypothesized relationship between anomie and suicide.

As a systematic attempt to demonstrate empirically that economic crises are associated with an increase in suicide, Durkheim's presentation has weaknesses. He did not list the criteria governing his data selection. Since his main focus is on France, figures for Vienna and Frankfort on the Main appear to have been included because they sustain the hypothesis. Limited to French data, Durkheim's case rests on only four instances, clearly an insufficient number to validate his hypothesis. Generally contented to show an increase during crisis periods, Durkheim largely failed to consider whether the impact upon suicide rates is a function of crisis severity;

TABLE 8.1　Suicide and Economic Crashes

Place	Date	Suicides (absolute numbers)	Percentage Increase over Preceding Year[d]
Vienna			
Year	1872	141	....
	1873[a]	153	8.5
	1874[a]	216	41.2
First four months	1871	48	....
	1872	44	....
	1873	43	....
	1874[a]	73	69.8
Frankfort on the Main	1873[b]	22[c]	....
	1874[a]	32	45.4
France			
Year	1847[a]		17
	1854[a]		8
	1861[a]		9
	1881	6,741	....
	1882[a]	7,213	7.0
	1883	7,267	....
First three months	1881	1,589	....
	1882[a]	1,770	11.4
	1883	1,604	....

SOURCE: Suicide (241–42).

[a]Denotes crisis period.

[b]When he described the crisis in Frankfort on the Main as "occurring at the same time" as that in Vienna, it is not clear whether Durkheim meant 1873 and 1874 or, rather, the period of greatest crisis in Vienna, the first four months of 1874. The latter seems more likely.

[c]This is the average number of suicides "in the years before 1874" (241). Durkheim used this average (covering an unspecified number of years) as his point of comparison.

[d]Percentages recomputed from data in Suicide (except 1847, 1854, and 1861 for France, which were given by Durkheim).

in his one such attempt, the figures show a negative relationship.

Prosperity. In another of those twists that make his work so interesting, Durkheim (242–46) went on to argue that economic prosperity has the same effect on suicide as sharp downturns, a contention that his figures sustain (table 8.2). He identified twelve years of prosperity; in nine of these, the suicide rate rose (the

TABLE 8.2 SUICIDE AND ECONOMIC PROSPERITY

Place	Year	Suicides (absolute numbers)	Percentage Change from Preceding Year[c]
Prussia	1849	1,527	....
	1850[a]	1,736	13.7
	1857	2,038	....
	1858[a]	2,126	4.3
	1859[a]	2,146	0.9
	1862	2,112	....
	1863[a]	2,374[b]	12.4
	1864[a]	2,203	-7.2
	1865[a]	2,361	7.2
	1866[a]	2,485	5.2
Bavaria	1847	217	....
	1848[a]	215	-0.9
	1849[a]	189	-12.1
	1850[a]	250	32.3
	1857	286	....
	1858[a]	329	15.0
	1859[a]	387	17.6
Average			7.3
Average, excluding 1848-49 for Bavaria			10.1
Average, excluding 1847-50 for Prussia and Bavaria			6.9

SOURCE: <u>Suicide</u> (242-43) unless otherwise noted.

[a]Denotes year of prosperity.

[b]Durkheim (243) cited figures for 1862 and 1866 only; other figures from <u>Suicide</u> (47).

[c]Percentages recomputed from data in <u>Suicide</u>.

average increase for all years was 7.3). Commenting on the exceptions represented by 1848 and 1849 in Bavaria, Durkheim (243) referred to his previous discussion of political society. Though failing to mention Prussia, his reference suggests the desirability of dropping it as well, since it had also experienced a political crisis during 1848 and 1849 that would affect suicide rates through 1850. During 1850, relative to 1849, a general relaxation and consequent lowering of level of integration in political society should cause an increase in suicide. Deleting this entire period (1847-50) for both Prussia and Bavaria produces an average yearly percentage increase of 6.9. Fortunately, concern over whether the hypothesis is best tested with the Prussia-Bavaria figures included or excluded is tempered by the small difference in the resulting averages (7.3 versus 6.9). Following Durkheim's suggestions on the impact of political crises, I used the 6.9 average and subtracted 2.3 percent (the estimated normal increase in suicide for the periods in question).[1] Thus 4.6 percent is the average yearly increase associated with periods of prosperity over and above the normal increase in suicide.

Altogether, Durkheim's data on prosperity share many of the shortcomings of his data on crashes. In particular, only five instances are given; only three, if the 1847-50 period is excluded. The paucity of instances alone prevents the analysis from being anything more than suggestive.

Having considered periods of prosperity, Durkheim (243) turned to "fortunate crises, the effect of which is abruptly to enhance a country's prosperity," and he endeavored to show that they "affect suicide like economic disasters."[2] His findings are summarized in table 8.3. The average yearly percentage increase in suicide for each of the acutely prosperous years is 5.4 (table 8.3, parts I and II). From this may be subtracted the average yearly increase in suicide (2.0 percent). Fortunate crises are thus associated with only a very small increase in suicide—3.4 percent.[3] This finding poses considerable embarrassment for the theory; it turns out that the average yearly increase associated with prosperity (4.6 percent) is greater than that associated with extreme prosperity (3.4 percent). The greater the disturbance, the smaller the impact upon suicide rates!

Durkheim's use of empirical indicators in this analysis poses difficulties. The wheat prices for 1850 and 1864 given in part I of table 8.4 represent the only instances in which Durkheim stated the value of an empirical indicator for a given year of prosperity. These two wheat prices plus that for the nonprosperous year of 1861 (table 8.4) thus constitute the only empirical indication that the period was, in fact, one of prosperity. Overall, the paucity of information on suicide rates and wheat prices makes it impossible to determine whether there is any correlation between magnitude of drop in prices and rise in suicide.

The indicators of extreme prosperity are not easily related to Durkheim's contention that such periods are associated with an increase in suicide (table 8.4, part II). There is no exact correspondence of years covered by suicide rates and economic indicators. In fact, the earliest years covered by indicators are the middle or latest years for which yearly increases in suicide rates are cited. While the

TABLE 8.3   SUICIDE AND EXTREME PROSPERITY ("FORTUNATE CRISES")

Part I

Place	Year	Suicides (absolute numbers)	Suicide Rate (per million)	Percentage Change from Preceding Year[a]
Italy	1870	....	29[c]	...
	1871[b]	....	31	6.9
	1872[b]	....	33	6.5
	1873[b]	....	36	9.1
	1874[b]	....	37	2.8
	1875[b]	....	34	-8.1
	1876[b]	....	36.5	7.4
	1877[b]	....	40.6	11.2
France	1877	....	....	....
	1878[b]	....	....	8
Paris	1888[d]	517	....	....
	1889[b]	567	...:	9.7
	1890	540	....	....
Average				5.9

Part II

Country	Period of Prosperity	Percentage Increase in Suicide Rate	Average Yearly Percentage Increase[e]
Italy	1877-89	28	2.3
Prussia	1875-86	90	8.2

Country	Per. Immed. Prec. Per. of Prosper.	Average Yearly Suicide Rate	Period of Prosperity	Average Yearly Suicide Rate	Average Yearly Percentage Increase (1861-65 to 1866-70)[f]
Prussia	1861-65	122	1866-70	133	2.2

SOURCE: *Suicide* (244-45) except where otherwise indicated.

[a] Most figures added.   [b] Denotes period of prosperity.

[c] Yearly average for 1864-70, which Durkheim used as a basis for comparison.

[d] All figures in this series (1888-90) are for the first seven months of each year (the months of the Exposition).

[e] Figures added.

[f] Figure added. Average computed using rate of 122 as rate for midpoint of 1861-65 interval, and 133 as rate for midpoint of 1866-70 interval.

1877-89 period for suicide rates overlaps with that of the indicators, there is no yearly breakdown of rates, and the average yearly increase in suicide during this period is too slight to sustain Durkheim's thesis. None of the economic indicators can be directly related to yearly increases in suicide rates since the former are not broken down by year. In brief, Durkheim's indicators do little to

enhance the credibility of the assertion that prosperity is associated
with an increase in suicide.

Poverty. Durkheim (245) completed his presentation of data by
arguing that, far from aggravating suicidal tendencies, "poverty

TABLE 8.4 SUICIDE AND INDICATORS OF PROSPERITY

Part I: Prosperity--Suicide and Wheat Prices in Prussia

Year	Wheat Price[a]	Suicides (absolute numbers)	Percentage Change from Preceding Year	
			Wheat Price	Suicides
1848	?	?	?	?
1849	?	1,527	?	?
1850[b]	6.91	1,736	?	14
1851	?	?	?	?
1852	?	?	?	?
1853	?	?	?	?
1857	?	2,038	?	?
1858[b]	?	2,126	?	?
1859[b]	?	2,146	?	?
1861	11.04	?	?	?
1862	?	2,112	?	?
1863[b]	?	?	?	?
1864[b]	7.95	?	?	?
1865[b]	?	?	?	?
1866[b]	?	2,485	?	?[c]

Part II: Extreme Prosperity (Italy)

Indicator	Years	Percentage Increase during Period	Suicide	
			Years	Percentage Change in Rate from Preceding Year
Steam boilers	1876-87	124	1870	...
			1871[b]	7
Horsepower (of steam boilers)	1876-87	209	1872[b]	6
			1873[b]	9
			1874[b]	3
Salaries	1873-89	35	1875[b]	-8
			1876[b]	7
Private wealth	1875-80 to 1885-90	20	1877[b]	11
			1877-89	2.3[d]

SOURCE: *Suicide* (242-44).

NOTE: ? denotes information not given.

[a]Wheat prices in marks per 50 kilograms.

[b]Singled out by Durkheim as a year of relatively marked prosperity.

[c]Durkheim (243) noted that suicide increased 17 percent from 1862 to 1866.

[d]Average yearly percentage increase from 1877 to 1889.

may even be considered a protection." He mentioned two countries (Ireland and Spain) and one Italian province (Calabria) that combine poverty with low suicide rates.[4] *Suicide* (245) also presents figures for French departments suggesting that as the wealth of a department increases, its suicide rate does likewise. The data are limited both in neglecting to exercise any controls and in failing to show whether wealthier individuals are more likely to commit suicide than the less wealthy.[5]

Interpretation and conclusion. Durkheim (246) concluded: "If therefore industrial or financial crises increase suicides, this is not because they cause poverty, since crises of prosperity have the same result; it is because they are crises, that is, disturbances of the collective order. Every disturbance of equilibrium, even though it achieves greater comfort and a heightening of general vitality, is an impulse to voluntary death." Disturbances of the collective order reduce social regulation, i.e., increase anomie. Consequently, they cause an increase in suicide. How well did Durkheim sustain his hypothesis that anomie and suicide vary proportionately?

Suicide (242) argues that "if voluntary deaths increased because life was becoming more difficult, they should diminish perceptibly as comfort increases." Testing this possibility, Durkheim argued that suicide increases during periods of economic prosperity. Consequently, he rejected the idea that increased hardship causes suicide and thereby accounts for the rise in suicide during economic crises. But does the conclusion logically follow? Because life is more readily renounced as it becomes easier does not preclude the possibility that it may also be renounced when it becomes harder. In this regard Durkheim (243) supplemented his first contention by arguing that "so far is the increase in poverty from causing the increase in suicide that even fortunate crises ... affect suicide like economic disasters." Not only does suicide increase during periods of prosperity, it even increases during periods of extreme prosperity when the general ease of life is even more markedly improved. Durkheim concluded by introducing another argument to dispose of what he saw as the main competitor to his own: if life is renounced as it gets harder, suicide should be frequent among the poor. In fact, however, those who live in poverty have low suicide rates; thus poverty "may even be considered a protection" against suicide (245). *Suicide* cites figures for those living in poverty. However, since the argument in question is couched in terms of the relationship between increasing hardship of life and suicide, Durkheim's conclusion is premature.

Perhaps Durkheim did not distinguish clearly between two different arguments. He successfully rejected the idea that suicide rates vary proportionately with the hardship of life, but this is not to say that he also rejected the different argument that increased hardship leads to suicide.

As important as his success in rejecting other explanations is his relative success in establishing his own. More than one aspect of his presentation undercuts it; often failing to cite his sources, he invariably failed to mention the criteria employed in selecting the figures presented. Knowing nothing about the representativeness of the data makes it difficult to have confidence in the findings. Generally, only a few examples are cited, and the average yearly percentage increase in suicide is frequently modest. The analysis suffers further from a lack of effective use of empirical indicators. Durkheim identified instances in which economic change is associated with an increase in suicide, but at no point did he systematically demonstrate that the magnitude of change in regulation corresponds with the magnitude of change in suicide rates. The treatment of prosperity indicates that it is actually associated with a greater increase in suicide rates than is extreme prosperity, a finding which suggests that regulation and suicide vary proportionately and not inversely as hypothesized.

Chronic Economic

Although modern sociology often treats the acute as the classic form of anomie, Durkheim (245) himself seemed to feel that chronic economic anomie is the more significant factor in high suicide rates. Given the importance he attached to it, the striking aspect of his analysis is its brevity. Only a single paragraph comments on the empirical evidence, which is itself almost wholly confined to table xxiv (258).

Durkheim (257) observed that industrial and commercial occupations are more afflicted by suicide than is "agriculture, where the old regulative forces still make their appearance felt most and where the fever of business has least penetrated." Durkheim's table permits seventeen comparisons between agricultural and industrial-commercial occupations for the same period in a given country; in all but two, suicide rates are lower in agricultural occupations. The overall average for agriculture is 184; that for the other three occupations, 449.

An additional aspect of the data is less supportive. For five of seven countries, variation within the industrial-commercial category exceeds that between one industrial-commercial occupation and agriculture, an indication that Durkheim ignored greater variability in these figures than that accounted for by the characterization of industrial-commercial occupations as anomic and of agriculture as relatively nonanomic.

Though Durkheim's case rests on the assumption that levels of social regulation in agriculture are higher than those in industrial-commercial occupations, he failed to employ indicators justifying this assumption. Even on the level of argumentation, Durkheim did little to sustain it. Thus his case ultimately rests on the unsupported assertion that agriculture is relatively nonanomic. The contention that levels of social regulation are higher in agriculture than in industrial-commercial occupations is plausible. However, Durkheim provided no empirically-based analysis using objective indicators of regulation to support his contention that in modern society, suicide varies proportionately with chronic economic anomie.

DOMESTIC ANOMIE

The analysis of domestic anomie (241–76) is the most difficult part of that section of *Suicide* devoted to establishing egoism, altruism, and anomie as the causes of suicide. Durkheim developed a long, complicated chain of reasoning. The involuted nature of the arguments requires that final assessment of an earlier link must sometimes be held in abeyance until the validity of later links has been determined. Compounding the problem, Durkheim was often less than explicit about his understanding of how a given empirical generalization relates to the theory. His general hypothesis relating suicide and anomie holds that the two vary proportionately,[6] but he complicated this formulation by postulating that the social regulation embodied in marriage affects men and women differently. Men need it; hence, their suicide rates go *down* as regulation increases. In contrast, women suffer from it, and their suicide rates go *up*. Consequently, as measured in terms of comparisons with single persons of the same sex, Durkheim hypothesized that married men's suicide rates vary inversely, and those of married women proportionately, with the degree of social regulation in marriage.

Durkheim's analysis will be easier to understand if certain themes concerning divorce are first identified; scattered throughout his analysis, these are often more implicit than explicit.[7] On the one hand, there is divorce itself and its attendant upheaval; on the other, divorce is one aspect of marriage. The stronger marriage, the more tightly it controls those living in it, the more strongly it resists disintegration through divorce, the fewer couples actually become divorced, and the lower the divorce rate is (263, 266, 269–71, 273). Thought of in this way, the higher the divorce rate, the weaker the regulatory power of marriage. These two aspects of divorce parallel the two types of anomie. Considered for the disruption it occasions, divorce may be seen as an indicator of acute anomie; considered as a breakdown of marriage, though, divorce rates are an indicator of chronic anomie. Though aware of the relationship between divorce and acute anomie, Durkheim employed divorce rates as the measure of social regulation in marriage.[8]

Acute Domestic

Treating first acute and then chronic domestic anomie, Durkheim (259) began by recalling his earlier treatment of widowhood. The sudden change occasioned by widowhood throws the survivor into a state of acute anomie. Durkheim presented no new data at this point; rather, a footnote (259n) cited his second chapter on egoistic suicide. Comparing the suicide rates of married and widowed persons for seven age categories in Oldenburg (table xx:177) and nine age categories in France (table xxi:178) gives the following average widowed/married suicide ratios for men and then women: Oldenburg, 2.69 and 1.86; France, 2.06 and 2.71 (or 1.78 excluding the extreme coefficient for widows in the fifteen-to-twenty age bracket). Durkheim never identified either the raw data or the specific empirical pattern relevant to his assertion that suicides of the widowed should be explained in terms of the shock of widowhood; presumably he would take these results as confirmatory evidence.[9] These figures have the merit of exercising a careful control for age; however, they do not control for presence of children. Figures employing this control present a similar picture (table 6.5). Married men with and without children have higher coefficients of preservation than do their widowed counterparts. For women with children, the married have a far higher coefficient of preservation than do the widowed. The arrow in the notation column (table 6.5) makes it questionable whether childless married women have a less extreme coefficient of aggravation than do childless widowed. Thus at least three, and perhaps all four, comparisons are consistent with Durkheim's assertion that the widowed have higher suicide rates than the married.

The attempt to identify acute anomie as primarily responsible for the high suicide rates among the widowed rests mainly upon Durkheim's brief descriptive characterizations of widowhood, e.g., "the shock of widowhood" (190; see also 259). Such characterizations are convincing at the theoretical level; at the empirical level, however, what is required are data relating suicide to the time elapsed since becoming widowed. In particular, if it could be shown that suicide rates are especially high for the recently widowed, Durkheim would have a strong empirical foundation for his interpretation. Indicating nothing about such relationships, however, the data do not rule out the possibility that suicide rates among the recently widowed are lower than among those who have been widowed for a longer time, a finding that would permit rejection of acute anomie as the relevant explanatory factor. Furthermore, the theory of egoism postulates an inverse relationship between familial integration and suicide, permitting it to be used also to predict higher rates for widowed persons than for married ones. Unfortunately, Durkheim failed to show how the effects of egoism are to be distinguished from those of anomie. Nothing in the data rules out the possibility that, as Durkheim maintained, high suicide rates among the widowed are to be attributed to acute anomie. At the same time neither is there anything to eliminate either chronic anomie or egoism as causes.

Chronic Domestic

Basic generalizations. Although he briefly mentioned widowhood, it quickly becomes apparent that Durkheim's main concern was with chronic domestic anomie. The empirical core of the analysis consists of six generalizations. (1) Suicide rates and divorce rates are positively correlated. (2) Suicide rates for divorced persons exceed those for the widowed. (3) Suicide rates of the widowed are a function of suicide rates of the married.[10] (4) Suicide rates of the divorced are a function of suicide rates of the married. (5) Coefficients of preservation for married men vary inversely with divorce rates. (Alternatively: the immunity to suicide of married men relative to single men varies inversely with divorce rates.) (6) Coefficients of preservation for men vary inversely, and those for women directly, with divorce rates. Also, coefficients for men vary inversely with those for women. To an important degree Durkheim's analysis stands or falls on the validity of these empirical generalizations.

Findings. Interpreting table xxv (259), Durkheim (260) opened with a statement of the empirical foundation of his entire analysis of chronic domestic anomie: "Throughout Europe the number of suicides varies with that of divorces and separations" ($r = .81$). As Durkheim pointed out, comparison of average suicide and divorce rates for each of three groups of countries classified in terms of relative frequency of divorce shows that higher divorce rates coincide with higher suicide rates. However, the positive correlation found by Durkheim is often reversed within his three categories. In his first category ("Countries Where Divorce and Separation are Rare"), inclusion of Russia is gratuitous.[11] Without Russia, divorce and suicide rank orders are perfectly inverse. Rank orders in the third category ("Countries Where Divorce and Separation are Frequent") are also inverse. In the comparison of countries with similar divorce rates, two of Durkheim's three categories display an inverse relationship between divorce and suicide.

Proceeding in characteristic fashion, Durkheim then attempted to replicate his original finding in data (table xxvi:260) for a single country ($r = .64$). The Catholic cantons in Switzerland bear him out ($r = .92$), as do cantons with mixed religious populations ($r = .86$). However, the Protestant cantons tell a different story; any tendency for cantons with higher divorce rates to have higher suicide rates also ($r = .01$) derives from Schaffhausen's exceptionally high suicide rate. Protestant cantons fall into two groups, those with divorce rates from 30 to 50 and those with rates of 80 and above. Removing Schaffhausen leaves five cantons—Neufchatel, Vaud, Bern, Basel (city), and Basel (country)—with an average divorce rate of 40.1 and a suicide rate of 350.4, versus three cantons—Outer Appenzell, Glaris, and Zurich—with an average divorce rate of 87.9 and a suicide rate of 209.3. *Eight of nine Protestant cantons, then, show an inverse correlation between divorce and suicide* ($r = -.55$), suggesting that in Protestant areas, divorce and suicide may be *inversely* correlated.

Suicide (261) presents additional data for France to demonstrate further that suicide and divorce are positively correlated. However, no source is cited; furthermore, no dates are given, nor is it certain that the suicide and divorce rates refer to the same years. No controls have been exercised for either alcoholic insanity, average size of family household, or average number of persons of independent means, all of which, Durkheim (78, 199, 245) argued, show strong correlations with the suicide rates of French departments when grouped as in the present instance. Divorce is given in terms of averages; neither the distribution of departments in each group nor the possible effects of extreme instances on the averages can be determined. There is no way to rule out an inverse relationship between divorce and suicide in areas with similar divorce rates, a pattern that emerges repeatedly in some of Durkheim's other data. Finally, Durkheim (261) classified departments "in eight categories according to the importance of their suicidal mortality," thereby treating suicide as the *independent*, and divorce as the *dependent*, variable instead of vice versa. Grouping by divorce might have produced different results.

Durkheim felt that his three sets of data, which individually display the same basic pattern, collectively demonstrate a positive correlation between divorce and suicide. However, the reassessment above shows that this conclusion is premature. In the one set of data permitting comparisons within a Protestant country, divorce and suicide are inversely related. Second, comparison of countries with similar divorce rates more often than not suggests that divorce and suicide are inversely correlated. Durkheim's analysis gets off to an empirically shaky start.

Having attempted to establish a positive relationship between suicide and divorce, Durkheim (262) then proposed to explain it in terms of "the intrinsic nature of divorce." His data pertain to Prussia, Baden, Saxony, and Württemberg. If he wished to show that the suicide rates of divorced persons exceed those of the unmarried, married, and widowed, the widowed-divorced comparison would be of particular concern. Being older, the widowed should commit suicide considerably more often than the divorced. In fact, however, it is the latter who commit suicide more frequently. "What is the explanation?" (262).

Both widowhood and divorce disturb the individual's relationship to his social environment and should therefore produce acute anomie. Divorce is often, probably typically, preceded by mutual recrimination and alienation building up over time; hence the divorce itself, while no doubt generally arousing mixed feelings, is in part a relief. In contrast, widowhood is typically undesired and the cause of immense grief (262). The crisis is *greater* for widowed persons, yet divorced persons display higher suicide rates. This "aggravation" in suicide rates of the divorced above and beyond those for the widowed does not "in any way" depend on the changed condition of the former (262-63). Having gone so far, Durkheim was content to drop this line of reasoning without explicitly drawing the theoretically relevant conclusion that later becomes clear: acute anomie may be rejected as the primary cause of divorced persons' high suicide rates. Because there are only two types of anomie, rejecting one type forces adoption of the other; in that case, chronic, not acute, anomie is responsible for the high suicide rates of divorced persons.

Ultimately, though, Durkheim was not concerned with the suicide rates of divorced persons per se but rather with what those rates reveal about marriage. Having "demonstrated" that suicide and divorce rates are positively correlated (the first generalization above), he began his explanation of this initial finding by calling attention to a second, namely, that the divorced have higher suicide rates than the widowed. Further explaining the first, he (263) recalled an earlier finding: "In a given society the tendency of widowed persons to suicide was a function of the corresponding tendency of married persons" (generalization three). Given this relationship between the suicide rates of married and widowed persons, it is reasonable to explain the rates of the latter by reference to aspects of the institution of marriage itself (197). By analogy, the same argument may be applied to the divorced (generalization four). Suicides of divorced persons, then, like those of the widowed, are to be attributed to the influence of the common life in marriage, an influence that persists beyond the marriage itself (263).

Durkheim's attempt to validate the fourth generalization is fraught with difficulties. Whereas data were offered to support his argument for the third, argument by analogy provides no such empirical demonstration for the fourth. Furthermore, Durkheim's proof of the third generalization, which appears in an earlier chapter (194-96) on egoism, flounders on the data. In his most precise statement of the relationship, Durkheim (196) stated that "the coefficient of widowed persons is about half that of married persons." Consequently, "the aptitude for suicide of widowed persons is a function of the corresponding aptitude of married persons."

Durkheim (196) argued that dividing the average coefficient of preservation (or aggravation) for the married by that for the widowed (table xxii:196) produces a ratio of about 2. (The average of the four ratios for the Seine and the provinces and of the two for France is 1.90). He presented the following averages of coefficients in support of his position:

$$\frac{\text{Husbands in provinces}}{\text{Widowers in provinces}} = \frac{2.59}{1.42} = 1.82$$

$$\frac{\text{Husbands in Seine}}{\text{Widowers in Seine}} = \frac{1.56}{0.76} = 2.05$$

$$\frac{\text{Wives in provinces}}{\text{Widows in provinces}} = \frac{1.50}{0.79} = 1.90$$

$$\frac{\text{Wives in Seine}}{\text{Widows in Seine}} = \frac{1.80}{0.94} = 1.91 \, [12]$$

The constancy of the ratios is indeed impressive. Durkheim further suggested that the same general pattern can be found in the figures for France (table xxɪ:178) and Oldenburg (table xx:177). For France the figures are:

$$\frac{\text{Husbands in France}}{\text{Widowers in France}} = \frac{2.44}{1.37} = 1.78$$

$$\frac{\text{Wives in France}}{\text{Widows in France}} = \frac{1.66}{0.85} = 1.95$$

Once again results sustain Durkheim. Finally, the figures for Oldenburg:

$$\frac{\text{Husbands in Oldenburg}}{\text{Widowers in Oldenburg}} = \frac{1.58}{0.90} = 1.75$$

$$\frac{\text{Wives in Oldenburg}}{\text{Widows in Oldenburg}} = \frac{1.82}{1.08} = 1.69$$

These results for Oldenburg provide only marginal support; however, as Durkheim (175) noted, they are based upon a small number of cases.

Checking Durkheim's results, I began with the total population (France, Ministère du commerce 1894: 101, 550-51, 554-55, 558-59, 562-63, 578-79, 582-83, 586-87, 590-91) for each of the unmarried age categories given in Durkheim's tables xxɪ (178) and

XXII (196). I then standardized the married and the widowed age distributions on that of the unmarried. Employing the suicide rates in Durkheim's two tables, I computed the absolute number of suicides using the standardized age distributions. I then divided the absolute number of suicides for unmarried by the absolute number of suicides for (1) the married and (2) the widowed to derive the coefficients of aggravation and preservation given in table 8.5. Compared to Durkheim's approach, this procedure avoids using

TABLE 8.5 COEFFICIENTS OF PRESERVATION AND AGGRAVATION FOR WIDOWED AND MARRIED, FOR STANDARDIZED AGE GROUPS

Place	Sex	Group	Suicide[a] (absolute numbers)	Coefficient
Provinces	Male	Unmarried Married	17,603 5,994	2.94
		Unmarried Widowed	17,603 12,871	1.37
	Female	Unmarried Married	4,096 2,587	1.58
		Unmarried Widowed	3,111 3,513	0.89
Seine	Male	Unmarried Married	2,759 1,584	1.74
		Unmarried Widowed	2,759 2,881	0.96
	Female	Unmarried Married	953 504	1.89
		Unmarried Widowed	953 779	1.22
France	Male	Unmarried Married	20,367 7,346	2.77
		Unmarried Widowed	20,367 15,605	1.30
	Female	Unmarried Married	5,332 3,017	1.77
		Unmarried Widowed	4,069 4,322	0.94

SOURCES: France, Ministère du commerce (1894:101, 550-51, 554-55, 558-59, 562-63, 578-79, 582-83, 586-87, 590-91) and Suicide (178, 196).

[a]Numerators for the same group sometimes differ owing to exclusions (see text).

an average for a series of coefficients above and below unity (see discussion in chap. 6 above) and effects a further control for age by employing standardized age distributions. Finally, some of the rates in Durkheim's two tables are unstable because they are based upon small populations. These frequently produce extreme coefficients which noticeably affect the average coefficients derived (see, e.g., the extreme coefficients for the fifteen-to-twenty age brackets in Durkheim's tables xxi and xxii). To reduce this instability, I excluded any age category for which an increment of one suicide increases the unmarried/married or unmarried/widowed suicide ratio by 0.25 or more. Specifically, all the fifteen-to-twenty age categories were excluded, except married women in France and in the provinces. Use of these results (table 8.5) produces the following married/widowed suicide ratios for the Seine and the provinces:

$$\frac{\text{Husbands in provinces}}{\text{Widowers in provinces}} = \frac{2.94}{1.37} = 2.15$$

$$\frac{\text{Husbands in Seine}}{\text{Widowers in Seine}} = \frac{1.74}{0.96} = 1.81$$

$$\frac{\text{Wives in provinces}}{\text{Widows in provinces}} = \frac{1.58}{0.89} = 1.77$$

$$\frac{\text{Wives in Seine}}{\text{Widows in Seine}} = \frac{1.89}{1.22} = 1.55$$

For France the results are:

$$\frac{\text{Husbands in France}}{\text{Widowers in France}} = \frac{2.77}{1.30} = 2.13$$

$$\frac{\text{Wives in France}}{\text{Widows in France}} = \frac{1.77}{0.94} = 1.88$$

Ranging from 1.55 to 2.15, these ratios fail to sustain the thesis (196) that widowed coefficients are about "half," or any other constant function, of those for the married. If rates for the widowed are not a function of rates for the married, then the entire empirical foundation for Durkheim's argument is undercut.

Durkheim (263) used the relationship between divorce and marriage (the fourth generalization) to explain his initial finding of a positive correlation between suicide and divorce. When the divorce rate is high, there must be many marriages "more or less close to divorce." Hence, rising divorce rates reflect an increase in "the family condition predisposing to suicide." Consequently, divorce and suicide "naturally vary" together.

Moving to the fifth generalization in his argument, Durkheim presented data (table xxvii:264) to show that divorce rates increase as the unmarried/married coefficient of preservation for men decreases. He failed to identify the basis on which he classified Prussia as an area in which divorce is common. If Prussia is excluded, there are but four countries (Italy, France, Baden, and Saxony) for which data are offered, and only two of them are outside of Germany. Moreover, there is only one country in each of two categories, and only two in the third. Though sustaining Durkheim, the data are of limited scope.

Attempting to replicate his finding, Durkheim (265) next cited figures showing that the divorce rate in the Seine is approximately four times that for all of France. He then referred to the data in his table xxii (196). With the exception of a reversal for persons aged twenty to twenty-five, the coefficients of preservation for husbands in the provinces are higher than for husbands in the Seine. The unmarried/married coefficient is 2.94 for the provinces, 1.74 for the Seine (table 8.5). These figures sustain his (fifth) generalization that compared to unmarried men, married men have less immunity to suicide where divorce is more frequent.

Durkheim (264) explicitly limited the stated relationship to men. Nonetheless, it is useful to consider data on women. While sketchy, Durkheim's data (267) show a tendency for married women's coefficients of preservation to vary directly with divorce rates. The figures for France (table xxii:196) show the same tendency. Holding age constant, eight comparisons can be made between wives in the provinces and those in the Seine. In five, the coefficient of preservation is higher for wives in the Seine. The unmarried/married coefficient for wives in the Seine is marginally higher than for wives in the provinces (1.89 versus 1.58, respectively; see table 8.5). The generalization that married persons' immunity (relative to that of single persons) varies inversely with divorce appears to hold for men, but not for women, as Durkheim (266-69) noted.[13]

Durkheim (266) next sought to establish one final generalization: "The coefficient of preservation of married women rises proportionately to the fall of that of husbands, or in proportion as divorces are more frequent and vice versa. The more often and easily the conjugal bond is broken, the more the wife is favored in comparison with the husband." Durkheim had already shown that coefficients of preservation for men tend to vary inversely, and those of women directly, with divorce rates (table xxvii:264 and table xxviii:267). As would be expected, the immunity of married men relative to that of married women increases as levels of social regulation in marriage increase (as measured by declining divorce rates). With France and Baden representing the only inversion, the data for France, Italy, and the three German states of Baden, Prussia, and Saxony sustain Durkheim (267).

He then proceeded once again to use table xxii. In place of the unmarried/married coefficients cited by Durkheim from that table, I have substituted the corresponding coefficients from table 8.5 above. Table 8.6 couples these coefficients with the divorce rates cited by Durkheim (265). Where the divorce rate is high, married

TABLE 8.6   DIVORCE AND COEFFICIENTS OF PRESERVATION FOR MARRIED PERSONS IN FRANCE

Area	Divorce Rate[a]	Unmarried/Married Coefficients		Ratio (Husbands/Wives)
		Husbands	Wives	
Seine	23.99	1.74	1.89	0.92
Provinces	5.65[b]	2.94	1.58	1.86

SOURCE: Divorce rates from Suicide (265), unmarried/married coefficients from table 8.5.

[a] Rate is number of divorces per 10,000 established households; Suicide (265).

[b] This is the rate "for all France" (265), presumably including the Seine.

women are relatively more protected; conversely, where divorce rates are low, men are more protected. Durkheim attempted to replicate this finding (for France) with Prussian data (267). However, since he failed to include coefficients of preservation for husbands, no conclusion can be drawn concerning the relative immunity of husbands and wives under varying conditions of regulation as measured by divorce rates.

Durkheim (268–69) concluded that "the following law may be regarded as beyond dispute: *From the standpoint of suicide, marriage is more favorable to the wife the more widely practiced divorce is; and vice versa.*" His data are limited to three countries (France, Germany, and Italy); thus, the finding must be framed with reference to them alone. The cross-national comparisons sustain the hypothesis, as does one replication for France.

To summarize briefly, the first generalization does not receive the kind of clear support desirable for one lying at the core of an entire argument. The third and fourth are not sustained empirically. Generalizations two, five, and six find some support in the data. On this simple accounting, Durkheim's case is neither convincingly sustained nor completely falsified by the data.

Discussion. Though important, the above results tell only one part of the story. These results must be coupled with additional analysis if a conclusive evaluation is to be reached. There are two aspects of Durkheim's presentation that fatally undermine his ability to convince the reader that chronic domestic anomie and suicide vary directly.

In attempting to explain the exceptionally high suicide rates of the divorced, Durkheim developed a widowed-divorced analogy. However, he (262) also noted that, though on the average younger, "divorced persons of both sexes kill themselves between three and four times as often as married persons." Indeed, a glance at his figures (262) shows suicide rates of married persons to be much lower than those for the widowed; hence, the suicide rates of the divorced exceed those of the married far more than they exceed those of the widowed. As applied to the divorced-married comparison, Durkheim's argument does not accord with his findings. In explaining suicide rates of divorced persons as a function of the institution of marriage, he emphasized that the crucial factor is the nature of marital society, *not* the divorce itself and the resulting disturbance. Such a line of reasoning cannot explain why suicide rates of the divorced exceed those of the married, much less why they should do so by such a wide margin. What the married and the divorced share, according to Durkheim, is exposure to marriage. In thus rejecting acute anomie (here produced by shock) as a crucial causal variable, Durkheim provided a rationale for believing that chronic and not acute anomie may be the relevant causal factor in accounting for high suicide rates among the divorced. In terms of his generalizations, the second and third supplement one another in that both undergird the fifth. As just noted, though, applying Durkheim's argument in the second (with its rejection of acute anomie) to the married-divorced comparison provides no key to understanding why suicide rates of the latter so far surpass those of the former.

Durkheim employed his theory in a highly selective fashion. Furthermore, his conclusions rest upon arbitrary decisions about the order in which to treat comparisons. The theory of acute anomie predicts that the widowed will have higher rates than either the married or the divorced and that the latter will have higher rates than the married. Durkheim (259) used acute anomie to explain why the widowed have higher rates than the married. Presumably, then, he would also want to test this theory on widowed-divorced and married-divorced comparisons. However, he did neither under conditions that would permit the theory's falsification. He implicitly acknowledged that the theory of acute anomie predicts that the widowed *should* have higher suicide rates than the divorced. Yet when the data showed that the reverse is true, he did not conclude that the theory was, to this degree, falsified. Rather, he concluded that chronic and not acute anomie is the operative factor. He failed to explain why acute anomie, held to be operative in the married-widowed comparison, no longer applies. Indeed, his only reason for deciding that acute anomie is no longer operative is the outcome of the suicide rates he was attempting to explain.

Obviously, acceptance of Durkheim's interpretation effectively precludes the possibility that his theory might be falsified. Following the lines of his conclusion from the divorced-widowed comparison, if married persons have higher rates than the widowed, this finding would only prove that chronic and not acute anomie is the operative causal factor. If the widowed have higher suicide rates than the married, it would prove the applicability of acute anomie. If the widowed display higher suicide rates than divorced persons, the applicability of acute anomie is proved; if divorced persons turn out to have higher suicide rates, then chronic and not acute anomie is operative. Whatever the comparison, whatever the outcome, the theory "explains" it. Because suicide rates themselves are used to determine which portion of the theory is applicable, the theory itself cannot be falsified.

Finally, the married-divorced comparison may be considered. The divorced have higher suicide rates than the married, just as the theory of acute anomie predicts. However, far from interpreting this result as sustaining the theory of acute anomie, Durkheim used the widowed-divorced comparison to reject it; that is, he used an empirical outcome to determine which of his two types of anomie was operative. It might, then, be anticipated that he would use the divorced-married comparison likewise. In fact, however, he did not and could not, for by this point he had used the divorced-widowed comparison to reject the applicability of acute anomie.

This rejection is strictly a function of the order in which he chose to consider comparisons. Although he compared widowed and divorced persons first in order to reject acute anomie, he could just as easily have first compared the divorced and the married to confirm the theory's applicability. Indeed, since he began with a comparison (married-widowed) suggesting the relevance of acute anomie, he might have attempted to seek the additional confirmatory evidence that he would have found in the divorced-married comparison. Instead, he turned to a comparison (widowed-divorced) that rejected acute anomie, and thus permitted acceptance of chronic anomie. From the standpoint of data support, Durkheim made a poor choice; the theory is compatible with results of one comparison (divorced-widowed) but incompatible with the other two (married-widowed, married-divorced). This choice, however, enabled Durkheim to protect his theory from falsification; he could selectively apply it to data that would sustain it and thereby build it through an arbitrary ordering of comparisons.

A second problematic aspect of Durkheim's argument is his use of sex as a variable. Having stated his fourth generalization, he did not attempt to establish it directly. First he developed the widowed-divorced analogy. Then he (264) argued that if his fourth generalization "is well founded, married persons in countries where divorces are numerous must have less immunity against suicide than where marriage is indissoluble," thereby creating the expectation that he would compare coefficients of preservation for the married to divorce rates. Instead, however, he related coefficients of preservation of married men to divorce rates. One might now ask: Which is the best test of his hypothesis, and what are the implications of this shift from all married persons to married men only?

The best test is the one he himself announced. If suicide varies inversely with social regulation and if higher divorce rates reflect weaker social regulation in marriage, then rates for married persons should vary proportionately with divorce rates. Since nothing in Durkheim's argument to this point makes any reference to sex as a variable, this deduction should be tested against data for both sexes. The data sustain the hypothesis for men but not for women. As discussed in Part I, Durkheim's theoretical attempt to explain this outcome is unsatisfactory on several counts. Furthermore, the data themselves create additional difficulties. Durkheim related divorce rates to married men's and married women's coefficients of aggravation and preservation. The accompanying argument—the *amount* men benefit, and women suffer, from marriage varies with level of social regulation—is developed *within* the boundaries of a more basic proposition: men benefit and women suffer because of their different biologically based needs. Table 8.7 gives Durkheim's unmarried/married coefficients for Oldenburg, plus the unmarried/married coefficients for France and for the Seine and the provinces from

TABLE 8.7   COEFFICIENTS OF PRESERVATION FOR MARRIED PERSONS IN OLDENBURG AND FRANCE

Place	Men	Women
Oldenburg	1.58	1.82
France	2.77	1.77
Seine	1.74	1.89
Provinces	2.94	1.58

SOURCE: Figures for Oldenburg from Suicide (table XX: 177); all French figures from table 8.5. The Oldenburg coefficients are averages; since I have recomputed both the individual coefficients and the resulting averages, the Oldenburg figures differ from those reported in Suicide.

table 8.5. Following Durkheim, these coefficients may be used to compare the two sexes in terms of which benefits most from marriage. For France generally and in the provinces men are better off, whereas in Oldenburg and the Seine women fare somewhat better. Durkheim (179, 194–97) himself emphasized that the sex that benefits most from marriage varies from region to region and from society to society. The patterning of the data suggests several hypotheses. The biological makeup of men (compared to that of women) in France and in the provinces is such that men have the greater need for social control in marriage. In Oldenburg and the Seine, on the other hand, women have the greater need. Such reasoning is not only inconsistent with Durkheim's contention that men have the greater need but also begins to sound incredible.

Furthermore, postulating regional variation creates the necessity of having to decide which sex benefits most in a given area. Durkheim gave no clue as to how such determinations are to be made other than by his example, i.e., he implicitly based them upon the suicide rates ostensibly being explained. All things considered, his appeal to the sexes' differential need for social regulation, and, hence, their different response to varying levels of social regulation in marriage, runs into severe theoretical and empirical difficulties. However imaginative, it has all the earmarks of an ad hoc, post-factum attempt to salvage the theory in the face of empirically embarrassing results.

Summary and conclusion. Important aspects of Durkheim's analysis are obscured in the intricate reasoning that links his six generalizations. First, in his attempt (198, 266, 269-76) to relate chronic domestic anomie to marital society, none of his data control for presence of children. Consequently, at no point was he able to distinguish empirically between marriage and the family, even though this distinction is basic to his entire endeavor. Second—rather strangely—his fifth proposition (suicide rates of married men and divorce rates are positively correlated) represents a specification of his first proposition (suicide and divorce are positively correlated). Here Durkheim's long chain of analysis concludes that a relationship held to be true of the population generally is also true of one of its major segments.

Finally, he presented only minimal evidence to support his basic proposition that suicide and anomie vary directly in modern society. In spite of what seems like a wealth of data, his case ultimately rests on a single table (table xxvii:264) which provides figures for three German states, Italy, and France, plus one replication (again for France). These figures demonstrate a relationship between anomie and suicide rates *only* for men, and then only for *married men.* In contrast to demonstrations at other points in *Suicide,* where he often attempted to show a given relationship in a variety of social contexts, Durkheim's empirical case rests largely on a relationship between divorce and suicide rates for married men in four states.

Following a passing reference to acute anomie, Durkheim developed his analysis of chronic domestic anomie by attempting to validate all six of his generalizations (see pp. 126-27). The evidence relevant to his first generalization is mixed. Durkheim next attempted to demonstrate that the suicide rates of divorced persons exceed those of the widowed. The data bear him out nicely. He used this finding to conclude that chronic anomie must be more important than acute, a conclusion that is less than convincing. It is based upon the presupposition that either chronic or acute anomie is an important causal factor in explaining suicide rates, a proposition validated neither in Durkheim's previous arguments nor by the overall analysis. In addition, the decision to choose chronic over acute anomie seems strained; while chronic anomie best explains the results of a comparison between suicide rates of widowed and divorced persons, acute anomie most satisfactorily explains the results of both married-widowed and married-divorced comparisons.

Generalizations two, three, and four share the same basic objective of demonstrating the relevance of chronic anomie. However, the theoretical payoff of these three propositions does not come until the fifth. If chronic anomie affects domestic society and if divorce is a good indicator of social regulation, then suicide rates for married men relative to those of single men should vary inversely with divorce rates. Although the data sustain this generalization, it nonetheless suffers from two important disabilities. On the basis of Durkheim's argument to this point, it would be assumed that the relationship between suicide rates for the married and divorce rates should apply to women as well as men. But the fifth generalization says nothing about women. In addition, his chapter on egoism states Durkheim's intent to save study of the special effects of marriage for the chapter on anomie. His figures, however, pertain simply to the married and permit no distinction between those with and without children, thus crippling his effort to fulfill his stated intention. Largely out of necessity, it would appear, Durkheim at this point introduced a questionable assumption. While varying levels of social control in familial society affect the two sexes similarly, biological differences cause them to react differently to varying levels of social control in marital society. The data sustain generalization six, and on this basis Durkheim concluded that chronic anomie affects marital, not familial, society. However, the underlying assumption about the different impact of regulation upon the sexes creates so many theoretical and empirical difficulties that generalization six does not aid in validating the theory empirically.

Each of Durkheim's propositions encounters severe difficulties. The attempt to demonstrate that suicide and divorce rates are positively correlated finds mixed results in the data. The second generalization is nicely supported; yet the inference drawn from it—that chronic anomie is more important than acute anomie—is incongruent with widowed-married and married-divorced comparisons. Generalization three is not sustained by the data, and *Suicide* offers no direct evidence at all in support of the fourth. Since four is based upon the validity of three, what evidence is offered for it flounders indirectly on the data. Although proposition five is confirmed and although everything in the theory to this point suggests that it should apply to both sexes, it is not sustained when rephrased to apply to women. The sixth generalization is congruent with the data but leads to the conclusion Durkheim draws from it only in conjunction with problematic assumptions about the differing, biologically determined needs of the two sexes.

I reject this appeal. Durkheim's analysis is based on the assumption that marriage represents a net increment of social regulation over the unmarried state. He hypothesized that suicide and social regulation vary inversely. The hypothesis is supported by data for men. Coefficients of preservation for married men vary inversely with divorced rates, and childless husbands (table 6.5) display a coefficient of preservation. For women the hypothesis is not sustained: coefficients of preservation of married women vary directly with divorce rates, and childless wives (table 6.5) have much higher suicide rates than do single women. Finally, Durkheim cited data to support his argument that men benefit, and women suffer, from the social regulation embodied in marriage. However, other data show regional differences concerning which sex benefits most from marriage. Though developed in one of *Suicide*'s most ingenious analyses, the theory of domestic anomie is not confirmed by Durkheim's data.

9 DURKHEIM'S VARIABLES AND THE VARIABILITY IN SUICIDE RATES

The preceding chapters in Part II have assessed the degree to which Durkheim's data sustain his theory. This analysis has intentionally adhered as closely as possible to the original in order to determine which conclusions could be sustained, given a systematic application of Durkheim's own analytic techniques. I now consider whether Durkheim used appropriate variables to explain variation in social suicide rates. I then assess the usefulness of Durkheim's theory in explaining the variation in suicide rates associated with his control variables.

POWER: THE CONTROLS VS. THE INDICATORS

Given *Suicide*'s purpose (explaining variation in social suicide rates), it might be expected that Durkheim would focus on those variables associated with the greatest variation in suicide. In fact, however, his control variables (sex, age, and geographic region) show far more potential explanatory power than do the variables employed as indicators of his two independent variables (integration and regulation).

The Control Variables

Fully aware of their powerful association with suicide, Durkheim consistently treated sex, age, and region as control variables.

Sex. Durkheim repeatedly found that suicide rates for men far surpass those for women. For instance, his table xxi (178) permits twenty-six French male-female comparisons, controlling for both age and marital status. Male/female suicide ratios greater than 4.0 are typical (4.8 is the average). Well aware of the relationship between sex and suicide, he (166; see also 72, 99, and table IV:71) indicated that in countries throughout the world, men are from four to six times more likely to kill themselves than are women.[1] Unfortunately, his appeals to sex as an explanatory variable occurred in ad hoc, post-factum attempts to account for empirical exceptions to his major propositions. Thus, his concern was not for sex per se as a variable.

Age. With a few important exceptions, there is a strong positive correlation between age and suicide, as Durkheim (73; see also tables xx:177, xxi:178, and xxii:196) well knew. Noting at one point (265n) that "the law of the effect of age on suicide is everywhere the same," at another he (324) indicated that the old are often ten times as likely to kill themselves as are the very young.[2] Yet, apart from occasional asides (215, 299), he made no effort to account for this "law."

Region. The variation in suicide rates by region is truly astounding. Rates for selected regions show an irregular, step-by-step progression from 1 to 602 per million (table 9.1). Denmark's rate is fifteen times that of Spain. Even more striking are variations within states. In Italy the rate for Bologna is 11 times that of Calabria; in France the rate for Marne is at least 28 times that of Corsica; the rate for Lower Austria is 18 times that for Dalmatia. Most striking of all is the variation within Switzerland, where Schaffhausen's rate is 602 times that of Lower Unterwalden. *Suicide* does not successfully explain these regional differences.

The Indicators

The variables Durkheim employed as indicators of differing levels of integration and regulation and which might have aided such an explanation, are not shown to be associated with great variability in suicide. For instance, *Suicide* fails to demonstrate that Catholics have lower suicide rates than Protestants. Similarly, if only impressionistically, wealth seems positively correlated with suicide. Yet, in his discussion of acute economic anomie and elsewhere, Durkheim considered the relationship between poverty and suicide only for the purpose of rejecting the former as a cause of suicide: "Poverty is not one of the factors on which the social suicide-rate depends" (181). While he (254) viewed wealth as more conducive to suicide than poverty, his underlying argument rejected both wealth and poverty as important causes in order to establish disturbance of the collective order as the primary cause. Durkheim made no attempt to show that regional variations in wealth explain regional differences in suicide.

Likewise, in his analysis of chronic economic anomie he (257–58) wished to show that agriculture as an occupation displays lower suicide rates than the (allegedly) more anomic commercial and

TABLE 9.1   SUICIDE RATES (PER MILLION) IN SELECTED REGIONS OF
EUROPE

Area	Years	Rate
Lower Unterwalden (Switzerland)	n.d.	1
Calabria (Italy)	1864-76	8
Valais (Switzerland)	n.d.	10
Hanover	1856-60	13
Dalmatia (Austria)	1872-77	14
Spain	n.d.	17
Corsica (France)	n.d.	18
Finland	n.d.	31
Holland	n.d.	36
England	1874-78	69
Bologna (Italy)	n.d.	88
Austria	1874-78	130
France	1874-78	160
Switzerland	n.d.	216
Lower Austria	1872-77	254
Denmark	1874-78	255
Saxony	1874-78	334
Marne (France)[a]	1887-91	above 500
Schaffhausen (Switzerland)	n.d.	602

SOURCE: Suicide (50, 74, 87-88, 137, 164, 259-60, 339,
351, and 394).

NOTE: n.d. = no date given.

[a]Appendix II in Suicide (394) is a map of France showing
suicide rates by districts (arrondissements) and departments. Because the map is poorly printed, interested
readers are referred to the originial in Le Suicide (124-25).
This map does not identify districts and departments by name.
However, it shows that sixteen districts have suicide rates
over 500, as do four departments: Seine-et-Marne, Marne,
Aisne, and Oise. (When a department was broken down into two
or more districts and all districts had rates over 500, only
the single department was listed; in addition, Seine-et-Marne
was included because four of five districts had rates in excess
of 500--the fifth was in the 400 to 500 category.)

industrial occupations. Similarly, in his first chapter on egoistic
suicide he (165–66) briefly treated occupational differences in suicide
rates to show that the liberal professions display high suicide rates.
Focusing on intranational comparisons in both instances, Durkheim
never attempted to use different occupational structures to explain
regional variations in suicide.

Suicide (135–38) assesses the role of urbanization only to reject the
idea that either it or the social environment of the city are themselves

causes of higher suicide rates. Consistent with this understanding, Durkheim did not attempt to use level of urbanization to explain variations—regional, national, or otherwise—in suicide; thus, urbanization, too, is largely treated only as a control variable. While Durkheim employed considerable cross-national data, cross-national variations in suicide were never the focal point of his analysis. Rather, he used such data either (1) to demonstrate that his hypotheses about a particular type of society (e.g., religious, domestic, military, political) or social condition hold in different regional settings, or (2) to *control* regional variations to show that they do not account for the differences he sought to explain. It is in this context that Durkheim's failure to account for regional differences in suicide must be understood.

As I have noted, Durkheim was rarely able to establish any consistent relationship between the variables he used to indicate varying levels of integration-regulation and suicide. Even when he achieved some success, the relationship between these variables and suicide proves weak when measured against the relationship between age, sex, region and suicide.

Implications

Durkheim focused upon less powerful variables, while neglecting to explain the variation associated with the more powerful. Indeed, his analysis is typically concerned with variations that appear inconsequential when measured against the total variation displayed in his own data. Related to this circumstance are many analytic difficulties. One obvious and potentially fatal consequence is his repeated difficulty in demonstrating systematic relationships between his independent variables and suicide. Related to this first difficulty are his attempts to magnify the differences he derived, and, probably, his sometimes arbitrary selection of data to support his generalizations.

The more powerful the variables, the more crucial is the adequacy of the controls exercised on them. Durkheim often controlled for the three variables I have shown to be powerful (region, age, and sex), sometimes skillfully, as in tables for Oldenburg (177) and France (178, 196) that show the relationship between marital status and suicide rates. Elsewhere, though, he was less successful. One example is his data on the presence of children, for which he used an inadequate age control. Another is found in his analysis of religion. Despite his contention that suicide and civilization are positively correlated, he never demonstrated that for countries at a given level of development, Protestant nations have higher suicide rates than Catholic nations. Similarly, his treatment of anomie included no attempt to control for variables that his earlier analysis of egoism had shown to be crucial. Had Durkheim focused upon more powerful instead of less powerful variables, in all probability he would have been more effective in demonstrating crucial empirical relationships, and shortcomings in his use of controls would not have so seriously undercut the success of his efforts.

Of course, Durkheim would not necessarily need to focus on sex, age, and regional variations in suicide, even if his ultimate goal were to develop a theory that would (among other things) account for them. He could begin by using other variables to establish the empirical validity of the asserted relationships between integration-regulation and suicide. Once the validity of his explanatory structure had been established thereby, he could then attempt to use his theory to explain age, sex, and regional differences in suicide.

Furthermore, it is not mandatory for a theorist to focus upon the most powerful variables. Obviously, a variable's power is only one relevant consideration; equally important is the relative ease with which it may be fitted into a coherent, theoretical framework. Whether Durkheim could have constructed an adequate theory employing age, sex, and region as primary variables remains an open question. The cogency of his present theory argues against the thesis that he could have done as well with a different set of variables; however, to reject that possibility may be to underestimate his skill as a theorist (a mistake not likely to be made by anyone who has fallen under the spell of *Suicide*). Nevertheless, a theory is, above all, an explanation. If it cannot explain fluctuations in its dependent variable, it is unsuccessful, whatever its excellence in other respects.

THE THEORY AND POSSIBLE EXPLANATIONS

I here examine whether Durkheim's theory explains the variations in suicide rates associated with age, sex, and region. For each variable, I note Durkheim's explanations; with age and sex, I also move beyond Durkheim's own analysis. Where data are employed, the analysis relies primarily, though not exclusively, on the data found in *Suicide*.[3]

Region

Durkheim (162-68) probably came closest to an explanation of regional differences in suicide when he used educational attainment as an indicator of free inquiry and, hence (ultimately), of integration.

In this argument he undertook to establish that suicide and educational attainment are positively correlated, both intra- and internationally. This argument was subordinated, however, to the larger purpose of demonstrating that Protestants have higher suicide rates than Catholics. Thus, however promising, the analysis is all too brief. Whether a fully developed analysis would have sustained Durkheim's conclusion that Protestants are more highly educated than Catholics, and that the more highly educated have higher suicide rates, remains unclear. [4]

Beyond this analysis, *Suicide* contains little explicit indication that the theory, as interpreted and applied by Durkheim, can explain regional differences in suicide. Many of the variables that Durkheim treated most extensively (e.g., marital-familial status, military-civilian status) are largely, if not wholly, irrelevant to an explanation of the regional differences in suicide revealed in table 9.1. Again, political and economic crises better explain rate changes over time in a given region than interregional variations, and Durkheim himself treated them accordingly. Differences in occupational structure or in levels of chronic domestic anomie could be used to explain regional differences in suicide; however, *Suicide* provides little empirical reassurance on the ultimate success of such attempts.

At minimum, successful use of Durkheim's theory to explain variation in social suicide rates would require developing new indicators of integration-regulation and then demonstrating that they vary systematically with social suicide rates. While this possibility remains open, it must be weighed against the following, interrelated considerations. First, a "best guess" concerning the theory's likely success must be based upon assessment of the theory's ability to explain the data Durkheim himself sought to interpret; here, as was demonstrated above, the theory is unsuccessful. Second, *Suicide* itself does not explain regional differences in suicide rates. Finally, Durkheim's work often focused upon variables that are largely irrelevant to explaining large regional differences in suicide. Thus, although an adequate test of the theory's ability to account for regional differences in suicide has yet to be undertaken, *Suicide* itself provides little grounds for optimism concerning the potential success of such an effort.

Age

While Durkheim (100-101, 211, 215, 299, 324-25) occasionally argued that age differences in suicide rates should be explained in terms of social causes, he made no sustained effort to do so, and he certainly made no sustained effort to demonstrate that such differences could be explained by varying levels of integration-regulation. The following discussion tests his theory in a way he did not.

Burdened by greater marital responsibilities and (for the vast majority) living within growing families, married men should be increasingly integrated into the family as they move from young adulthood through middle age. Later, as children grow up and leave home, family size and, consequently, levels of integration should decrease. At a still later age, retirement should constitute a new source of diminished regulation. However, the graph for French males fails to reflect this hypothesized pattern; instead, it depicts a steady *increase* in suicide from the early twenties on through old age (fig. 9.1).

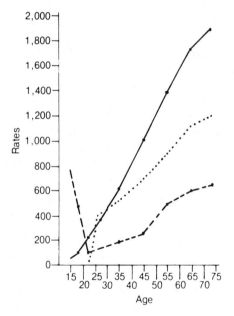

Fig. 9.1. Suicide rates (per million) in France for unmarried, married, and widowed men (1888–91). From *Suicide* (178). Unmarried =————; married =--------; widowed =.......

Presumably, married women's lives center more exclusively on home and family than do those of men. Thus, their suicide rates should decrease during the child-rearing years as their family sizes and responsibilities increase. Instead, their rates increase steadily up to about age forty-five, at which point they increase at a more rapid rate (fig. 9.2). It could be held that this steeper rate of

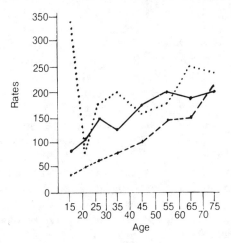

Fig. 9.2. Suicide rates (per million) in France for unmarried, married, and widowed women (1889–91). From *Suicide* (178). Unmarried =————; married =- - - - - - -; widowed =........

increase from the middle forties to the middle fifties reflects a lowering of social integration as family size decreases, but the reason why the rates flatten so noticeably between the middle fifties and the middle sixties remains unclear. However well the theory may apply to women fifty-five and over, it does not appear congruent with the steady increase in actual suicide rates up to the middle fifties.

Theoretical expectations concerning the unmarried are less clear. Men forty-five years old have a suicide rate three times that of men aged twenty-five; yet, there is no obvious reason to hypothesize the steady, marked diminution of integration required to make Durkheim's theory explain the relationship between age and suicide among unmarried men. Unmarried women, in turn, reverse the general upward trend of suicide rates with a marked decline from the middle twenties to the middle thirties, and a slight decline between the middle fifties and middle sixties. Why single women alone should experience these reversals, and why they come at precisely the points indicated, is also unclear.

Sex

Durkheim occasionally focused on male-female suicide rate differences, but these references occur as brief, scattered, inconsistent, and inconclusive asides; at times they even involve him in an approach he roundly rejected elsewhere, namely, biological reductionism (166, 215-16, 272, 299, 385-86; see also the discussion of male-female differences in Part I). Reminiscent of the situation with respect to age: (1) *Suicide* does not even begin to show that suicide differences by sex can be explained in terms of the varying levels of integration-regulation in the social milieu of men as compared to women; (2) *Suicide*'s failure in this regard typifies the problems encountered in any attempt to use Durkheim's theory to explain the differences displayed in the data.

Employing Durkheim's data now for analyses that he never reported reveals that men's suicide rates regularly exceed those of women; in France, on the average, men's rates are about five times as high. This difference poses complicated questions for theoretical interpretation. Among the married, both men and women spend considerable time within the family. Beyond that, men hold jobs, while women are more likely to remain within the familial milieu. Durkheim sometimes interpreted membership in any group as subjecting the individual to the sui generis forces constituting its social reality and, hence, as an increment in the sum total of social control to which he is subject. On this basis it could be predicted that men's suicide rates should be *lower* than women's. However, even if it were determined that women's rates should be lower, given that both men and women spend considerable time together in the family, it is hard to account for a five-to-one male-female ratio.

Alternatively, treating the time that both spend in the family as a constant, the integration that women experience from spending additional time in the family may be compared with that men experience on the job.[5] This analysis requires comparing family and job, something *Suicide* does not do. However, one can compare differences in integrative forces to which men and women are subject. In some situations the family-work difference appears slight—in the agricultural context, for example, particularly in the family-farm setting. Here men and women spend considerable time together in the same kinds of activities; moreover, the men do not go off to work in an industrial or commercial setting in which anomie has replaced the regulatory forces still present in agriculture. It could be predicted, then, that male-female suicide differentials would reach a peak when men work in industrial-commercial occupations, and fall to insignificance in agricultural settings.

Durkheim (71) gave suicide rates by sex for seven European states. From these data, male/female suicide ratios have been computed and compared with figures for percentage of labor force in agriculture (table 9.2). There is a moderate positive correlation (*r* = .52) between percentage of labor force in agriculture and male/female suicide ratios instead of the negative correlation predicted. *Suicide* does not present the necessary figures for a similar

TABLE 9.2 PERCENTAGE OF LABOR FORCE IN AGRICULTURE AND MALE/FEMALE SUICIDE RATIOS IN SELECTED EUROPEAN STATES

Country	Year	Percentage in Agriculture	Years	Ratio
England	1881	11.5	1863-67	2.74
Saxony	1882	19.2	1871-76	4.18
Prussia	1882	42.8	1871-76	4.41
France	1881	47.7[a]	1871-76	3.74
Denmark	1880	51.1[b]	1870-76	3.32
Italy	1881	57.4[a]	1872-77	4.00
Austria	1890	62.4	1873-77	4.59

SOURCES: Male-female suicide ratios computed from Suicide (71). When more than one set of figures for the same country was given, the latest figures are used. Labor force figures are from the following sources: England (Booth 1886:324); Saxony and Prussia (Keltie 1886:166); France (Tracy 1964:80); Denmark (Howard 1935:50); Italy and Austria (Clark 1940:200-01).

[a] Includes fishing and forestry.

[b] Includes fishing.

comparison for France. Official government figures show that there is a negligible relationship (*r* = .03) between percentage of labor force in agriculture and male/female suicide ratios for the eighty-six French departments.[6] Male/female suicide ratios do not increase in nonagricultural settings.

Changes in male/female suicide ratios for married persons may also be considered (table XXI:178; see also figs. 9.1 and 9.2). Presumably the social environment of married men who move beyond middle to old age becomes more like that of married women as the men retire and spend a larger proportion of their time in the family. Thus, men aged sixty and older should increasingly show suicide rates more like those of women than do young-adult or middle-aged males. In fact, however, male/female ratios are higher among the old than among young adults, with a single exception (very young husbands fifteen to twenty). In a related vein, among those aged 40 to 50, 50 to 60, 60 to 70, 70 to 80, and above 80 male suicide rates are 3.2, 3.4, 4.0, 3.4, and 7.0 times higher, respectively, than those for women. It is hard to imagine that differences in social-control levels within their respective social environments can explain these sex differences.

Perhaps the theory of acute anomie should be introduced at this point to help explain the higher male/female ratios found among the old. Compared with women, who presumably experience less sudden discontinuities as they age, retirement may throw men into a state of acute anomie. I assume that unmarried, married, and widowed men retire at the same age. However, the highest male/female suicide ratios are not found at the same age intervals for all; they occur in the seventy-to-eighty age bracket for unmarried and widowed persons, and in the above-eighty brackets for the married. Moreover, these brackets are probably too late in life to be affected by retirement. The theory of acute anomie is of little help in accounting for the previously identified discrepancies which arise when Durkheim's theory is applied to male/female suicide ratios for married persons.

Conclusion

Even though Durkheim did not do so, an attempt may be made to use his theory to explain the great variability in suicide rates by age, sex, and region; indeed, one test of a theory is its ability to incorporate new variables successfully, especially powerful ones. Unfortunately, Durkheim's theory does not pass the test. Severe difficulties surface when attempts are made to apply it to variations by sex and age, nor are there reassuring signs that it can explain regional variation in suicide. Certainly an adequate test of the theory's ability to handle these "new" variables would require far more extensive analysis than that provided above, and Durkheim himself might succeed where I have failed. Indeed, he seldom admitted his inability to explain a finding that he considered relevant. Nonetheless, until it has been shown that Durkheim's theory adequately interprets the kinds of variation just considered, we must conclude that, at best, he explained only a minute fraction of the total variation displayed in his own data.

III DURKHEIM'S SOCIAL REALISM

Durkheim (1965b:3) considered science the study of reality. He (1965a:223) saw all reality as "a system of forces." Phenomena possess two variable, reality-conferring attributes: power and irreducibility. The reality of a force is proved by demonstrating its effects: the more powerful the force, the greater its effects; the greater the effects, the more powerful the force. Similarly, the degree to which the investigator can show that given effects are attributable to force X rather than to some other force, Y, and, hence, that a given force has its own power and not simply derived or borrowed power, also varies. The more powerful a system of forces and the greater its irreducibility, the more real it is. In characterizing phenomena in these terms, Durkheim referred less to sheer existence than to the strength and irreducibility of the system of forces that together constitute a given reality.

Suicide's underlying purpose was to establish sociology as a legitimate scientific discipline on a footing equal to that enjoyed by such recognized fields as physics and biology. Any such discipline must study its own distinctive reality. In the case of sociology this reality is social phenomena in general, society in particular. Durkheim (38, 310) felt it necessary to demonstrate that social forces exist as forces in their own right, and do not derive their power from physical, biological, or other natural forces. Therefore, much of *Suicide* is devoted precisely to (1) demonstrating the power of social forces and (2) showing that their effects cannot be attributed to nonsocial forces. In short, *Suicide* attempts to legitimize sociology as a science by proving that society is real.

This particular aspect of Durkheim's thought has been identified by various terms. Alpert (1961:131-66) referred to Durkheim's social realism; Tiryakian (1962:11-21), to his sociologism; Benoit-Smullyan (1948:499-537), to his sociologism and his angelicism. Others have noted Durkheim's sociological reductionism. In using such phrases, authors have identified what they see as the central, distinctive component of his perspective. To a degree, such determinations depend on a given author's interpretation; hence, it cannot be presumed that these various terms denote exactly the same thing. All are similar, however, in stressing Durkheim's emphasis upon the primacy of the social and on society as a reality. This aspect of his thought—here termed social realism—is the focus of Part III.

11   SUICIDE AND NONSOCIAL FACTORS: ARGUMENT BY ELIMINATION

If the social factor is to be the object of its own branch of science (sociology), its reality must be proved. This task requires demonstrating that social phenomena cannot be explained by non-social factors. Therefore, in the first book in *Suicide* (55-142) Durkheim treated successively the relationships between suicide and psychopathic states, race and heredity, cosmic factors, and imitation.

INSANITY, NEURASTHENIA, AND ALCOHOLISM

In his first chapter ("Suicide and Psychopathic States") Durkheim (57-81) attempted to show the inadequacy of existing attempts to explain suicide as a function of mental abnormalities (neurasthenia, insanity, or alcoholism). The mental phenomena he discussed fit on a normality-abnormality continuum. At one end is normality (perfect mental equilibrium); at the other, various psychopathic states. Durkheim treated two of these states, insanity (mental alienation) and alcoholism. Milder mental abnormalities or nervous degeneration are called neurasthenia or neuropathology. Although the chapter title refers to "psychopathic states," *Suicide* also treats these milder forms of mental disorder.

Insanity (Mental Alienation)

The theory that suicide results from mental alienation has commonly been defended by viewing suicide as either (1) a sui generis disease in itself or (2) simply an event of one or more varieties of insanity (58). The first proposition treats suicide as a restricted delirium or monomania (a monomaniac being an individual with normal mentality except for a single false idea or extreme emotion that gradually possesses his entire mind; 59). Durkheim (60-62) held that the concept of monomania postulates an independence of the various psychic functions, making it possible for one such function to be impaired while the others function normally. However, since such a conception is completely incompatible with the commonly accepted view of the interdependence of psychic functions, it may be concluded that "there are no monomanias" (62). Thus monomania may be rejected as a cause of suicide.

Turning his attention to the second possibility, Durkheim (62-66) proposed to classify the suicides committed by insane persons as (1) maniacal suicide, (2) melancholy suicide, (3) obsessive suicide, and (4) impulsive or automatic suicide. While these types are alike in that such suicides are devoid of motive (or at best accompanied by a purely imaginary motive), nevertheless most suicides are accompanied by real motives (66). Durkheim phrased the problem as that of learning "whether *all* suicides are insane," and concluded that "numerous" suicides are "not connnected with insanity" (67; italics added). From this conclusion he (67) immediately produced another: "Since the suicides of insane persons do not constitute the entire genus but only a variety of it, the psychopathic states constituting mental alienation can give no clue to the collective tendency to suicide in its generality." In concluding only that many suicides have no connection with insanity, Durkheim left open the possibility that some large but unspecified proportion do. To the degree that insanity itself is a social phenomenon, this possibility does not necessarily undermine his larger purpose of dismissing nonsocial factors in suicide. Although insanity is treated under "extrasocial factors," a footnote (58n) states that "actually it is partly a social phenomenon." Unfortunately, this suggestion is not followed up. Because he did not indicate either the degree to which insanity is a social (as opposed to individual) phenomenon or the proportion of suicides not attributable to insanity, Durkheim's initial argument makes only a modest beginning toward rejecting nonsocial factors in suicide.

Neurasthenia

Durkheim (67-77) next considered neurasthenia. Sensitive to the slightest stimulus, the neurasthenic is easily upset and lives in a state of more or less continuous agitation (69-76). In all probability the most common type of mental disorder found among suicides, it is becoming increasingly common (68-69). Obviously, its relationship to suicide is of the first importance. The problem is that neurasthenia has not been studied statistically, so its variations cannot be directly compared with those of suicide (69). Since, however, "insanity is only the enlarged form of nervous degeneration . . . the number of nervous degenerates varies in proportion to that of the insane," thus making it feasible to use the latter as the measure of the former (70). Moreover, using insanity as a measure permits assessment of the relationship between suicide and the total of all kinds of mental abnormalities.

Durkheim wished to demonstrate that suicide and insanity rates do not necessarily vary proportionately. He did, however, cite two instances in which they are positively correlated. Both are more common in cities than in the country—a coincidental, not causal, relationship deriving from the circumstance that both result from the development of "urban civilization" (70). Later he (76) noted the temptation to see a causal relationship in the regular increase in both rates over a century, but he rejected such a conclusion on the grounds that, even though suicide is sometimes frequent in lower societies, insanity is rare. Yet he failed to cite evidence on insanity rates in lower societies, and, since the empirical evidence on suicide rates in lower societies is inadequate, his argument is therefore unconvincing. Furthermore, even if suicide and insanity rates in primitive society were precisely as Durkheim claimed them to be, this situation would scarcely eliminate the possibility of a causal relationship in modern society. The nature of suicide (as Durkheim's own theory holds), the nature of insanity, or both might be very different in modern society; likewise, their mutual relationships might be different.

Having acknowledged these two instances in which suicide and insanity rates vary proportionately, Durkheim then cited others in which, he argued, these two rates do not show the positive relationship hypothesized by those who would explain suicide as a function of mental disorder. He (70-71) began with national, male/female insanity and suicide ratios which show that whereas the ratio of male to female insanity is approximately one to one, the suicide ratio is four to one. His conclusion—that the two show no tendency to vary proportionately—appears well founded.

With regard to the "tendency to insanity among the different religious faiths" in eight German states and one Swiss canton, *Suicide*'s table v (72) reveals that without exception, Jews have noticeably higher insanity rates than do either Catholics or Protestants. Catholic-Protestant differences tend to be relatively slight. Average rates (per 1,000) are: Protestants, 1.29; Catholics, 1.25; and Jews, 2.52. Durkheim (72) concluded that "*suicide varies in inverse proportion to psychopathic states,* rather than being consistent with them." My analysis in Part II shows that Catholic and

Protestant suicide rates are substantially similar. Since their insanity rates given here are also very similar, the data do not preclude the possibility that suicide and insanity vary proportionately. Durkheim's data permit few comparisons of suicide and insanity rates for the same groups in a given state at one point in time. Supplementing his insanity statistics (table v:72) with suicide rates from Morselli (1882:table xvi:122) reveals instances of both proportional and inverse variation. The data are inadequate to validate any generalization pertaining to Europe as a whole. Overall, then, Durkheim's argument that suicide and insanity vary inversely is poorly founded empirically.

Relating insanity and suicide by age, Durkheim (73) asserted that insanity is minimal "when the suicide-rate is maximal, and prior to that no regular relation can be found between the variations of the two." However, he presented no empirical evidence relating age to insanity. Only if one *assumes* the adequacy of the existing data can this conclusion be accepted. Finally, Durkheim (74) presented data on insanity and suicide by country and noted that far from varying together, there is, if anything, an inverse relationship ($r = -.24$).[1]

On the basis of these findings, Durkheim (76) concluded: "The social suicide-rate therefore bears no definite relation to the tendency to insanity, nor, inductively considered, to the tendency to the various forms of neurasthenia." His argument seems to be as follows: comparing suicide and insanity rates for different groups of people reveals varying patterns. Sometimes the rates are positively correlated, sometimes negatively; in still others there is no clear relationship. Therefore, no "definite" (i.e., consistent) relationship between the two exists.

To this point Durkheim's argument is well founded. However, granting this much does not settle the larger question of whether the relationship between insanity and suicide permits retaining the hypothesis that the two phenomena are causally related. Indeed, an argument for a causal relationship could be made as follows. As Durkheim (73) noted, "statistics of mental alienation are not compiled accurately enough for . . . international comparisons to be very strictly exact." Furthermore, no controls are employed. The figures relating insanity and religion are not consistent and too limited to be very significant. Two of the more revealing patterns in the data are those that *Suicide* either slights or explains away, namely: (1) the positive correlation between insanity and suicide rates revealed in the century-long increase in both, and (2) the "fact that suicide, like insanity, is commoner in cities than in the country" (70). These positive correlations reveal a less-than-accidental relationship that must be explained. One explanation might appeal to the progress of civilization generally and its greater development in urban areas. At the same time it would be equally possible to hypothesize a genuine cause-and-effect relationship: the roughly equal male-female insanity rates and the greater likelihood that men will commit suicide demonstrate the impact of biological factors, either directly or through their influence on mental makeup, and, hence, propensity to insanity/suicide. Reference to biologically determined differences is, of course, consistent with Durkheim's own use of them to explain the different responses of men and women to social regulation. Much the same kind of argument may be applied to the data relating suicide and insanity rates by age.

In assessing Durkheim's lengthy discussion of insanity and suicide, one may lose sight of his underlying argument. When he first introduced insanity rates, he had *already* rejected the possibility that suicide might be explained by insanity. It is true that he (70) used insanity to measure the incidence of "mental abnormalities of every kind," and that he was also interested in the relationship between insanity in its own right and suicide. But, eliminating alcoholism (treated at a later point) and insanity, it is the relationship between suicide and neurasthenia that constitutes the focal point of his analysis. Though he wove back and forth between an interest in insanity itself, its use as a measure of all types of mental aberrations, and its use as a measure of the incidence of neurasthenia, the context clearly shows that his primary goal was to assess the relationship between neurasthenia and suicide. Such a focus is entirely reasonable. After all, insanity is rare; neurasthenia, common. For his purposes it was more important to reject neurasthenia than insanity as a cause of suicide. As for the tendency to switch focuses, since insanity is employed as an indicator, Durkheim would naturally want to point out the implications of his empirical findings for his earlier conclusion that insanity is not an important cause of suicide.

Insanity is an unusual kind of indicator. By definition, the neurasthenic is *not* insane. Rather, Durkheim (70) argued that "since insanity is only the enlarged form of nervous degeneration," it should vary "in proportion" to neurasthenia. This assumption is questionable. *Suicide* does not claim that the two are in any way causally related, nor is evidence provided that shows an empirical

relationship. Apart from the supposition that they represent more
and less severe mental abnormalities, Durkheim provided no theoretical reason to suppose that they should vary proportionately. But
if this contention is not accepted, Durkheim's assertion that neurasthenia and suicide do *not* vary proportionately is deprived of its
empirical basis, as is his empirically based attempt to reject mental
disorder as an important factor in suicide. Indeed, coupling his
suggestion that neurasthenia is not uncommon with his assertion
that it "may predispose to suicide" (76) reveals that this conclusion
is compatible with other elements in *Suicide* itself.

Alcoholism

Durkheim's consideration of alcoholism concluded the chapter on
psychopathic states. To what could easily stand as *Suicide*'s motto—
"facts are unanswerable"—Durkheim (77) added: "Let us test
them." He began with four maps of France (Appendix I:393), each
of which depicts rates for one of the following: suicide, prosecutions
for alcoholism, alcoholic insane, and alcoholic consumption. The
maps show each department, shaded from white to black according
to a six-point scale: the darker the shading, the higher the rate in
question.[2] Comparing suicide with prosecutions for alcoholism,
Durkheim (77) observed little connection between them. His commentary is summarized in table 11.1. Durkheim found that those
areas highest on suicide are not highest on alcoholism; inversely,

TABLE 11.1 PROSECUTIONS FOR ALCOHOLISM AND SUICIDE IN FRANCE

Area	Suicide	Alcoholism
Ile-de-France and eastward	High	Not high[a]
Marseilles to Nice	High	Not high[a]
Normandy (especially Seine-Inférieure)	Most of the area below average	High
Finisterre and Breton departments	Low ("Brittany almost immune")	High
Rhone and neighboring region	Rhone not above average[b]	High

SOURCE: Suicide (77-78).

[a]Durkheim did not identify these areas as high on alcoholism; hence, by
implication, they should be categorized otherwise.

[b]Durkheim did not comment on the Rhone and the neighboring region, but
only on the Rhone.

those highest on the latter tend to be average or low on suicide. Such an analysis demonstrates some independent variation between the two phenomena. At the same time there are many areas that combine low suicide and alcoholism rates, others that are average on both, and still others high on both. Specifically, using Durkheim's scales to define categories, thirty departments are low on both suicide and alcoholism, seven are average on both, and another six are high on both. This finding indicates the basic limitation of his analysis: by focusing on only one extreme (those highest on either alcoholism or suicide), Durkheim ignored most of the information contained in his own figures and, in so doing, failed to rule out the possibility that alcoholism and suicide show a significant tendency to vary proportionately.

Durkheim (78) turned next to figures for France relating suicides to the alcoholic insane. His procedure—grouping departments into eight categories in order to compare average rates for suicide and alcoholic insane—suffers from the limitations identified in Part II. In addition, departments are grouped according to suicides, thereby treating the suicide rate as the independent, and the alcoholic insane rate as the dependent, variable. Durkheim thus did not rule out the possibility that grouping departments according to alcoholic rates might reveal a more regular relationship between suicide and alcoholism. His commentary focused upon those aspects of the data consistent with the conclusion that suicide and alcoholism are unrelated. In fact, the figures show some positive relationship. Durkheim closed with a reference to his maps, inspection of which also shows that the two rates are far from perfectly correlated. However, it is not clear what, if anything more, they demonstrate. If, as Durkheim (78) suggested, these maps are consistent with the implications of the figures just considered, then presumably they display some positive relationship between alcoholic insanity and suicide.

Beginning his examination of the final indicator, Durkheim (78) noted that at first glance, the relationship between alcoholic consumption and suicide seems closer than that between suicide and alcoholic insanity. Suicide rates are highest in the northern departments, the same region where the most alcohol is drunk (78–79). But the relevant maps indicate that the areas of highest incidence of alcoholic consumption and of suicide do not coincide perfectly. As before, though, Durkheim's analysis focuses on the degree of overlap between areas highest on both suicide and alcoholism; he

thus ignored most of the available information and failed to reject
the possibility of an overall tendency for suicide and alcoholic
consumption to covary. Indeed, the maps suggest the existence of a
positive correlation. As Durkheim noted, there is a tendency for
highest rates of alcoholic consumption and of suicide to appear in
northern (as opposed to southern) France. Partly overlapping with
this configuration is a wide path from central France down to the
Mediterranean coast that tends to be low on both alcoholic consumption and suicide. Thus, if suicide and alcoholism obviously
vary somewhat independently, they nonetheless appear to be positively correlated.

With regard to national comparisons, *Suicide* (79) gives figures
for six countries north of France, where, contrary to Durkheim's
interpretation, a high correlation exists between alcoholic consumption and suicide ($r = .94$).[3] (See table 11.2.) By demonstrating the
lack of any positive correlation in these countries, Durkheim hoped

TABLE 11.2   ALCOHOL CONSUMPTION AND SUICIDE RATES (PER
MILLION) IN NORTHERN EUROPE

| Country | Consumption | | | | Rank Order | |
	Liters per Inhabitant	Date	Suicide Rate		Alcohol	Suicide
Holland	4	1870	35.5 (n.d.)[a]		1	1
Belgium	8.56	1870	68		2	2
England	9.07	1870-71	70[b]		3	3
Sweden	10.34	1870	85		4	4
Denmark	16.51	1845	258 (1846-50)[a]		5	5

SOURCE: *Suicide* (79) unless otherwise noted.

NOTE: Durkheim gave years for alcohol consumption; suicide rates refer to
"corresponding periods" (79).

[a]Durkheim cited no rates. These suicide rates are taken from elsewhere in
Suicide (74, 259) and are for the dates indicated.

[b]*Suicide* gave alcohol consumption for England and suicide rate for Great
Britain. There seems to be little difference between the suicide rates for
the two regions for the period indicated (50, 74).

to support his contention that the conjunction between high rates of
both alcoholic consumption and suicide in northern France is
accidental. By his own logic, however, the positive correlation shown
by data for France and the other countries does more to suggest than
to reject the possibility of a causal relationship between alcoholism
and suicide. Durkheim (80) also cited German data, but they are

inconclusive and fail to sustain his conclusion that they show no positive relationship between alcoholism and suicide in Germany. In short, none of Durkheim's data sets rules out a positive relationship between suicide and alcoholism. To the contrary, analysis reveals numerous instances of appreciable correlation between the two. More broadly, Durkheim's treatment of neurasthenia, insanity, and alcoholism also fails to establish that these phenomena, individually or collectively, play no important causal role in the incidence of suicide.

RACE AND HEREDITY

Durkheim (Chapter 2 of Book 1:82-103) next considered normal psychological states, in which he included race and heredity.

Race

The concept. Durkheim (82–85) displayed acute awareness of the problems encountered in using the concept of race. One implication of his discussion was that until a more precise definition is achieved and until scientists successfully demonstrate the empirical reality to which the concept refers, the burden of showing its potential usefulness lies with those who support it rather than with those who wish to discount its influence. Durkheim's discussion suggested that his willingness to consider race as a possible causal factor was an attempt to meet his opponents more than halfway. It represented a bow in the direction of then-current interpretations of suicide, a gesture required by widespread belief in the importance of race. This bow might have been unnecessary if all scientists had been as aware as Durkheim of the difficulties encountered in using race as a scientific concept. *Suicide* reveals his awareness of the handicap under which he labored in his efforts to refute explanations of suicide that were based on an ill-defined concept.

The data. Durkheim (84) defined race as a group of individuals who have resemblances that are transmitted hereditarily. Having identified the difficulties in employing the concept of race, he (85) continued: "Yet let us agree that there are certain great types in Europe the most general characteristics of which can be roughly distinguished and among whom the peoples are distributed, and agree to give them the name of races." Without indicating how such a classification was originally derived, Durkheim (following Morselli) distinguished four, in order of decreasing aptitude for suicide:

Germanic, Celto-Roman, Slav, and Ural-Altaic. Given the small number of its representatives in Europe, the last group is mentioned only as a courtesy. The theory attributing differences in suicide rates to race is tenable only to the degree that members of a given race display an equally strong aptitude for suicide (85). In fact, however, different nations of the same race show great variations in suicide (85–86). (See table 11.3.)

TABLE 11.3   RACE AND SUICIDE RATES (PER MILLION) IN EUROPE

Racial Group	Rate
Germanic Type	
Scandinavian	
Denmark	268
Norway	74.5
Sweden	84
Anglo-Saxon	70
Flemish	50
Celto-Roman	
France	150
Italy	30
Spain	"still fewer" than Italy
Slav	
Bohemia	158
Moravia	136
Carnida	46
Croatia	30
Dalmatia	14

SOURCE: Suicide (86).

Having noted the great variability within each racial group, Durkheim (86) shifted his focus to the Germanic race, for which four of five instances (table 11.3) show a suicide rate from 50 to 84. On this basis it might be considered that the Germanic race displays relatively low suicide rates. However, Durkheim wanted to reject the generalization that the Germanic type displays *high* suicide rates. Given his assumption that rates in Germany are high, this may explain the rather curious circumstance that no rates for any German state are included under the Germanic type. The figures he did include permitted him to reject the notion that German rates are high and to stress their overlap with those of both the Celto-Roman and Slavic races. He (86) also noted that although Denmark's rate is high, those for Norway and Sweden are not, making it impossible to attribute Denmark's "suicide-rate to race, since it produces opposite effects in the two countries [Norway and Sweden] where this race is purest." His findings permitted him to conclude that of all Germanic peoples, only the Germans themselves are strongly inclined to suicide. He (86) continued:

> If then the terms were strictly used, it would be a question not of race but of nationality. Yet, since the existence of a German type in part, at least, hereditary, has not been disproved, the sense of the word may be stretched to the extreme extent of saying that suicide is more developed among the peoples of German race than among most Celto-Roman, Slavic or even Anglo-Saxon and Scandinavian societies. . . . In any case, this is the only instance where a certain influence of ethnic [racial] characteristics might possibly be suspected.

Durkheim (86) observed that to establish the influence of race requires more than just demonstrating high suicide rates in Germany, for these might be due to the social environment. Rather, a specifically Germanic aptitude for suicide must be shown to persist even where the social environment has changed. Only then could high suicide rates be regarded as a racial product. He (87) proposed to "see whether the German retains this sad primacy outside Germany, in the midst of the life of other peoples and acclimatized to different civilizations. Austria offers us a complete laboratory for answering this question. In differing proportions in the various provinces, the Germans are mixed with a population of totally different ethnic origins." Durkheim analyzed the data in table VII (87), using language to distinguish between races.

He grouped the fifteen Austrian provinces into four categories, according to percentage German in each, in order to compare their average suicide rates. This procedure and the accompanying commentary, together with two strategic omissions, reinforced the thrust of his analysis. His first three averages show an inverse relationship between percentage German and suicide rates. However, his average for the first group excluded Lower Austria, whose inclusion would raise the group average from 106 to 143. Durkheim also omitted altogether the average of the last group, thereby eliminating the basis for a comparison with other averages incompatible with his interpretation. Contrary to the tenor of his commentary, rank orders for proportion German and suicide rates correspond perfectly from one to four, except that groups two and three are interchanged. Collapsing the figures into two categories produces the following results: provinces having a German majority show an average suicide rate of 135; those with a German minority, 86.

Selvin's analysis of table vii is revealing. He (1965:119) observed that it is the five contiguous provinces comprising the eastern part of present-day Austria that have high proportions of Germans and disproportionately few suicides. Following his lead, table 11.4 divides Austrian provinces into eastern and western groups. The

TABLE 11.4 GERMANIC RACE AND SUICIDE RATES (PER MILLION) IN AUSTRIAN PROVINCES

Province	Number of Germans per 100 Inhabitants	Rate	Rank Order Percentage German	Suicide Rate
Western				
Salzburg	100	120	1	1
Upper Austria	100	110	1	2
Transalpine Tyrol	100	88	1	5
Carinthia	71.40	92	4	4
Styria	62.45	94	5	3
Nonwestern				
Lower Austria	95.90	254	1	1
Silesia	53.37	190	2	2
Bohemia	37.64	158	3	3
Moravia	26.33	136	4	4
Bukovina	9.06	128	5	5
Carniola	6.20	46	6	8
Galicia	2.72	82	7	7
Cisalpine Tyrol	1.90	88	8	6
Littoral	1.62	38	9	9
Dalmatia	.....[a]	14	10	10

SOURCE: Suicide (table VII:87).

[a]Durkheim's use of dots here presumably means either that a precise figure is unavailable or that the number does not differ appreciably from zero.

latter are marked by relatively similar suicide rates. The 106 average for the all-German provinces (Salzburg, Upper Austria, and Trans-alpine Tyrol) versus that of 93 for the two other western provinces suggests a moderately strong relationship between race and suicide. In contrast, "the Spearman rank correlation for" the nonwestern "provinces is 0.95, indicating an almost perfect relation between the suicide rate and the proportion of German-speaking people" (Selvin 1965:119). When all Austrian provinces are taken together, a noticeable relationship between suicide and race emerges. Dividing Austria geographically reveals that race and suicide stand in a different relationship in two separate regions. In view of the relationship between suicide and race in Austria generally, and particularly in view of the nearly perfect relationship which exists in nonwestern Austria, it is impossible to concur with Durkheim's conclusion (87) that the data reveal "not the least trace of German influence" upon suicide rates.

Turning next to figures for Switzerland in order to compare the German and the Latin races, Durkheim (88) observed that the fifteen cantons that are wholly or partly German have an average suicide rate of 186. This figure is hard to interpret. The cantons are not identified, nor is any source given. The four suicide rates cited indicate that Durkheim was not using the figures in his table xxvi (260). The reference to "wholly or in part German" leaves the proportion vague. There is no evidence to rule out the possibility that the cantons in question show the same kind of near-perfect correlation between proportion German and suicide rates found in nonwestern Austria.

Durkheim (88) emphasized that the average suicide rate of 255 for five cantons with French majorities surpasses the 186 for the fifteen German cantons, a comparison undermining the contention that the German race is associated with higher suicide rates than is the Latin. One problem with these data is the small number of French cantons examined. If the figures in table xxvi (260) are any guide, their average would be 23.7 percent less if the single canton with an exceptionally high rate (Neufchatel) is excluded. Reducing the French canton average of 255 by 23.7 percent gives 195, a figure similar to the German average of 186. The hypothesis to which Durkheim was addressing himself is that German rates should be relatively high. In fact, however, there is nothing in the data presented to indicate that they should exceed the French; in table

11.3 the French suicide rate is 170 to 300 percent higher than for four of the five examples of the Germanic type. It remains unclear whether German rates should exceed French, or vice versa. This failure presents another problem. What is the significance of Durkheim's observation that among the French cantons, the one with the lowest suicide rate (Valais, 10) had the highest proportion of Germans, whereas those with an "almost wholly" Latin population display rates ranging from 321 to 486. About all that can be said, if anything, is that in the French cantons, suicide rates vary inversely with the proportion of Germans. Overall, then, Durkheim does not successfully reject the hypothesis that race is causally related to suicide.

To "eliminate the religious factor," which might obscure the racial factor, "if there is one," Durkheim (88) concluded his analysis of the Swiss cantons with the following suicide rates: German Catholics, 87; French Catholics, 83; German Protestants, 293; and French Protestants, 456. These figures support his hypothesis that Protestants have a higher social suicide rate than do Catholics, but they do not require qualification of the conclusions just derived from the analysis of figures for Switzerland.

Having eliminated (to his satisfaction) the possibility that "Germans commit suicide more than other peoples ... because of their blood," Durkheim (89) turned to figures for France, observing that the French are a mixture of two principal races, the Cymries and the Celts. Since the two groups are distinguishable by height (the Cymries are taller), the percentage of drafted soldiers exempted for insufficient height is used as an indicator of race. After placing French departments into six groups, Morselli had found suicide and height to be positively correlated. Unfortunately, in lieu of the actual figures, *Suicide* (89) included only a reference to Morselli. Durkheim acknowledged that "so exact a correspondence" as that reported by Morselli must be attributable to race, yet he dismissed Morselli's finding on the grounds that his comparison used Broca's classification of racial groups. Acknowledging the authority of Broca, Durkheim nevertheless rejected his classification as ultimately founded on too many unverifiable conjectures. The reader of *Suicide* is left in a quandary. Presumably Broca, and Morselli following him, believed that the former's classification had merit; yet Durkheim rejected it without giving either the classification itself or Broca's rationale for deriving it. The reader thus has no grounds for rejecting a correlation which Durkheim (89) himself admitted can "scarcely be explained by anything but the action of race."

Moving beyond Broca's "systematic but somewhat overingenious scheme" (90), Durkheim presented table viii (91), which shows average suicide rates of French departments divided into six groups according to height. He emphasized those features of the results which undermine the contention that stature and suicide are positively related. For instance, among the three taller groups, "the first group with highest stature has fewer suicides than the second and scarcely more than the third," whereas the three shorter groups show approximately equal suicide rates "however unequal in respect to height" (90). Interestingly, though, each of the taller groups has a far higher suicide rate than does any of the shorter groups. Following a procedure employed throughout *Suicide,* I compared averages. Doing so shows that the average suicide rate of 191 for the taller groups is about double that of 93 for the shorter groups (excluding the Seine; see *Suicide* 90n). It might be anticipated that Durkheim would acknowledge the existence of the relationship between suicide and stature. Instead he asserts that "the coincidence" between stature and suicide "is only broadly and generally accurate." Furthermore, "these two progressions are not exactly parallel" and do "not appear in the detailed variations shown by the two subjects compared." Thus, "once the coincidence has ... been reduced to its true proportions, it is no longer a decisive proof of the ethnic [racial] elements." Rather, "it is merely a curious fact inadequate to prove a law" (90-91). To the contrary, however, if the relationship is far from perfect, it is strong enough to be treated as more than "merely a curious fact."

A footnote (93n) at the very end of the discussion briefly treats the relationship between height and suicide in four Italian provinces. No source was identified, but the figures given for average height are the same as those found in Morselli, which, with Durkheim's earlier reference to *Il Suicidio,* suggests the latter as his source. Morselli (1882:103) cited data showing that Italian departments with less than twenty suicides per million have an average suicide rate of 14.4 and an average stature of 1.616; those with twenty-one to forty suicides, 30.9 and 1.635; and those with over forty suicides, 46.5 and 1.643. (The correlation between suicide and stature by department, using the 1866-71 figures for stature, is $r = .45$; see Morselli 1882, table xiv:103.) Morselli interpreted these figures as revealing the influence of race, while Durkheim's interpretation emphasized the effects of civilization. Although offering an alternative explanation, Durkheim never explained why the differences in suicide associated with stature might not be caused by race. Insofar as height indicates racial differences—a possibility Durkheim explicitly entertained for France—the data suggest that differences in suicide are systematically associated with racial differences in both France and Italy.

Interpretation. Attempting to overcome Morselli on the latter's own grounds, Durkheim adopted the classification of races employed in *Il Suicidio.* The reader of *Suicide* is told nothing about the derivation of that classification and hence is in no position to evaluate it. Another classification might produce a different picture.

Durkheim did not treat Morselli's classification of the four basic racial types as exhaustive of all relevant racial differences. As presented in *Suicide* (85), Morselli's classification identified France as one illustration of the Celto-Roman race. The classification does not clarify whether all Celto-Romans—the French, Italians, and Spaniards—are to be treated as one race or whether each of these groups represents a distinct race. In any case, Durkheim (89) himself divided the French into two principal races (the Cymries and the Celts). If the French constitute *two* races, however, presumably many of the groups identified in table 11.3 as different examples of a single race are themselves sufficiently distinct to qualify as separate races. Given Durkheim's definition of race in terms of hereditarily transmitted differences, height is a reasonable indicator (Durkheim used it as such), and the variation in suicide associated with height differences is significant. The average suicide rate for the French departments with tallest average stature is double that for those with the shortest. In Italy, departments with tallest average stature have an average suicide rate of more than three times that of those with the shortest. If the racial differences *between* countries are greater than those within countries, then they might well "explain" the variation by race in suicide rates.

Altogether, the data do not support any one-sided conclusion about the relationship between race and suicide. On the one hand, the three (or four) great racial types do not display any marked tendency toward a constant suicide rate clearly distinguishable from that of the other types (table 11.3). There is noticeable variation within racial types, and most comparisons between two types reveal overlapping rates. On the other hand, these findings do not necessarily rule out the importance of race. If each one of the instances represented under each of the four great types constitutes a distinct race, then variability within these four types does not undermine the hypothesis that each race has a distinctive suicide rate. On the contrary, if it were granted that each instance represents a more or less distinct racial type, then these racial differences might account for the variation in suicide rates.

Durkheim began his analysis with a sophisticated treatment of the problems encountered in scientific use of the concept of race. Once he attempted to validate the lack of any empirical correlation between race and suicide, however, he met with difficulties. He opened with figures (for three of the four great races in Europe) that seem to provide convincing support for his contention, but reexamination of them in the light of his analysis suggests that the variation displayed could be attributed to racial differences. His data show a near-perfect correlation between suicide and proportion German for the greater part of Austria. With height as an indicator of race, the evidence also reveals a noticeable correlation between race and suicide in France; figures for Italy show an even more pronounced correlation. Thus, the data for nonwestern Austria, Italy, and France—all of which show that race and suicide covary—must be placed against Durkheim's generally unsuccessful attempts to demonstrate that suicide and race do not vary proportionally.

Durkheim recognized that correlations do not necessarily demonstrate a causal relationship, and certainly *Suicide* gives no indication that proponents of a racial explanation of suicide have done more than attempt to demonstrate an empirical correlation; none has provided an accompanying theoretical explanation for the correlation. This failure put Durkheim at a disadvantage because he could only attack the empirical correlation and not the explanation of it. At the same time (consistent with his own approach, which tests for the existence of a cause-and-effect relationship by determining whether two phenomena vary systematically together), he (89) was apparently willing to grant that a close correlation between suicide and race could, as in France, "scarcely be explained by anything but the action of race."

Perhaps—here I can only speculate—Durkheim was willing to meet the racial hypothesis more than halfway because he knew he would reject it empirically. More generally, there is no doubt that he felt most comfortable when he could refute an explanation not only theoretically but also empirically. If one theoretical argument can be countered with another, "facts are unanswerable." In the present instance, despite the convincing nature of Durkheim's opening statement on the problems of using race to explain variations in social phenomena, the facts are more congruent with the hypothesis that race is a causal factor in suicide than with his own contention to the contrary.

Heredity

"The theory that sees race as an important factor in the inclination to suicide also implies that it is hereditary; for it can be an ethnic [racial] characteristic only on this condition." Proof that "the tendency to suicide is genetically transmitted" would prove that "it depends closely on a definite organic state" (93). Durkheim began with some general observations that are not decisive either theoretically or empirically because, as he (95) noted, the necessary data were unavailable. The following discussion concerns the relationship between suicide on the one hand and sex and age on the other, for which more systematic evidence was available.

Durkheim held that the suicide-sex relationship is inconsistent with the hypothesis that suicide is hereditary because this hypothesis implies that suicide should occur with equal frequency for both sexes. He (99) argued that "as suicide by itself is in no sense sexual, there is no reason why inheritance should afflict men rather than women." But, as is revealed in evidence presented throughout *Suicide*, men commit suicide much more frequently than women. Only Durkheim's argument remains unconvincing. It is reasonable to hypothesize that the biological differences between men and women are associated with or give rise to additional differences that are not themselves "sexual." Durkheim's theory of domestic anomie appeals to just such differences. The finding that men have higher suicide rates, even when other variables, including social ones, have been controlled, is consistent with the hypothesis that biological differences are causally related to suicide.

Concluding his presentation of evidence with the data in table IX (101), Durkheim distinguished between phenomena that can appear at virtually any age and those that appear only after the individual has reached a given age. Placing suicide in the first category, he asserted that all such characteristics should become apparent at a very early age, for "the longer it takes in appearing, the more clearly must heredity be considered only a weak stimulus to its existence" (100). Suicide is rare during childhood, increasing steadily until it reaches greatest frequency in old age (101). Contrary to Durkheim, however, various hereditarily transmitted diseases (even those such as Huntington's chorea that are so debilitating as to lead to suicide) do not appear until adulthood. The very constancy of the relationship between age and suicide favors rather than denies the hypothesis that aging as a biological phenomenon may be causally related to suicide. Thus, *Suicide* falls far short of demonstrating that the striking relationships between suicide and both sex and age undermine rather than sustain the hypothesis that hereditarily transmitted characteristics play an important causal role in suicide.

Cosmic Factors

Durkheim (104) next analyzed the relationship between suicide and cosmic factors, observing that even "if individual predispositions are not by themselves the determining causes of suicide, perhaps they are more active in combination with certain cosmic factors." Two such factors, climate and seasonal temperature, are considered.

Climate

Climate was treated briefly. Durkheim (105) cited the following data for Europe: between 36° and 43° north latitude, 21.1 suicides per one million inhabitants; 43°–50° north, 93.3; 50°–55° north, 172.5; and beyond 55° north, 88.1. There is no indication of the longitudes in question, why these particular divisions of latitude were chosen, or how other divisions might affect the relationship of climate to suicide. Durkheim (105) observed that suicide is at a minimum in the south and north of Europe and at a maximum in the center, adding that Morselli had identified the area bounded by 47° and 57° north latitude and 20° and 40° east longitude as that most favorable to suicide; this zone coincides approximately with the most temperate region of Europe. Longitude is not given in terms of the current system (which uses Greenwich, England as the prime meridian).[4] Not only, then, is it difficult to identify the region in question, but Durkheim cited no specific rate for it. Finally, no map is provided, thus making it difficult to place these figures in terms of European geography.

Durkheim (105) then cited reasons for believing that the relationship between high suicide rates and the temperate region of Europe is not causal. He stated that suicide has flourished in all climates, including India and ancient Rome, but offered no supporting data save a footnote reference to his chapter on altruistic suicide (in which there is certainly no confirmatory empirical evidence). Even if true, Durkheim's claim that suicide flourished in these two areas does not reject the possibility that internal or internal-external comparisons using these areas would reveal a positive correlation between less extreme climatic conditions and suicide.

Durkheim next observed that the zone of high suicide rates does not coincide with a clearly defined climatic region but rather shows up as two distinct areas, one centering on Ile-de-France, the other on Saxony and Prussia. He included no suicide rates, no maps, nor even any references at this point, leaving it largely up to the reader to determine the nature of the overall relationship between climatic zones and areas of high suicide rates. The regions closest to the central area of frequent suicide display the next highest rates (105). Durkheim might easily have interpreted this pattern as indicating a causal relationship; yet he (106) argued that proximity to the temperate climate cannot be held accountable. To discount the influence of climate when it is found to vary together with suicide, solely on the grounds that there is no reason to believe it *is* of importance, is to draw a conclusion about the relationship being investigated and then to use that conclusion to deny the significance of the empirical relationship.

Durkheim (106) then asked whether it is not more probable that the social milieu causing high suicide rates in northern France and northern Germany reappears, albeit with less intensity, in neighboring countries having a somewhat similar way of life. However, there are substantial barriers separating the regions in question (e.g., the English Channel separates southern England from northern France; the Alps, southern Germany and northern Italy). In addition, particularly in the instance of Germany, the regions of highest suicide rates are separated from the areas they are supposed to influence by areas of relatively low suicide rates. It is hard to see how the influence postulated by Durkheim could manifest itself in this leap-frog fashion.

The final set of evidence (table x:106) showing suicide rates for the north, center, and south of Italy during three periods is more convincing. The differences between northern and central Italy diminish and are finally reversed, despite unchanging climatic conditions. When compared to those for the center or the north, however, suicide rates for the south are consistent with the assertion that in countries outside the central European zone, suicide increases with proximity to the zone.

Durkheim's conclusion (106) was unequivocal: "One need dwell no further on an hypothesis proved by nothing and disproved by so many facts." Nevertheless, his evidence supports the hypothesis that temperate climate is positively associated with suicide.

Temperature and Length of Day

Accepting the existence of a strong relationship between seasonal variations in temperature and suicide, Durkheim (106) observed that the facts are clear but subject to various interpretations. His presentation centered on the attempt to show that suicide and the seasons are related only because collective life itself varies with the seasons. This demonstration is perhaps the most systematic and ingenious in all of *Suicide*.

The data. In all countries the six warmest months of the year show more suicides than the six coldest (107). Even the proportion of suicides committed in the warmest months versus those committed in the coldest remains relatively constant from one country to another. Referring to findings of Morselli (comparing thirty-four different periods in eighteen European states), Durkheim (108) delineated the relationship more precisely. The seasons fall in the following order of most to fewest suicides in twenty-six of thirty-four comparisons (76 percent): summer, spring, autumn, winter.

Durkheim (108) noted that from these findings, some observers have concluded that temperature directly influences the tendency to suicide. However, if temperature is the basic cause, it should vary with suicide. In fact, this is not the case in the data for France and Italy (111). Contrary to the hypothesis that higher temperatures are associated with higher suicide rates, considerably *more* suicides occur in spring than in autumn, even though spring temperatures are marginally lower. Durkheim (111) also pointed out that the difference between spring and summer is slight for suicides, but relatively great for temperature.

Indicating that a finer breakdown of the data reveals even more clearly the lack of any tendency for suicide rates to vary proportionately with temperature changes, Durkheim presented another table (xii:112) to show that monthly variations obey the following law, found to be true for all European countries: *"Beginning with January inclusive, the incidence of suicide increases regularly from month to month until about June and regularly decreases from that time to the end of the year"* (111). Temperatures are highest in July and August, but suicide rates peak in June. Except for a December-

January tie in Prussia, suicide rates are lowest not in January (the coldest month), but in December. Furthermore, in a given country, months with nearly the same temperature may have a very different proportion of the annual total of suicides, while those with nearly the same proportion of suicides may have very different temperatures. If Durkheim (113) characteristically overstated his conclusion in holding that thermometric variations and suicide show no relationship, he nonetheless showed that in monthly comparisons, suicide and temperature often do not covary.

Furthermore, if temperature had the influence attributed to it, the hottest countries should have the highest suicide rates (113). In fact, however, suicide is infrequent in southern Europe; Italy, Spain and Portugal all have low rates. Also, in France the only large area with low suicide rates comprises the departments south of the Loire.[5] Although he applied it to the French data only, his observation (113) that results are "inconsistent with the theory that heat is a stimulant to suicide" is applicable to these international comparisons as well.

Durkheim (113) next turned to the contention (attributed to Lombroso and, following him, Morselli), that it is not so much the intensity of heat but rather the contrast between the departing cold and the advent of the hot season that causes suicide. The data permit unequivocal rejection of that hypothesis. Rather than rising most sharply during the period of sharpest temperature increase (March to April), suicide rates at that time rise no more than they do between January and February. Later, modifying his earlier contention that the Lombroso-Morselli thesis suggests constant rates during the autumn, Durkheim (114) held that their view implies that the onset of cold weather should have the same deleterious effects as the onset of the first warm weather. Summarizing some of Morselli's data on Europe that are not reproduced in *Suicide*, Durkheim (115) concluded that in 67 percent of the cases, suicide rates decrease regularly from September through December.

Durkheim (115-16) next examined the relationship between "the proportional share ... in the total of annual suicides" and the average length of the day for each month. The r of .97 between suicide and length of day in France (table XIII:115) is barely short of Durkheim's "perfect" parallelism (116). Coupled with his desire to demonstrate the closeness of this correspondence was his wish to show that it is closer than that between monthly variations in temperature and suicide. The r's for average monthly temperature and suicide are as follows: Naples, .59; France, .60; Rome, .64; and Prussia, .84 (table xii:112). Far from displaying no relationship as Durkheim (113) claimed, the correlations range from moderate to high. This quibble aside, the correlation between length of day and suicide is still far higher than those for temperature and length of day, and, equally important, it is virtually perfect. Here Durkheim's data provide convincing support.

He (116) followed with suicide data for Paris by time of day. Unfortunately, they are reported in vague categories (e.g., early morning, middle of the day) rather than by hour. They show that four-fifths of all suicides occur during the daytime or evening and three-fifths during the daytime alone. Additional data on Prussia (table xiv:117) display a similar pattern. Durkheim noted the preponderance of suicides by day, which makes an earlier finding of his—the longer the day, the more suicides—understandable. The question (117) remains: "But what causes this diurnal influence?"

Durkheim's explanation (117) is that daytime "is the time of most active existence, when human relations cross and recross, when social life is most intense." He presented additional data for Paris and France that show a drop in suicide in the interval between 11 A.M. and noon (Paris) or noon and 2 P.M. (France), compared with immediately preceding and succeeding periods of the day. Durkheim interpreted these drops in suicide as corresponding to a decrease in social interaction. Countering an alternative interpretation, he also pointed out that these data for Paris and France, as well as those for Paris and Prussia, fail to reflect any influence from heat and sun because fewer suicides are committed during the middle of the day than either immediately before or after. Though *Suicide* (117) identifies the middle of the day as "the moment of greatest heat," no supporting evidence is offered. Data giving temperatures taken at six different times each day (except Sunday) in Paris for 1870 show that while the noon temperature exceeded the 3 P.M. reading 20 percent of the time, the 3 P.M. temperature was higher 77 percent of the time. Even apart from these data, Durkheim's rejection appears premature. Presumably the crux of the matter is not simply the heat of the day but how hot individuals feel or actually become. The decrease in activity during the noon hour should prevent individuals from becoming overly hot, and they probably also seek relief from excessive heat. Certainly, many people remove themselves from direct exposure to a very hot sun, thus mitigating its influence. Appeals to the influence of heat and the sun thus are not necessarily inconsistent with the finding that suicide rates drop during the middle of the day.

Results based on the analysis of 6,587 French suicides classified according to the day of the week on which they occurred (table xv:118) are interpreted as providing additional evidence that fluctuations in suicide follow those of social life generally. As would be expected, given the "prejudices" concerning Friday that are known to retard public activity, "suicide diminishes toward the end of the week beginning with Friday" (118). The Saturday rate reflects the slackness commencing on Saturday afternoon. On the following day economic activity stops altogether so that, were it not replaced by other activity, the Sunday decrease could well be even greater than it is. Women's share of suicides is proportionally greatest on Sunday, the very day when they mingle most with others (118-19).

Durkheim (120) presented a final argument. Because of occupational differences (city people being engaged in trade, industry, art, and science; country people, in agriculture) and use of artificial lighting in cities, the difference in total amount of collective activity by season should be less in cities than in the country as a whole (table xvi:121). "Whereas in France, Prussia, Austria and Denmark there is a difference of 52, 45 and even of 68 per cent between the minimum and the maximum, at Paris, Berlin, Hamburg, etc., this averages from 20 to 25 per cent and even reaches 12 per cent (at Frankfurt)" (121). The data sustain the thesis that there is a greater difference between seasons in these states as a whole than in their major cities.

Conclusions. Durkheim's purpose was to establish that collective activity, and not temperature or other cosmic factors, is causally related to social suicide rates. This analysis is complicated because temperature and collective activity are positively related not only to each other but also to suicide. His approach was to demonstrate that temperature and suicide are related only through the former's relationship to social life. The logic of his presentation required demonstration that even though two variables correlate with suicide, systematic breakdown of the figures shows one to be so much more closely related as to distinguish it alone as the causal variable.

The analysis opened with a brief treatment of the relationship between suicide and climatic zones. Although Durkheim concluded that there is no appreciable association, his analysis does not support him; in fact, most of the data reflect a noticeable correlation between geographic zone and suicide rates. The key portion of his analysis demonstrates that length of day is more closely related to suicide rates than are temperature variations. Interpreting length of day as a measure of collective activity, he buttressed his case with additional data revealing a positive correlation between social interaction and suicide. Altogether, the demonstration of a positive relationship between collective activity and suicide is one of the most imaginatively developed and compelling analyses in *Suicide.*

Nonetheless, Durkheim's findings produce a discrepancy. Integration and regulation vary proportionately with collective activity (social interaction). Durkheim held that in modern society, suicide is *inversely* related to integration and regulation. Hence, his argument that suicide and collective activity vary proportionately runs counter to his theory of suicide. Only a finding that suicide rates go *down* as involvement in collective activity goes up would have supported his theory. Ironically, Durkheim's success in showing the correlation between collective activity and suicide advances his case for a sociological explanation of suicide while simultaneously calling into question the adequacy of the particular sociological explanation offered in *Suicide.*

IMITATION

The last chapter (123-42) of Book I was given to ruling out a final nonsocial factor in suicide, namely, imitation. Durkheim (124-27) excluded situations in which reciprocal influence and fusion of individual states generate a sui generis collective reality acting as a force that impinges upon individuals in a crowd, causing them to act, think, and feel alike. He also ruled out the sui generis pressure exerted by society upon the individual, causing him to conform to prevailing manners and morals. Rather, Durkheim (123) restricted imitation to individual psychological phenomena ocurring "between individuals connected by no social bond." The act occurs automatically in a mechanical, reflexive manner, without benefit of mental activity to link the stimulus (act copied) and the imitative response (123-30).

Durkheim delineated the conditions that must prevail if suicide is to be attributed to imitation. Suicide (133) must radiate out from centers that necessarily display its maximum intensity. These centers can be identified according to specific criteria. First, by definition (133), they must display the highest rates in the area. Second, they must exist as a "cynosure for outlying districts" (134). Since people's eyes can be "thus fixed only on a point of importance to the regional life ... phenomena of contagion are bound to be most pronounced near capitals and large cities" (134). Finally, given that the power of example weakens with distance, "surrounding regions should be less afflicted the further they are from the focal hearth, and inversely" (134).

Durkheim's empirical analysis rests on the contention that if suicide is a result of imitation, mapping would reveal it to be "grouped more or less concentrically around certain centers from which it radiates more and more weakly" (137). But *Suicide* does not present figures for concentric zones; rather, rates for principal centers are compared to those prevailing in neighboring districts. These comparisons do not employ rates for the cities in question but for the entire district in which the city is located. Although *Suicide* also fails to indicate what proportion of all residents in these districts actually live in the cities (on the assumption that these cities contain the vast majority of the districts' residents, thereby largely determining their suicide rates), the procedure is adequate.

Durkheim (134) noted that the customary French maps are of little value because the suicide rates of cities are obscured by being averaged with those of their respective departments. Consequently, he presented a map (Appendix II:394) by district. Most noticeable (134-35) is a large northern area of high suicide rates which covers the region of the former Ile-de-France, running deep into Champagne and extending into Lorraine. There is only one noticeable center in the area; thus, if imitation were the cause, Paris would have to be the focal point (135). In fact, however, the district (the Seine) including Paris has a suicide rate of 471 per million, whereas neighboring districts invariably have higher rates (134-35). Also mentioned are nine additional departments in which the district containing the principal town does not display the highest suicide rate of all districts in that department. However, the situation in the remaining French departments is not considered. Thus the analysis may show that for areas with high rates, suicide does not radiate from principal centers; but it has not ruled out another possibility, namely, that in areas of moderate or low rates, suicide does radiate.

Durkheim (136) observed that it would be interesting to compare communes. Without amplifying, he noted that a map of communes cannot be constructed for the entire country, although one was compiled for the department of Seine-et-Marne by Dr. Leroy, who classified communes by both population and suicide rates. *Suicide* cites figures for only eight communes (136-37). Durkheim (137) then noted that of the twenty-five communes with the highest suicide rates, all but two have very small populations. These results are presented in the form of a long quote from Dr. Leroy. As a consequence, perhaps, some points are unclear. For instance, it is not stated where the communes mentioned rank in terms of size, compared to all communes in the department. Nor is it indicated whether, as seems to be implied, the eight communes are an exhaustive listing of all those ranging in population from 3,468 to 11,939 persons. Finally, there is no indication of the relationship between size of population and rate of suicide for other communes. Overlooking these problems, it might be concluded at this point that comparing suicide and population rank orders reveals no tendency for the larger towns to have higher suicide rates.

However, there is another problem with the data. With small populations, one suicide has a drastic impact upon rates. For instance, a single case in a town of 630 inhabitants raises the suicide rate from 0 to 1,587 per million (which, incidentally, is a rate cited by Durkheim). Overcoming this problem requires a larger base population, which can be obtained by grouping towns of approximately the same size and treating them as a single instance. Such a procedure has an averaging effect, and its use on the commune data might well drop the twenty-three high-suicide communes far down the rank order list.

Durkheim held that the French pattern he found prevailed elsewhere, but his documentation is sparse. *Suicide* indicates that the highest suicide rates for German states are 311 for the Kingdom of Saxony and 303 for the Duchy of Saxe-Altenburg, while that for Brandenburg is only 204. Without citing additional rates, Durkheim (137) observed that "neither Dresden nor Altenburg set the tone for Hamburg or Berlin." Of all Italian provinces, Bologna and Livorno have the highest suicide rates (88 and 84, respectively), while "Milan, Genoa, Turin and Rome follow only at a distance."

The specific criteria applied in identifying the centers from which suicide should radiate are not always clear. Durkheim (134) spoke of cynosures—areas "of importance to the regional life"—and identified large cities and capitals as examples. However, he did not always indicate whether the centers in question are necessarily either the largest in the regions or capitals, or how they may be otherwise identified, though he did employ the unambiguous criterion of size.

It may be questioned whether the concentric zone pattern bears any necessary relationship to the hypothesis that imitation is an important factor in suicide. There is little reason to assume, as

Durkheim did, that rates of suicide must be higher in some such center of importance; the only requirement is a model that can be imitated. A single instance of suicide provides such a model and, if sufficiently visible, could give rise to virtually any number of imitative acts. Indeed, Durkheim's own commentary stresses the crucial nature of such qualitative questions as the extent to which a center exists as a cynosure for surrounding districts. In short, there is no reason to assume that imitated centers of suicide must necessarily display high suicide rates. To the extent that this assumption is granted, Durkheim's empirical analysis is largely irrelevant as an attempt to rule out imitation as a factor in suicide.

CONCLUSION

Durkheim attempted to demonstrate that suicide cannot be explained by nonsocial causes. However, he did not distinguish systematically between absolute incidence and variation in rates. At times he argued that a given nonsocial factor does not cause suicide; elsewhere he emphasized that, given existing relationships between variations in an independent variable and in suicide rates, the variable in question cannot be considered a cause of *variation* in suicide rates. A hypothetical example suggests the importance of the distinction. Imagine a situation in which all suicide is caused by two variables, A and B. A is a constant and causes two hundred suicides per year; B, a variable, causes from none up to fifty suicides per year. If one asks which factor is the most important cause of suicide, the answer is A. However, if one is trying to explain variation in rates, then B is the decisive factor. More broadly, if it were possible to show that some variable, C, accounts for all suicide, then an alternative factor, D, may be ruled out as a cause. However, Durkheim never successfully identified any such causal factor. Consequently, his argument against nonsocial factors as important causal elements vis-a-vis the absolute incidence of suicide may be rejected. The main thrust of Book II, however, is the attempt to explain variation in social suicide rates. Hence Book I is best assessed in terms of Durkheim's success in ruling out nonsocial factors as causes of *variation* in rates.

Durkheim's data often suggested the importance of nonsocial factors because they covary with social suicide rates. Moreover, he was unable to demonstrate that variation in his two independent variables, integration and regulation, is systematically related to variation in suicide rates. According to the logic of Durkheim's analysis, then, it must be concluded either that nonsocial factors are more important than the social or that integration and regulation are not the crucial social variables.

Durkheim was not above employing a double standard. For example, noting two exceptions to a generalization, he (107) ruled them out partly on the grounds that the base figures were too uncertain (totaling only 387 and 755 instances of suicide). Elsewhere (e.g., suicide rates of small towns), though, he accepted far smaller numbers. In assessing the importance of insanity, he (67) identified the problem as that of learning "whether *all* suicides are insane" (emphasis added). Concluding that not all are, he ruled out insanity. However, he never even tried to demonstrate that all suicides can be attributed to a specific social variable. Acknowledging the existence of a noticeable correlation between race and suicide, he (90–91) rejected any causal connection on the ground that their "progressions are not exactly parallel"; yet he presented no data on integration-regulation that would not be ruled out by such a standard. In considering the relationship between race and heredity, he (95) noted that "it is not enough to cite certain facts favorable to the thesis of heredity." They must also (1) be numerous enough not to be attributable to accidental circumstances, (2) not permit another explanation, and (3) not be contradicted by other facts. These criteria are applied with a vigor that is lacking in the analysis of data offered in support of his theory. In short, Durkheim applied a double standard to the disadvantage of nonsocial explanations of suicide.

For the most part Durkheim did not consider interaction between and among the nonsocial factors that he rejected as causes of suicide. Usually, he dismissed such factors one by one, without considering whether two or more in combination might not have an effect that is unnoticed when each is treated separately. Another possibility is even more serious. Durkheim typically attempted to discount the importance of nonsocial variables by showing that they are less important than the sum of relevant social variables. Following Durkheim, one might assume that taken together, the social variables explain more variation than does any single nonsocial variable. Together social variables might explain, say, 30 percent of the total variation, whereas each nonsocial variable, being less important, might explain only a third as much. Because there are many nonsocial variables, collectively they might be more important than the social factors. Thus seven nonsocial factors may explain 70 percent of the variation, social factors, only 30 percent. Given the consistent tendency of Durkheim's nonsocial factors to correlate with variation in suicide rates, this possibility is quite realistic.

Finally, Durkheim argued by elimination. Two factors may affect social suicide rates, social ones and nonsocial ones (52, 57). Eliminating the nonsocial leaves the social (145). This type of argument is convincing to the extent that the complete universe of relevant nonsocial causes has been identified. Unfortunately, Durkheim did not explain how to assure that the complete universe had been covered; instead, he examined only those nonsocial factors current in what he treated as the relevant literature. Logically, this procedure weakened his analysis because he provided no reason to believe that he had exhausted the universe. Psychologically, however, his approach was stronger; by implying that he had covered the relevant literature, he created a void predisposing the reader to entertain his theory.

On the basis of *Suicide*, it must be concluded that nonsocial factors have not been incorporated into a theoretical structure that convincingly links them to suicide. However, Durkheim argued that nonsocial factors are less systematically associated with variation in social suicide rates than are social factors generally or his two independent variables—integration and regulation—in particular. This argument must be rejected because nonsocial factors are often much more closely linked to variation in social suicide rates than are integration and regulation. Quite apart from the problems inherent in using argument by elimination, Durkheim did not successfully reject nonsocial factors as possible causes of suicide. *Suicide* thus provides little reason for proponents of various nonsociological explanations to acknowledge the inherent superiority of a sociological approach to suicide.

DURKHEIM'S CASE FOR
   SOCIAL REALISM

Both Durkheim's sociological theory of variation in social suicide rates and his attempt to deny the significance of nonsocial causes constitute essential aspects of his case for social realism. But even beyond these, *Suicide* is permeated with arguments for social realism, centering on the doctrine of emergence. He also held that suicide statistics demonstrate the existence of a reality—society—that needs to be analyzed. Interaction is identified as the process that creates society, and Durkheim attempted to delineate society, an exercise that found him flirting with a group mind doctrine. He weighed social against nonsocial reality in order to conclude that the former was the more powerful. Finally, applying these perspectives to the specific subject matter of his book, Durkheim assessed the role of social and nonsocial factors in suicide.

EMERGENCE

The Doctrine of Emergence

Suicide attempts to demonstrate that social phenomena are real. The reality of phenomena is not a question of the way in which they are conceived by the observer. The scientist does not create different realities by describing the same phenomena in different ways. Rather, the reality is prior to and exists independently of the way in which it is conceived. Conceptions, scientific or otherwise, are only more or less accurate reflections or "representations" of reality itself. Durkheim was a realist, not a nominalist.

Durkheim felt that insofar as the structural arrangement (or the interconnectedness, interaction, combination, or fusion of parts) gives rise to something qualitatively different, more complex, and greater than the parts themselves, it may be said that "the whole is greater than the sum of its parts." Though he sometimes took this statement as a self-evident doctrine of science, elsewhere he argued in favor of it. Specifically, there are instances in which a whole cannot be described in terms of, or explained from, knowledge of its parts. To the extent that this is true, the whole is emergent relative to its parts.

Although Durkheim often stated the argument in this general form, he typically applied it in contexts that feature additional conditions. Wholes and their constituent elements may stand in a special relationship: the parts exist at one level (or order) of nature; the emergent whole constitutes another, higher level of reality. Thus physical elements combine to form emergent chemical phenomena; chemical elements, emergent biological phenomena; the biological, psychological phenomena; and, most important, psychological and individual phenomena, emergent social phenomena. Durkheim (320, 325n) held that the emergence found at other levels of reality also applies to the social. However, since *Suicide* assumes (but never attempts to demonstrate) the emergent nature of phenomena at these lower levels of reality, Durkheim's argument by analogy rests upon an unproven assumption.

Stated in its most general form—the whole is greater than the sum of its parts—the argument is difficult to evaluate because it is subject to numerous interpretations (Nagel 1961:380–97). I therefore use an example that is often cited in this context. When the chemical elements oxygen and hydrogen combine to form water, the properties of water are emergent relative to those of oxygen and hydrogen because water's properties cannot be explained from knowledge, however complete, of the elements alone.[1] Though this argument has immediate intuitive appeal, it cannot withstand close scrutiny.[2] If the theory in question excludes reference to the properties that oxygen and hydrogen manifest upon combining (e.g., heat capacity, density), then Durkheim's claim will hold. However, if the theory predicts such properties and they are indeed observed, then it cannot be said that new, unexplained phenomena have appeared. Of course, unpredicted properties may occur. But far from meaning that such properties are inherently emergent, such an event merely demonstrates the theory's inadequacy. Phenomena are thus not inherently either emergent or nonemergent. Rather, they become so only relative to given theories.

It is not a proper part of science to assert that wholes cannot be explained in terms of parts, or that phenomena at a given level of analysis can be explained only in terms of other phenomena at that same, and no other, level. If a scientist explains wholes in terms of parts, or phenomena at a higher order of reality using variables at a lower level, the scientific community must accept the explanation. If otherwise satisfactory, it certainly cannot be rejected on the grounds that it is reductionist. Indeed, many current advances in science are reductionist in form (e.g., the reduction of biology to biochemistry or chemistry, and that of chemistry to physics), thereby implicitly undermining Durkheim's emergence argument.

To assert the legitimacy of reductionist explanations is not to argue (as some have) that reductionism is the preferred mode of explanation. A scientist is free to develop such explanations as he chooses. Thus Durkheim's stance that social phenomena may be explained in terms of other social facts is wholly acceptable. Only his more extreme claim—that social phenomena are inherently emergent and, consequently, can be explained only by other social phenomena[3]—is questioned here.

Inferences from Demographic Statistics

The doctrine of emergence is supplemented by arguments based on over-time data on the rates and incidence of suicide for various European countries. Durkheim (46–52) argued that these data themselves demonstrate the sui generis (emergent) nature of society. Short-run figures for given countries display considerable stability, thereby suggesting that, far from varying randomly, they reflect some relatively stable reality or set of causes. Indeed, suicide rates show greater stability than rates derived from "leading demographic data" (e.g., general mortality; 48). Relatively large, short-run variations reflect the exceptional crises that occasionally affect a society. Larger, long-term changes only prove that society has undergone structural change. Finally, various societies display quite different rates, as is to be expected given their individual character. Altogether, suicide rates display precisely the combination of stability and variability expected if it is assumed that, as socially caused phenomena, these rates reflect the state of the reality, society, itself.

Taken as justification for developing a sociological theory of variation in suicide rates, Durkheim's arguments are convincing. But Durkheim also wanted to demonstrate the illegitimacy of nonsociological approaches, and here he is less convincing. The suicide statistics in question purportedly show all suicides in a given society. Consequently, there is no basis for characterizing the rates as purely social suicide rates unless it can be demonstrated that suicides resulting from individual (as opposed to social) causes have no appreciable impact on the empirically given rates. As was shown above (Chapter 11), Durkheim's most systematic attempt (55–142) to prove this assertion was unsuccessful.

Durkheim (51; emphasis added) argued that "*many* of the individual conditions" causing suicide "are not general enough to affect" national suicide rates, but this argument does not reject the possibility that, taken cumulatively, individual factors do have a significant impact. Furthermore, "many" is not all, and it would take only a few or even just one widely prevalent individual cause to affect national suicide rates. Durkheim (147–48) himself observed that "alcoholic suicides evidently exist . . . in great numbers." In stressing the individual nature of nonsocial causes, which may lead "this or that separate individual to kill himself," Durkheim (51) employed a verbal "sleight-of-hand." By focusing on the individual and stressing that what affects a given individual cannot have appreciable effect upon the total number of suicides in a given country, Durkheim directed attention away from the possibility that a single individual cause affecting numerous individuals might, indeed, have a decisive impact.

Durkheim (46–52) focused on variation in the rates (or incidence) of suicide in different countries over time. Given that society is the unit to which the rates apply, it is sensible to attribute variation in those rates to variable aspects of society itself. However, to attribute this variation exclusively to social causes requires ruling out all other causes. Because Durkheim's data did not distinguish socially caused suicides from those otherwise caused, he was unable to present such a demonstration. Neither Durkheim's doctrine of emergence nor his argument from national suicide data demonstrate that society is a sui generis reality or that suicide is socially caused.

Interaction as the Emergence-Creating Process

Durkheim identified association (interaction) as the process that creates emergent social phenomena. Part I (above) identified interaction as a key causal variable, and Durkheim's emphasis on its importance is found throughout *Suicide*. In analyzing the relative importance of temperature versus social life, Durkheim (117, 121–22) identified interaction as determining the strength of social life. It is the characteristically high rates of interaction in crowds that explain their powerful control over the individual (124, 126; see also below). The same emphasis is found in a key chapter in *Suicide* (297–325) that delineates the all important "social element of suicide." There Durkheim (310) stated that it is through the association of individuals that something new is created in the world. More specifically, as individuals interact, their individual consciousnesses combine to form collective sentiments, or collective representations. (The latter is a concept that Durkheim first introduced at about the time he wrote *Suicide* and that had become central to his theory by the time he wrote *The Elementary Forms.*) Further, "it is clear that essentially social life is made up of [collective] representations" (312). The higher the rate of interaction, the greater the fusion of individual consciousnesses into collective representations and, consequently, the stronger the latter. Durkheim here explained why both integration and regulation vary proportionately with interaction, which is decisive not only as the process through which the "essential" social component (collective representations, sentiments) is created but also as the determinant of the social factor's strength.

Though the process is responsible for generating social phenomena, Durkheim treated the specifics of fusion-through-interaction only in brief, scattered, and vague comments. As a result, he left many basic questions unanswered. For example, *Suicide* expresses uncertainty on how the process works, how individual consciousnesses come into contact, and where their synthesis (collective sentiments) is located empirically. Durkheim (130) noted that he had been successful in supplying "only a conjectural and approximate description ... of the complex process whence come collective sentiments." A footnote added: "For we must confess that we have only a vague idea of what it is. Exactly how the combinations occur resulting in the collective state, what are its constituent elements, how the dominant state is produced are [complex] questions. . . . Manifold experiments and observations would be required and have not been made. We know little as yet how and according to what laws mental states of even the single individual combine; much less do we know of the mechanism of the far more complicated combinations produced by group-existence. Our explanations are often mere metaphors."

The Emergent Result: Society

What is it? Though everywhere using the term and addressing himself to its basic nature, Durkheim (somewhat curiously) nowhere defined society. Perhaps a simple oversight, this lack may also result from his failure to identify, and then consistently adhere to, a single conception of society. Reflecting his social realism, he often spoke of society as a whole. The constituent elements of this whole are variously identified as individuals, groups, communities, common beliefs and practices, collective forces, collective states, collective or social states of mind, collective representations, functions, or organs (160, 170, 213-14, 249, 310-13, 320-21, 366, 375-84). *Suicide* (313) even asserts that "material things" are part of society. But just what whole these disparate elements together comprise is never specified.

Durkheim's conception exhibits great "displacement of scope" (Wagner 1964:571-84). He treated France as a society; he also referred to a married couple as a society. In terms of its abstractness, Durkheim's conception is reminiscent of "collectivity" as employed by contemporary sociologists (see, e.g., Parsons 1961:30-79). Although Durkheim clearly understood society as a compound composed of parts that, either through fusion or structural interconnectedness, give rise to emergent phenomena, his identification of the elements does not lead to any sharply etched image of the compound itself. Durkheim's conception of society is abstract, inclusive, and ultimately elusive.

A group mind? Durkheim's characterization of society must be understood in the context of his underlying attempt to legitimize sociology. He felt that psychology was the science most threatening to sociology because (nonsocial) psychological explanations represented the strongest competition to sociological explanations of social phenomena. In addition, his highly ideaistic conception of society (e.g., as "collective sentiments" or "representations") meant that considerable care was needed to avoid defining society in terms suggesting that it might be reduced to individual psychic states. Durkheim (312) himself noted that he had "no objection to calling sociology a variety of psychology, if we carefully add that social psychology has its own laws which are not those of individual psychology." His stress on both the emergent and the psychic natures of society led him to formulations that suggested the existence of a group mind.

Durkheim (37-38, 302, 313) felt that social phenomena are external, constraining forces that exist independently of individuals. The ability of collective forces to control the individual demonstrates their independence of him (39, 309-10). These formulations are consistent with those in another of his major works, *The Rules of Sociological Method,* published just two years before *Suicide.* In it Durkheim (1950:1-13) argued that, in relation to the individual, social factors are defined by exteriority and constraint.

Durkheim (319) denied that the substratum of collective psychic phenomena is the individual consciousness; he held rather that it is the emergent, collective phenomenon "formed by all the individual consciences in union and combination." Here, and elsewhere (51, 125–26, 214), Durkheim seemed explicitly to postulate the existence of a group mind; e.g., "society may generalize its own feeling as to itself, its state of health or lack of health" (213), or "religion is ... the system of symbols by means of which society becomes conscious of itself" (312).

Although Durkheim emphasized that social realities are exterior to and independent of the individual, before writing *Suicide* he (1960:350) held that "there is nothing in social life which is not in individual consciences." After *Suicide* he (1965a:389; see also 253, 383) asserted that "society exists and lives only in and through individuals.... It is real only in so far as it has a place in human consciousnesses, and this place is whatever one we may give it." In *Suicide* he (310) held "that society has no other active forces than individuals" and that he (320) never intended to imply "that society can exist without individuals, an obvious absurdity we might have been spared having attributed to us." Indeed, he had good reason to be indignant because he repeatedly noted that individuals are the elements of the compound society and that it is through the combination of individual phenomena (e.g., individual sentiments) that social phenomena (e.g., collective sentiments) come into being. Without individuals, society would cease to exist.

In holding that the collective consciousness is independent of and exterior to the individual, yet is to be found in and exists only through the individual consciousness, Durkheim had in mind different consciousnesses. The collective consciousness is exterior to the nonsocial individual with his nonsocial consciousness; in contrast, the collective consciousness is to be found in and lives through the social individual and his social consciousness. Though Durkheim did not put the matter in this way, such an interpretation reduces the apparent inconsistency of his various formulations.

Durkheim's interpreters have often considered it important to determine whether he was guilty of employing a group-mind concept, as though he were on trial. Hostile critics have emphasized this concept's "fallacious" nature and, taking it as representative of his work generally, have used its appearance in *Suicide* to justify rejection of Durkheim's theories. In the face of such an approach, admirers have naturally been anxious to deny group-mind connotations. All too frequently a question decisive in the present context has been overlooked: What difference does the group-mind concept make to Durkheim's theory of suicide? The answer is: Not much. Though Durkheim used the group-mind concept (213-14), particularly in explaining how differing levels of egoism account for variation in social suicide rates, it could easily be eliminated from his theory without incurring explanatory loss. Today, sociologists reject the notion of a group-mind, yet they still feel quite comfortable using a somewhat modified version of Durkheim's theory of egoistic suicide.

Durkheim's appeal to society as a self-conscious entity became more, rather than less, central to his general theory as it developed during the course of his intellectual career (Pope 1975a). Thus it certainly cannot be held that the group-mind doctrine was a temporary aberration later eliminated from his work. Furthermore, as is suggested by its increasingly integral position in his theoretical structure, Durkheim may have been far less willing to part with this concept than some of his admirers have been. So long as society is to be explained in terms of individual interaction and reciprocal influence, Durkheim would argue that this entails explaining the whole by its parts, the compound by its elements, society from the individual. But "to explain the complex by the simple, the superior by the inferior, and the whole by the part ... is a contradiction in terms" (Durkheim 1953:29). If interaction not only transforms men (no small effect) but also creates emergent social phenomena that obey their "own laws" (312), then the whole can no longer be explained in terms of its parts, and the issue is resolved in favor of society as a distinct reality. To deny that individual phenomena fuse empirically—that individual sentiments and representations combine to form collective sentiments and representations—would undercut what Durkheim viewed as a powerful argument in favor of the sui generis nature of social phenomena. He insisted strongly on this point; to reject it would, in his eyes, seriously undermine *Suicide's* central argument, namely, that because society is real, sociology is a legitimate scientific discipline.

Social control. Though his basic purpose was to explain how society develops, shapes, and controls the individual, Durkheim never clarified how social control occurs. He (318-19, 335) conceptualized the relationship between society and the nonsocial individual as one of forces in opposition. In these terms, the more powerful society is as a system of forces, the better able it is to control the opposing force represented by the unsocialized individual. Though this conceptualization explains why level of social control is a function of societal power, it says little about the manner in which control is realized. *Suicide* asserts that by their very nature, collective phenomena possess a force and moral authority that the individual respects and before which he must bend. For instance, *Suicide* refers to collective currents that "have, by virtue of their origin, an authority which they impose upon the individual" (214) and to "the obligatory nature and special prestige investing collective beliefs and practices by virtue of the very fact of their being collective beliefs and practices" (130: see also 127, 159). At times this mode of explanation threatens to become tautological (collective beliefs and practices are powerful because they are powerful) or circular. On the one hand, collective phenomena are widespread because they are powerful; on the other, proof that they are powerful is found in the fact that they are widespread. *Suicide* (212, 258, 287, 320, 335) employs a primitive notion of internalization but does not contain an adequate account of the social psychology of internalization.

In sum, Durkheim placed an extraordinarily heavy explanatory burden upon collective realities, particularly society. Society is everywhere held to be a major (if not the only) cause of the effects that interested him. However, his success in completing parts of the implied explanatory structure is uneven. *Suicide* specifies the conditions under which society exercises different levels of control over the individual; it also describes at length the effects of different levels of social control. (Indeed, *Suicide* is largely an account of the consequences, for both the individual and society itself, of varying levels of social control.) Interaction is identified as the process through which emergent realities are created. Simultaneously, though, Durkheim acknowledged uncertainty as to the nature of this process. Furthermore, he failed to define society adequately or to provide a satisfactory account of how collective realities control the individual. Given that *Suicide* is a pioneering work, it would be absurd to require that Durkheim develop a complete theory of society. Yet willingness to accept his explanations must await completion and evaluation of those parts of the causal structure that *Suicide* only implied.

THE INDIVIDUAL AND THE SOCIAL

"It seems hardly possible to us that there will not emerge ... from every page of this book ... the impression that the individual is dominated by a moral reality greater than himself: namely, collective reality" (38). In addition to trying to demonstrate the emergent nature of social phenomena, Durkheim also devoted considerable attention to its other reality-conferring attribute, namely, its power. His conceptualization of the social and the nonsocial components of man as forces in opposition proved exceptionally convenient for his attempt to demonstrate the primacy of the social. If the individual and the social factors were mutually reinforcing, it would be difficult to separate their respective effects in order to determine which effects should be attributed to which causes. Since they are opposed, their respective effects and, thereby, their relative importance can be assessed simply by determining which prevails in a given situation.

Suicide argues convincingly that the individual is transformed by his social existence. However, the explanation of this fact does not require an appeal to emergent social realities. Durkheim often noted that society is much more powerful than the individual, but this statement simply shows that the many are more influential than the one. Nor does Durkheim's perspective adequately explain situations in which an individual is more powerful than the many (e.g., when a great charismatic leader is able to transform an entire society).

Durkheim felt that the more vividly he demonstrated the individual-social opposition, and the more clearly he established the relative power of the social, then the more convincing would be his argument for society's reality. His favorite examples were various types of collective gatherings—for example, the collective religious ceremonies analyzed at length in *The Elementary Forms*, and the crowd in *Suicide* (125-26, 201-2). Collective gatherings are well chosen because in terms of his theoretical perspectives, they should be strongly integrated. Compact grouping encourages high rates of interaction, and a common focus of attention insures that individuals are acting and reacting in common. A comparison of what individuals do in such settings (where they are dominated by collective realities) with what they do in other settings (where individual forces are relatively more powerful), can reveal the impact of the social factor.

That people act differently in a crowd—"the mutual reactions of men in assembly may transform a gathering of peaceful citizens into a fearful monster" (126)—does not necessarily prove the reality of some supraindividual social factor. Crowd and noncrowd settings are different, and this difference alone many account for behavioral variations. Though none of them has ever committed murder, individuals may join a lynch mob; simple safety in numbers may account for this fact (acting alone, an individual might have to stand trial for actions that a mob can take with impunity).

There is a second point. Durkheim's general argument is that people act differently in highly social settings and that this fact demonstrates the reality of social forces. Acknowledging the influence cited by Durkheim, it is nevertheless possible to deny the necessity of attributing that influence to some supraindividual, sui generis social factor. Whatever occurs may be simply the result of many closely gathered people mutually influencing and responding to each other. To the extent that this explanation holds, the difference between crowd and noncrowd behavior does not demonstrate the reality of an emergent social factor. Finally, in presenting these general arguments to demonstrate the power of the social factor, Durkheim generally eschewed systematic assessment of explanations not based on appeal to an emergent social factor; consequently, he failed to show the inherent inadequacies (if any) of the latter. Where he (e.g., in Book I) did systematically attempt to reject nonsocial explanations of a social phenomenon (in this instance, suicide), he was unsuccessful.

INDIVIDUAL AND SOCIAL FACTORS IN SUICIDE

Etiological and Morphological Typologies

As the preceding discussion indicates, *Suicide* proceeds on many fronts simultaneously. Nonetheless, its specific goal is to explain variation in social suicide rates. Durkheim identified the social causes of suicide and named the types of suicide accordingly (see Part I above). He realized that there is considerable "distance" between a given social condition as a cause and the act of suicide as an effect. Consequently, he identified the subjective states that constitute the otherwise missing linkage. These subjective states, themselves effects of given social conditions, impel the individual to suicide. In short, by linking different subjective states to different social conditions, Durkheim (277–94) derived a morphological classification to supplement the previously established etiological-sociological one: "The egoistic suicide is characterized by a general depression, in the form either of melancholic languor or Epicurean indifference" (283). Anomic suicide is accompanied by anger, disappointment, irritation, and exasperated weariness (284), while the altruistic suicide may experience a calm feeling of duty, the mystic's enthusiasm, or peaceful courage (293).

Social causes are linked to their respective subjective states deductively, through "logical implication" (278). Durkheim (278) recognized the limitations of this approach, observing "that a deduction uncontrolled by experiment [empirical evidence] is always questionable." Though he (284) made brief reference to the results of a study of papers left by 1,507 suicides, he did so only illustratively, in order to indicate some of the reasons cited by suicides for their behavior. Durkheim (278) used literary sources (e.g., Lamartine's *Raphael*) for ideal-type accounts of the subjective states presumably linked to particular sociological types of suicide. However, nowhere is evidence presented to demonstrate that some or all suicides of a particular sociological type actually experience the subjective states attributed to them. Although Durkheim characterized the egoistic suicide as apathetic and the anomic as angry, there is no evidence for rejecting the reverse possibility. In short, Durkheim offered virtually no empirical evidence to link his etiological classification with his morphological one.

Individual and Social Factors as Causes of Suicide

Durkheim discounted the importance of individual factors as causes of suicide. But beyond this, do individual factors play any autonomous role, or are they simply the epiphenomena of underlying social causes? Durkheim's statements on this matter are inconsistent. He did not always distinguish between such individual factors as the subjective states of individual actors and neurasthenia, to which he attributed a carefully delimited role as a factor in the origin of suicide. Furthermore, when he discounted individual factors, it is not always clear whether he was referring to absolute incidence or to social suicide rates; and, when reference is to the latter, whether to variation in these rates or to the sum total of suicides constituting them.

The main argument of Book I (55-142) postulates that if individual causes account for some suicides, the total number is so small as to be negligible. Some passages in *Suicide* (299, 305) seem to rule out individual causes altogether. At one point Durkheim (102) attributed some importance to individual factors by acknowledging that even though they do not cause suicide, they may play a role in preventing it: "Doubtless, suicide is impossible if the individual's constitution is opposed to it." Furthermore, two interrelated types of individual factors must be given their due. One is specific contingencies (e.g., bankruptcy or widowhood) that affect one person rather than another; the second is the subjective states (e.g., sorrow or frustration) to which these contingencies give rise. Durkheim (151, 287, 299-300) viewed both the contingencies and the resulting subjective states as products of underlying social conditions. At minimum, then, individual factors cause no variation in social suicide rates; at most, they play little if any role in determining the absolute level of suicide exhibited in given social environments.

Since it is both widespread and acknowledged to predispose individuals to suicide, neurasthenia is treated as the most important individual cause of suicide. Having struggled with the complex relationship between individual and social factors in suicide and having, in effect, ruled out all individual factors other than neurasthenia (or nervous degeneration generally), Durkheim (323) then declared that "the role of individual factors in the origin of suicide can now be more precisely put." If in the same social environment "certain individuals are affected and certain others not, this is . . . because the formers' mental constitution . . . offers less resistance to the suicidogenetic current." But does this statement not imply that individual factors *do* play a part? The answer depends upon the conceptualization of suicide as a dependent variable. If this variable is a rate, Durkheim answers no: variation in nonsocial, individual characteristics *do* make people differentially prone to suicide, but only a few individuals act; hence, in order to achieve their effect, social causes need few candidates upon which to operate. Considering nervous degeneration to be the most widespread individual factor causing a predisposition to suicide, Durkheim (324) observed that "no society exists in which the various forms of nervous degeneration do not provide suicide with more than the necessary number of candidates. Only certain ones are called." In the sense that social causes produce the full complement of which they are inherently capable, because there are more than the necessary number of people with nonsocial, individual characteristics predisposing them to suicide, individual factors play no part in determining the suicide rate. (Presumably, though, Durkheim would acknowledge that individual factors such as neurasthenia play a role in the limited sense that, were they to disappear, suicide rates would drop.)

From another perspective—identifying which individuals in a given group will kill themselves—Durkheim's stance makes individual factors decisive. Ruling out the social environment as a constant leaves only individual factors as variables that may explain why some persons kill themselves and others do not. The price Durkheim paid for his insistence upon discounting individual factors, then, is the inability to explain who among the many possible candidates in a given social environment will actually commit suicide. Although Durkheim vacillated in his estimation of the applicability of his theory, sometimes considering it as a complete explanation of suicide and, again, regarding it rather as a theory of variation in social suicide rates, it is best understood as the latter. Fortunately, his more extreme assertions in favor of social realism overstep the mark. There is no reason sociological theories cannot be supplemented by social psychological and nonsocial explanations as scientists attempt to develop an ever more complete theory of suicide.

13   EPILOGUE

I have examined Durkheim's theory, the relationship between his theory and his data, and his case for social realism. *Suicide* partly realized its goals, achieving some important successes but also suffering some important failures. Durkheim's theory contains one pervasive ambiguity resulting from the fuzziness of the integration-regulation distinction. Since these are Durkheim's central independent variables, ambiguity therefore exists at the core of the theory. Indeed, the overlap between the theory of egoism and that of anomie is virtually complete. Including the latter makes Durkheim's theory of suicide far more difficult to falsify; however, it adds no explanatory power. Consequently, there is a strong case for equating egoism and anomie and, hence, integration and regulation, thus resolving the most problematic aspect of Durkheim's theory without cost.

Although different parts of the theory inevitably find different degrees of confirmation or refutation in the evidence, few of the data are confirmatory; the overwhelming bulk are either neutral or negative. The data themselves are of varying quality; cumulatively, they constitute a limited but nonetheless meaningful test of the theory. Hence, their failure to conform to theoretical expectations seriously undermines the theory. What has hitherto been widely considered one of *Suicide*'s great strengths—the way in which Durkheim marshaled confirmatory empirical evidence—must now be judged a major weakness. However inadequate, though, the empirical test offered in *Suicide* remains, three-quarters of a century after its publication, the best test of his theory. Nonetheless, by contemporary standards neither the data nor the methods of analysis are satisfactory; a definitive test of Durkheim's theory of suicide is still needed.

Suicide presents a complex, multifaceted case for social realism. First, Durkheim endeavored to cite evidence proving the inadequacy of nonsocial explanations of suicide. Judging by the materials offered, his efforts were doubly handicapped: the relevant data were largely unavailable, and the explanations in question were often not theories but empirical correlations. Examination shows that contrary to Durkheim's own conclusion, the data cited in *Suicide*—evidence frequently consistent with the very explanations Durkheim attacked—do not permit rejection of nonsocial explanations. Second, Durkheim argued that the whole is greater than the sum of its parts and that emergent phenomena appear at successively higher orders of nature. Whether phenomena are inherently emergent (as Durkheim argued) or emergent only relative to given theories (as I maintain) is a question still unsettled by Durkheim's arguments for social realism, nor will it be settled by the discussion presented above.

The third major component of Durkheim's case for social realism is his theory of suicide itself. Judged by Durkheim's own standard— compatibility with the data—this theory is inadequate. Moreover, it is often less compatible with the data than are some of the nonsocial explanations that Durkheim rejected. Therefore, if *Suicide* is evaluated for its success in explaining suicide (or for the empirical adequacy of Durkheim's theory relative to competing, nonsocial explanations of suicide), it must be judged a failure. However, such a conclusion flies in the face of *Suicide*'s status as a classic. Turning instead to Durkheim's more fundamental purpose—to legitimize sociology as a scientific discipline—or judging the book in terms of contemporary perspectives, one comes to a different evaluation.

In order to legitimize sociology, Durkheim wanted to present a compelling example of the sociological approach. *Suicide* attacks nonsocial explanations of suicide in order to replace them with his own seemingly adequate theory. This work and his others, coupled with his academic influence, made him the founder of academic sociology in France (Clark 1968; Lukes 1972; Shils 1972) and, with Max Weber, the dominant influence on contemporary sociology. The widespread acceptance of sociology as an academic and scientific discipline is perhaps more attributable to Durkheim than to any other single sociologist, and *Suicide* is an essential source of that influence.

Beyond its role in establishing sociology, *Suicide*'s standing may be assessed from a contemporary perspective. Such an evaluation necessarily depends in part upon assessment of the assumptions identified with *Suicide*. Durkheim's underlying objective, based on his conceptions of science and reality, was to legitimize sociology as a scientific discipline by proving that society is real. He believed that science is the study of reality. Every science studies its own distinctive realities; for Durkheim, sociology's distinct reality was social reality, understood as an emergent system of forces.

Today one can reject Durkheim's perspectives as too restrictive. The debate over emergence promises to continue. Whatever the ultimate outcome of this debate (if, indeed, it is ever resolved and not dropped as unproductive), it will probably have little impact upon sociology. As Stinchcombe (1968:vi) has observed: "There is a good deal of nonsense talked in the social sciences about 'assumptions,' 'approaches,' '*sui generis*,' . . . and the like. Mostly this nonsense does not interfere with the work of the discipline, but this is because exceptional men trust their intuition rather than their logical and philosophical prejudices." The discipline of sociology is here to stay, regardless of ultimate evaluations of the validity of arguments for emergence like those proposed by Durkheim.

Similarly, there is no need to lend to sociology the mechanistic tone imparted to it when social reality is conceptualized as a power, current, or force. Thus Lukes (1972:216) observed that Durkheim's "aggressively sociologistic language . . . was altogether less suited to what he wished to say than the language of 'social bonds,' attaching individuals to social goals and regulating their desires." Since the language of force was integral to Durkheim's expression, removing it would alter his work; however, nothing of value would be lost. Hence, however basic to his thought, Durkheim's conceptualization of social reality as an emergent, irreducible system of forces may be rejected without diminishing appreciation of *Suicide*.

Consistent with his view of the social as an emergent reality, Durkheim denied that the phenomenon of interest could be even partly explained by nonsocial causes. He wished to make his theory as strong as possible, relative to its competitors. If his theory was excellent and all others (especially the nonsocial) more or less worthless, then there could be no question concerning either their relative merits or the validity of sociology's claim to scientific status. Hence, Durkheim attempted to build up his own work by tearing down that of others. Today, scientists recognize that explanatory resources may assume varied forms and that these resources are too valuable to be lightly discarded. Consequently, rather than evaluating theories in the context of a zero-sum configuration, they often attempt to make competing theories mutually supplementary. Thus *Suicide*'s success in rejecting nonsociological explanations of suicide is a matter of far less moment today than it was for Durkheim.

Much has changed since *Suicide* was written, and much that was basic to it in 1897 may be rejected without appreciably lowering one's estimation of the book. Final evaluation rests upon a determination of what in *Suicide* is worth emulating. First, this work is theoretical. Durkheim constructed a coherent, powerful, and highly developed explanation, persuasively presented. *Suicide* is also empirical, containing a variety of data. Of particular value is the way in which Durkheim joined theory and fact by systematically interrelating the two. Furthermore, *Suicide* has been widely accepted as the most successful sociological theory of suicide to date. Here, however, caution must be urged lest *Suicide* be honored not only for its genuine but also for its presumed accomplishments. *Suicide*'s data do not sustain the theory. Yet given the theory's coherence, power, and influence, it deserves a more definitive empirical test than Durkheim provided.

Suicide is a sufficiently ambitious work to command respect in spite of its failure to achieve all of its immediate goals. In terms of both its influence and its continuing relevance as a model for integrating theory and data, *Suicide* remains a monument. In it Durkheim attempted to explain variation in social suicide rates, reject nonsocial explanations of suicide, and state an impregnable case for social realism; but these battles were simply episodes in the greater effort to establish sociology as a scientific discipline. Though *Suicide* largely lost the battles, it has been instrumental in winning the war.

NOTES

CHAPTER TWO

1. Succeeding references to *Suicide* cite page numbers only.

2. For a lengthy discussion challenging the reliability and validity of official suicide statistics, see Douglas (1967:161-231). For an empirical study concluding that "national and international suicide statistics are sufficiently reliable to be of scientific value, although they need to be interpreted critically," see Sainsbury and Barraclough (1968:1252). Having reviewed the literature, Gibbs (1971:277, 278) concluded that "all things considered, present knowledge precludes an adequate evaluation of official statistics. . . . We can conclude only that the question of the reliability of suicide statistics remains unsolved." Clearly the reliability of official suicide statistics is an open question.

CHAPTER THREE

1. Prisons (141, 345-46, especially 346n) and monastaries (227-28) also appear to exemplify altruistic society. Durkheim (228n) further observed that "probably the frequent suicides of the men of the [French] Revolution were at least partly due to an altruistic state of mind."

2. In *Suicide* Durkheim assumed that individuals in close physical proximity take advantage of the opportunity to interact; however, he did not explain why they should do so. More explicitly, *Division* (Durkheim 1960:54-55) asserts that like attracts like. Given that people in primitive society are alike, their very similarity serves as a source of mutual attraction; hence they do, in fact, interact at a high rate. *The Elementary Forms of the Religious Life* (Durkheim 1965a; hereafter referred to as *The Elementary Forms*) cites an additional reason why primitive societies are characterized by high rates of interaction. Society, realizing that its continued existence depends on the regenerative effects of interaction, requires its members to interact accordingly (Pope 1975a).

3. I question the consistency of Durkheim's statement. On the one hand, he argued that greater restraint helps men; on the other, that the lessened restraint resulting from less strict enforcement of monogamy benefits them.

4. Here the contrast between fatalism and altruism is marked. Notwithstanding that altruism causes suicide, Durkheim's accounts of military and primitive society reflect a full appreciation of its virtues, which include subordination of the individual to that sui generis source and goal of all morality, society. Had he treated fatalism more fully and extended his range of empirical examples, he might have modified his view and, as with altruism, noted its more favorable aspects.

CHAPTER FOUR

1. Similarity of sentiments and ideas is absolutely decisive in Durkheim's theoretical structure, because *only* those that are alike fuse to form the common or collective conscience (*Division*), collective sentiments (*Suicide*), or collective representations (*The Elementary Forms*). In contrast to common ideas, which in fusing strengthen the collective conscience, dissimilar ideas conflict, thereby weakening it. Given Parsons's own recurring stress on common values as the basis of social integration, it is ironic that he missed this essential component of Durkheim's theory.

2. Johnson sometimes argued that egoism and anomie "are merely two different names for the same thing" (1965:882), sometimes that "anomie is one aspect of egoism" (1965:883). The first interpretation is preferable because there is little reason to subsume either under the other. For instance, arguing in favor of the second interpretation, Johnson (1965:883) identified "no common conscience" as part of Durkheim's definition of egoism but not of anomie. In fact, however, a weak collective conscience is clearly implied in Durkheim's analysis of anomic suicide (241-76, especially 248-57 and 270-76). Actually, the basic difference between egoism and anomie lies in the explanatory purposes assigned to each.

3. Johnson's justification (1965:880-81) for eliminating fatalism partly overlaps with that for eliminating altruism. Given fatalism's marginal status in *Suicide,* I concentrate on altruism.

4. The company in which Durkheim (215-16, 299) placed women is instructive. He identified the following pairs, contrasted according to the degree to which they are biological (as opposed to social) beings: animals versus humans, women versus men, children and the aged versus young and middle-aged adults, primitive man versus modern man. That is, Durkheim grouped women with animals, children, the aged, and primitive man.

CHAPTER FIVE

1. Durkheim used an unusually large number of terms to refer to the social factor. Any of several (e.g., moral rules, collective force, moral realities, collective beliefs, common sentiments, society, moral order) could be employed instead of collective sentiments.

CHAPTER SIX

1. For the convenience of English-speaking readers, all references to Morselli are to this English translation. Durkheim referred to the original Italian work (Morselli 1879).

2. Durkheim did not discuss whether weighted or unweighted averages constitute the best test of his hypothesis. Insofar as his target population is Western Europe, averages weighted by population size deserve consideration. The weighted average for the countries in table 6.2 is 93 for Protestant countries, 97 for Catholic. Excluding Saxony drops the weighted Protestant average to 75. With or without Saxony, then, weighted averages do not sustain Durkheim. The population figures used to compute weighted average suicide rates are for 1876 except Scotland, 1858. All figures are taken from Banks (1971:6-44) except: Austria and Scotland (Martin 1880:20, 246); England and Saxony (Keltie 1885:151, 258); and Finland (Keltie 1890:891).

Ironically, Durkheim's own prior research undercuts *Suicide*. In an early article on suicide and birth rates he (1888:448) considered suicide rates in seventeen European countries. Of these, one (Rumania) was predominantly Greek Orthodox, and five (Switzerland, Prussia, Bavaria, Hungary, and Holland) were in the mixed religious category. Excepting only Saxony (included in table 6.2 but not listed in Durkheim 1888), the other eleven countries are the same as those in table 6.2 (although Durkheim 1888 lists England and Wales; table 6.2, only England). The 1888 list is instructive because it is presumably free of any attempt to demonstrate a thesis concerning Protestant-Catholic suicide differentials. Had Durkheim coupled his 1888 list with the rates cited in *Suicide*, he would have derived a Protestant average of 91.8 versus 84.6 for Catholics.

3. Following Durkheim, I use "unmarried" (or "single") to refer to single, never-married persons.

4. Durkheim (177) specified only that the comparisons be made between groups of the same age. In practice, however, comparisons are invariably between groups of the same sex. I therefore identify both age and sex as controls.

5. *Suicide* does not give the numbers of cases in the individual cells of tables XX–XXII, nor does it indicate when dots are substituted for rates. Given that (1) one rate is based upon only four cases (computed from data on p. 178) and (2) there is no reason to believe that any rate has been withheld because it was based upon too few cases, I assume that rates based on even a single instance of suicide are included.

6. Durkheim (39, 175) constructed the tables from documents of the Ministry of Justice. He did not further identify the "unpublished documents" (175) constituting his raw data. Presumably, the table is based upon death certificates. The preface notes (39) that "the records of some 26,000 suicides had to be studied to classify separately their age, sex, marital status, and the presence or absence of children." Mentioning 26,000 here, he (175) later noted classifying "about 25,000 suicides." He did not say what happened to the remaining 1,000 cases. Presumably, they represent instances lacking information necessary for classification. The figures, then, represent a relatively complete enumeration of suicide as recorded in census data for the years 1889–91.

7. Herein lies an unanswered question about *Suicide*. Referring to tables XXI and XXII, the preface (39) asserts that age, sex, marital status, and "the presence or absence of children" would be considered. In the tables themselves, though, this control is absent. As will become increasingly apparent, this omission is highly regrettable because it vastly complicated the analysis, forced Durkheim to use procedures of doubtful validity, and ultimately precluded the relatively decisive test of his basic hypothesis relating family size and suicide rates that would otherwise have been possible. Although table XXII is of some value, controlling for presence of children would have been far more useful for testing the theory of egoism than the control for region. As to why the control was not exercised, one can only speculate that the importance of children became apparent only after much of Durkheim's work on these tables had been completed.

8. The English translation is inaccurate and therefore confusing at this point. The third sentence of the first full paragraph on page 204 should read: "But in Paris the *coup d'etat* of Louis Bonaparte has the usual effect." In the translation "France" is substituted for "Paris." For the original passage see Durkheim 1930:216.

9. On Saxony compare Durkheim (207n): "In Saxony the reduction of 1870 . . . is not continued in 1871."

10. The reference to "full" moral effect implies that the decrease in suicide for the urban population exceeded that of the rural population. Actually, the figures (208) show an increase in rural suicide.

11. Durkheim's reference (203) to the "sudden rush of suicides" accompanying the French Revolution suggests acute anomie more than egoism.

CHAPTER SEVEN

1. However, Durkheim (76, 368) also expressed some uncertainty about the universality of high suicide rates in primitive societies.

2. Although the context suggests reference to Hindus, Durkheim's figure (for which no reference is cited) appears to be that for all widows. (However, if 2,366 is considered as the total for Hindu widows, the suicide rate for that group is still only 231.) Because data were not available for all years, I estimated the figures for 1821 for total population, Hindu population, widows, and Hindu widows as follows: total population was assumed to increase at a constant rate from 1800 (Mamoria 1959:3) to 1850 (Carr-Saunders 1936:37). Thus, of the total population increase from 1800 to 1850, 21/50 had occurred by 1821. The proportion of Hindus was assumed to be the same as in 1871 (.73; see Great Britain 1875:394), the first year for which statistics are available. Similarly, the proportion of widows was assumed to be the same as in 1891 (.09; see Great Britain 1893–94:786), the first year for which these figures were available. Hindus are assumed to have been widowed in the same proportion as the total population.

3. *Suicide* uses army and military interchangeably, although the ambiguous reference to the military may sometimes subsume additional branches of the armed forces. In any case, Durkheim's analysis suggests that his interpretation applies to military society generally, with the focus on the army a function of the availability of the data.

Durkheim used the word "soldier" both to designate those who were not officers (either commissioned or noncommissioned) and to refer to any member of the army. Generally, the context makes his meaning clear. I shall use the term army personnel to designate any member of the army, reserving use of soldier, noncommissioned officer, and officer to distinguish ranks.

4. Much of Durkheim's analysis centered on military coefficients of aggravation. Like those found at other points in *Suicide*, these coefficients employ the unmarried as a referent (control) group. Generally, a coefficient is the ratio of the suicide rate of the control group to that for some other group. For instance, coefficients for married men are derived by dividing the suicide rate of unmarried men by that for married men. In the present instance, however, Durkheim computed his coefficient as the suicide rate of the group in question (military personnel) divided by that for the control group (unmarried male civilians). He usually termed coefficients above unity "coefficients of preservation"; those below unity, "coefficients of aggravation." Here his terminology is reversed; ratios above one are called coefficients of aggravation. As computed in the chapter on altruism, coefficients above unity show how many times *more* frequent suicide is among army personnel than among civilians.

5. *Suicide* is vague about the ages in question. The table (228) shows no age for either group. Durkheim's most explicit statement is found in a footnote (229n): "For the United States we have assumed that the average army age was from 20 to 30 years as in Europe." Apparently, then, civilian rates are for those twenty to thirty. Even assuming that the average age for army personnel is twenty to thirty, however, it is

less than certain that civilian rates refer to civilians in this age group. Elsewhere, in selecting civilians of the "same" age as army personnel, Durkheim (229) employed not a twenty-to-thirty age bracket for civilians but rather the twenty-to-twenty-five age bracket. If the same procedure was followed here, the strong correlation between age and suicide would account for some of the civilian-military suicide differential. Durkheim may also have used figures from various sources whose civilian suicide rates may not all have referred to the same age bracket, twenty-to-thirty or otherwise. The data in table XXIII should not be accepted at face value.

6. The coefficient of preservation for childless husbands is 1.51 (table 6.4). On this basis, it can be argued that a control for marriage as well as for presence of children should be exercised. However, in view of Durkheim's observation (275n) that "it is even probable that marriage in itself produces a prophylactic effect [on men] only later, after the age of thirty," a control for marriage does not seem mandatory.

7. For the period 1867-74, the suicide rate for noncommissioned officers was 993 (229). Not knowing the suicide rate for unmarried civilian men for that period, Durkheim used the 1889-91 average of the rate for the twenty-five-to-thirty and thirty-to-forty age groups, 510.5, to derive a coefficient of aggravation of 1.95 for noncommissioned officers. On the grounds that "the number of suicides ... almost doubled" between 1867-74 and 1889-91, Durkheim (230) felt the coefficient may be roughly doubled. Actually, his figures (230) show that the French suicide rate rose from 140 in 1867-74 to about 215 in 1889-91, an increase of 53.6 percent. On the assumption that rates for unmarried civilian men rose in equal measure, their suicide rate in 1867-74 may be estimated as 332. Dividing the rate of 993 for noncommissioned officers by 332 produces a coefficient of aggravation of 3.0 for noncommissioned officers compared to unmarried male civilians.

8. Specifically: (1) The median year of the period for the officer suicide rate is 1870; that for civilians, four and one-half years earlier. (2) Even though officers are but three months shy of thirty-eight, they are compared with civilians aged thirty-seven. (3) He (230) mentioned that suicide rates for civilians are "a little more than 200." How much more, he neglected to say, nor did he indicate why he employed 200 in preference to the actual rate.

9. Suicide rates for unmarried men aged twenty-two and thirty are derived from figures in *Suicide* (table XXI:178).

10. Durkheim (231-32) also considered rates for soldiers, noncommissioned officers, and officers, while rejecting disgust and validating integration as the variable best explaining differences in military suicide rates. He referred to figures for France, Italy, Prussia, and Austria. The treatment is cursory and unsystematic, citing rates for different groups in each country. In addition, no controls are exercised for either age or marital status. Altogether, these brief references do little to validate his thesis that military suicide rates vary proportionately with level of altruism.

11. *Suicide* (232) also includes some data showing that the frequency of suicide increases with age at a higher rate for military personnel than for civilians. Durkheim (231) cited these primarily to reject "the cause most often suggested" as the explanation of military coefficients of aggravation, namely, "disgust with the service." It is not clear whether he also interpreted these data as sustaining his hypothesis on suicide and integration. In any case, just as a lower rate of increase for the military would not undercut his hypothesis, a higher rate of increase does not sustain it.

12. Compare Durkheim (238): "When he puts on his uniform, the soldier does not become a completely new man; the effects of his education and of his previous life do

not disappear as if by magic; and he is also not so separated from the rest of society as not to share in the common life."

13. Three countries (Württemberg, Saxony, and Denmark) in table 7.3 stand apart in that their military rates refer to a period about thirty years earlier than that of the other countries. They have been included because the hypothesis being tested relates civilian and military rates, holding that they should vary inversely. The central concern, then, is that military and civilian rates for a given country (but not necessarily for all) refer to approximately the same period. However, even if one excludes these three countries, the product moment correlation between military and civilian suicides is .28 (or .69 if Austria is also excluded). Once again the hypothesis is not confirmed.

14. Durkheim's analysis of religious society might lead one to expect that he would rank Catholic countries as most integrated, those with mixed religious affiliation next, and Protestant countries last. Instead, Durkheim here placed two Catholic countries (Italy and Austria) and one Protestant country (England) in the relatively integrated group. One Protestant country (Saxony), one mixed (Prussia), and one Catholic (France) appear in the relatively unintegrated group. (Although he considered Prussia to be Protestant, it was only 65 percent Protestant; Morselli 1882:128.)

15. Durkheim (236–37) contrasted individualism and egoism with traditionalism and altruism. Beyond that, he referred to altruism in civilian society. Taken literally, this would mean that integration and suicide are positively related. Elsewhere, however, Durkheim treated suicide and integration in civilian social structures as inversely related. Hence, in the present case it seems best (particularly if the theory is to be put in testable form) to interpret the reference to altruism to mean relatively highly integrated and not to mean altruism in the more literal sense.

In this regard it should be remembered that Durkheim did not typically think of his theory as diagrammed in figure 5.1. Thus he did not always take into account that in crossing the mid-point of the integration continuum, the relationship between integration and suicide changes from negative (egoism) to positive (altruism). In addition to the present instance, another example is *Suicide*'s analysis of the Jews (see pp. 72–76).

16. As a "final proof" (237) of the law (236) that "the causes of military suicide are . . . in inverse proportion to, the most determining causes of civilian suicide" Durkheim (237–38) noted that military suicide is decreasing while civilian suicide is increasing. The military rates cited (237–38) for seven countries, which refer to periods of widely varying duration, show that military suicide decreased from the 1860s, the 1870s, or the 1880s to the early 1890s. In two instances (England and Austria) the average yearly percent decrease (0.33 or less) is minute. Durkheim provided no civilian rates covering the same time intervals, and, with the exception of Prussia and France, they are not to be found in *Suicide;* thus, it is impossible to determine whether, as the theory would predict, the magnitude of increase in civilian rates is proportional to that of the decrease in the military rates. Altogether, this brief analysis in *Suicide* made no appreciable contribution toward the empirical grounding of the theory.

Chapter Eight

1. To derive an estimate of the average yearly increase in suicide, I used the yearly average for the decade immediately preceding and following the crisis periods, omitting only the years identified as years of crisis (computed from data on page 47).

2. Durkheim did not elaborate on the distinction between prosperity and "fortunate crises." Presumably, the latter occur more suddenly and entail greater change, but Durkheim did not identify a common indicator that would permit direct comparisons between them. Furthermore, tables 8.2 (prosperity) and 8.3 (extreme prosperity) do not indicate that extreme prosperity comes about more suddenly or represents greater overall change. Whatever the more specific differences, there is no doubt that Durkheim judged the key difference to be the greater overall disturbance of the collective order caused by extreme prosperity.

3. I computed the normal yearly percentage increase in suicide as the average during the decade immediately preceding and following the crisis periods themselves (table 8.3). Unfortunately, I could not obtain data for all the periods. Consequently, this average is based upon figures for only the following periods: Italy, 1864-69; France, 1867-77 and 1879-89; and Prussia, 1865-74, 1887, and average for period 1896-1900. (The period 1896-1900 was used for Prussia in the interests of consistency, even though, of course, it extends beyond the 1897 publication date of *Le Suicide*.) Rates and absolute figures are respectively employed where Durkheim used them. Figures are from *Suicide*, except the following: Italy, 1864-69 (Morselli 1882:28); France, 1867-77, 1879-89 (Deshaies 1947:44); Prussia, 1896-1900 (Webb 1911: 597); Prussia, 1865-74, and 1887 (Ferri 1895:256a).

4. Spain and Calabria were Catholic, while Ireland was 76.6 percent Catholic (Morselli 1882:128). In terms of Durkheim's theory, Catholicism is also relevant in explaining the low suicide rates.

5. To infer from the data given that relatively well-to-do individuals are more likely to commit suicide would be, of course, to commit the ecological fallacy.

6. In contrast to his analysis of the relationship between egoism and suicide (208-9), Durkheim never explicitly stated that suicide varies proportionately with anomie. Rather, he concentrated on showing that suicide rates in less regulated milieus are higher than those for the more regulated. But if never made explicit, the contention that change in suicide rates is proportional to change in strength of social regulation is clearly present.

7. Throughout this section (following Durkheim), I use divorce to subsume both divorce and separation.

8. Durkheim saw divorce both as the effect of certain "ideas and customs" (384) and as a cause of suicide through its effect on marriage (270, 273). He (271, 273) treated divorce rates as reflecting the state of marriage as an institution; specifically, the level of social regulation embodied therein.

Durkheim apparently viewed the relationship between divorce and marriage as parallel to that between free inquiry and integration. Free inquiry generally develops only after social integration has been weakened (158-59). Once established, however, "it may battle in its own name" (169). Similarly, he seems to hold that divorce does not appear except where marriage as an institution has been weakened. Once established, divorce may react upon marriage to weaken it still further.

9. On the assumption that widowed persons experience greater shock than those who are single, the theory of anomie would predict that suicide rates for the widowed would be higher. However, the data in Durkheim's tables (177-78) show no such consistent tendency. Related to the theory of anomie, these results constitute negative evidence. The problem is that the theory of egoism predicts the higher rates for single persons, while the theory of anomie predicts the higher rates for the widowed. The theory of anomie could be tested against widowed-single comparisons if it were possible to exercise a control on integration. However, since Durkheim's treatment of

egoism and familial society takes marital status itself as the indicator of level of integration, attempts to control for integration while making single-widowed comparisons would, at minimum, be difficult.

10. The attempt (194–97) to validate this generalization empirically is located in a chapter on egoistic suicide. I include it here because it is integral to the analysis of domestic anomie.

11. With the exception of altruistic suicide in primitive societies, Durkheim's analysis focused on Western Europe. Data for Russia and other countries (79, 228) are included only when they support Durkheim's explanations.

12. Because I have recomputed all of his coefficients and the resulting averages, the figures here sometimes differ from those reported in *Suicide*.

13. In attempting to establish the relationship between divorce rates and suicide rates for the married, Durkheim did not directly compare the two rates. Rather, he employed his unmarried-married coefficient. It is possible for these coefficients to vary inversely with divorce rates, as Durkheim said they should, *even though* the suicide rates of married persons go down as divorce rates go up. Consider the accompanying example employing hypothetical figures for men.

	Suicides per Million		Unmarried/ married Coefficient	Divorce Rates
Country	Single	Married		
A	150	100	1.5	20
B	400	200	2.0	10

Durkheim (263) stated that if his fourth generalization was well founded, married persons' suicide rates would rise as the divorce rate rose. In the above example the *lower* the divorce rate, the *higher* the suicide rate of married persons. Durkheim's coefficients, however, are consistent with his hypothesis because the lower the divorce rate, the higher the immunity of married persons as measured by the unmarried-married coefficient of preservation. His coefficient in effect controls for the level of suicide prevailing in a society, as measured by the suicide rates of single persons. It thereby measures the immunity to suicide conferred by marriage, which, after all, is the focal point of his analysis. Similar considerations apply to the coefficients for married women. Durkheim, then, was interested in the relationship between the *relative*, not the absolute, immunity of married persons and the divorce rates.

CHAPTER NINE

1. Durkheim (166) identified one exception (England) and one (166n) possible exception (Spain).

2. This estimate is conservative. Using rates derived from figures for France in *Suicide* (table XXI:178) permits derivation of much higher ratios. For instance, unmarried males seventy-five years old are *thirty-nine times* as likely to kill themselves as those aged fifteen. Assuming the correctness of Durkheim's observation (172) that suicide rates regularly increase with age, even among children, comparing rates for children with rates for the very old produces ratios of one hundred to one and higher.

3. As a matter of convenience I use the terms "egoism" and "anomie" in those contexts in which *Suicide* used them; however, this use should not be taken as an indication that there is, in fact, a viable theoretical sociological distinction between them.

4. Of course, even if Durkheim's conclusions are empirically valid, they must still be reconciled with *Suicide's* failure to demonstrate that Protestants have higher suicide rates than do Catholics (see chapter 6).

5. The many considerations relevant to this point make prediction difficult, as may be seen by comparing two men identical in every respect, except that the first works and the second does not. Does the first suffer a net loss or gain in social regulation on the job? Clearly, the individual is subject to greater social regulation in an agricultural than in an industrial or commercial endeavor (257-58), but this consideration does not by itself show whether, in this relatively anomic setting, the individual suffers a *net* gain or loss of regulation at work. Further, it is necessary to compare this gain-loss with that which the individual foregoes when he spends time on the job rather than with his family. Unfortunately, Durkheim's theory provides few guides to an answer. Thus one can derive different answers to these questions and, hence, different predictions concerning the relative suicide rates of men who do and do not work.

6. Suicide ratios were computed for 1876 from absolute number of suicides and male-female population sizes. These figures were taken from *Annuaire Statistique de la France* (1968:30-33, 26-29, 111-12). Percentage of labor force in agriculture was taken from the same source (34-37).

Chapter Eleven

1. Durkheim's table VI (74) is broken down into parts A and B, between which there is some overlap. The *r* for insanity and suicide in Part A is -.14; in Part B, -.39. The *r* for the entire table, using the most recent data, is the -.24 noted.

2. The maps in the English translation of *Suicide* are reduced facsimiles of those in the French edition (9th ed.) and are difficult to read.

3. Durkheim (79) also mentioned Russia. Given his usual focus on Western Europe, this reference appears gratuitous. Indeed, the Russian figures are the only non-Western European ones anywhere in Book I. Furthermore, Russia hardly fits Durkheim's specification of countries north of France. Beyond these considerations, comparing figures for suicide and alcoholic consumption for all Russia with those for St. Petersburg produces results that contradict Durkheim's denial of a positive relationship between alcoholism and suicide (79, 259).

4. More than one consideration leads to this conclusion. Employing the Greenwich standard, in today's Europe 20° east longitude passes through Albania, Yugoslavia, Hungary, Czechoslovakia, Poland, Sweden, and Norway, while 40° east cuts through Russia. Not only is this generally outside the area of Durkheim's primary concern, but all available figures in *Suicide* indicate that rates in this area are low, not high. Finally, this area does not include either of the two regions specifically identified by Durkheim as falling within the area in question, Ile-de-France and the German states of Prussia and Saxony.

Durkheim, of course, followed Morselli (1882) who did, in fact, refer to the longitudes identified by Durkheim. Table 1 in Morselli (see maps following his index) included a map of Europe showing intensity of suicide. On this map, 20° east longitude cuts through central France, while 40° east passes through Baltic Russia and Hungary. Curiously, even this area includes only half of Ile-de-France, plus a vast area far to the east of Prussia and Saxony, where suicide rates, far from being high, are rather low.

5. One of Durkheim's maps of suicide in France (Appendix I:393) shows a second large area (the northeast corner of France) that also had low suicide rates. Durkheim may have had in mind his map in Appendix II (394), which conforms more closely to the pattern he described.

Chapter Twelve

1. This example indicates that emergent wholes do not necessarily exist at some higher order of nature than do the parts. Oxygen and hydrogen may be conceptualized as chemical phenomena; water, in terms of its physical properties. In this case, upon combining, the parts give rise to phenomena at a *lower* order of nature than themselves.

2. The argument that follows is heavily indebted to Nagel (1961:366-80).

3. "We have shown that a social fact can be explained only by another social fact" (Durkheim 1950:145). For Durkheim's stance on sociological explanation see Chapter V, "Rules for the Explanation of Social Facts." In this chapter he (1950:110) held that "*the determining cause of a social fact should be sought among the social facts preceding it and not among the states of the individual consciousness.*" The statement reflects Durkheim's concern to reject any reductionist explanation of social phenomena, particularly the psychological.

REFERENCES

Alpert, H.
1961   *Emile Durkheim and his sociology.* New York: Russell
            and Russell.

Aron, R.
1967   *Main currents of sociological thought.* Vol. 2. *Durk-
            heim / Pareto / Weber.* Translated by R. Howard
            and H. Weaver. New York: Basic Books.

Banks, A. S.
1971   *Cross-polity time-series data.* Cambridge, Mass.: MIT
            Press.

Benoit-Smullyan, E.
1948   The sociologism of Emile Durkheim and his school.
            In *An introduction to the history of sociology,* ed.
            H. E. Barnes, pp. 499–537. Chicago: University of
            Chicago Press.

Bierstedt, R.
1974   *The social order.* 4th ed. New York: McGraw-Hill.

Booth, C.
1886   Occupations of the people of the United Kingdom,
            1801–81. *J. Statistical Soc.* 49:314–435.

Carr-Saunders, A. M.
1936   *World population: Past growth and present trends.*
            Oxford: Clarendon Press.

Clark, C.
1940   *The conditions of economic progress.* London: Mac-
            millan & Co.

215

Clark, T. N.
1968   Emile Durkheim and the institutionalization of sociol-
               ogy in the French university system. *Eur. J. Soc.*
               9:37-71.

Coser, L. A.
1971   *Masters of sociological thought: Ideas in historical
               and social context.* New York: Harcourt Brace Jovan-
               ovich.

Dahlgren, K. G.
1945   *On suicide and attempted suicide: A psychiatrical and
               statistical investigation.* Lund, Sweden: Lindstedts.

Deshaies, G.
1947   *Psychologie du suicide.* Paris: Presses Universitaires
               de France.

Douglas, J. D.
1967   *The social meanings of suicide.* Princeton: Princeton
               University Press.

Durkheim, E.
1888   Suicide et natalite: Etude de statistique morale. *Revue
               philosophique de la France et de L'étranger* 26:
               446-63.
1930   *Le suicide: Etude de sociologie.* 2nd ed. Paris:
               Librarie Felix Alcan.
1950   *The rules of sociological method.* Translated by S. A.
               Solovay and J. H. Mueller. New York: Free Press.
1951   *Suicide: A study in sociology.* Translated by J. A.
               Spaulding and G. Simpson. Glencoe: Free Press.
1953   *Sociology and philosophy.* Translated by D. F. Pocock.
               Glencoe: Free Press.
1960   *The division of labor in society.* Translated by G.
               Simpson. Glencoe: Free Press.
1964   The dualism of human nature and its social condi-
               tions. In *Essays on sociology and philosophy,* ed.
               K. H. Wolff, pp. 325-40. New York: Harper Torch-
               books.
1965a   *The elementary forms of the religious life.* Translated
               by J. W. Swain. New York: Free Press.
1965b   *Montesquieu and Rousseau: Forerunners of sociology.*
               Translated by R. Manheim. Ann Arbor: University of
               Michigan Press.
1973   Individualism and the intellectuals. Translated by
               M. Traugott. In *Emile Durkheim on morality and
               society,* ed. R. N. Bellah, pp. 43-57. Chicago: Univer-
               sity of Chicago Press.

Ferri, E.
1895   *L'omicidio-suicidio: Responsabilità giuridica.* 4th ed.,
            expanded. Turin: Fratelli Bocca.

France, Institut national de la statistique et des études economiques
1968   *Annuaire statistique de la France: Deuxième année—
            1879.* Nendeln, Liechtenstein: Kraus.

France, Ministère du commerce, de l'industrie, des postes et des
télégraphes
1894   *Résultats statistiques du dénombrement de 1891.*
            Paris: Imprimerie nationale.

France, Ministère du travail et de la prévoyance sociale
1907   *Résultats statistiques du recensement général de la
            population effectúe le 24 Mars 1901, tome V.* Paris:
            Imprimerie Nationale.

Gibbs, J. P.
1971   Suicide. In *Contemporary social problems,* ed. R. K.
            Merton and R. A. Nisbet, pp. 271–312. 3d ed.
            New York: Harcourt Brace Jovanovich.

Gibbs, J. P., and Martin, W. T.
1964   *Status integration and suicide: A sociological study.*
            Eugene: University of Oregon Books.

Giddens, A.
1971a   The suicide problem in French sociology. In *The
            sociology of suicide: A selection of readings,* ed.
            A. Giddens, pp. 36–51. London: Frank Cass.
1971b   *Capitalism and modern social theory: An analysis of
            the writings of Marx, Durkheim and Max Weber.*
            London: Cambridge University Press.

Great Britain. Parliament. House of Commons
1875   Memorandum on the census of British India of 1871–
            72. *British Sessional Papers,* 54:379–443.

Great Britain. Parliament. House of Commons
1893–94   General report on the census of India, 1891. *British
            Sessional Papers,* 64:531–857.

Halbwachs, M.
1971   The causes of suicide. Translated by A. Giddens.
            In *The sociology of suicide: A selection of readings,*
            ed. A. Giddens, pp. 28–35. London: Frank Cass.

Hendin, H.
1964   *Suicide in Scandanavia: A psychoanalytic study of
            culture and character.* New York: Grune and
            Stratton.

Henry, A. F., and Short, J. F., Jr.
1964   *Suicide and homicide: Some economic, sociological, and psychological aspects of aggression.* Glencoe: Free Press.

Homans, G. C.
1950   *The human group.* New York: Harcourt, Brace and World.

Howard, L. E.
1935   *Labour in agriculture: An international survey.* London: Oxford University Press.

Hyman, H.
1955   *Survey design and analysis: Principles, cases and procedures.* New York: Free Press.

Inkeles, A.
1959   Personality and social structure. In *Sociology today: Problems and prospects,* ed. R. K. Merton, L. Broom, and L. S. Cottrell, Jr., pp. 249-76. New York: Basic Books.
1963   Sociology and psychology. In *Psychology: A study of a science.* Vol. 6. *Investigations of man as socius: Their place in psychology and the social sciences.* ed. S. Koch, pp. 317-87. New York: McGraw-Hill.

Johnson, B. D.
1965   Durkheim's one cause of suicide. *Am. Soc. Rev.* 30:875-86.

Keltie, J. S., ed.
1885   *The statesman's year-book: Statistical and historical annual of the states of the civilised world for the year 1885.* London: Macmillan and Co.
1886   *The statesman's year-book: Statistical and historical annual of the states of the civilised world for the year 1886.* London: Macmillan and Co.
1890   *The statesman's year-book: Statistical and historical annual of the states of the world for the year 1890.* London: Macmillan and Co.

LaCapra, D.
1972   *Emile Durkheim: Sociologist and philosopher.* Ithaca: Cornell University Press.

Lukes, S.
1967   Alienation and anomie. In *Philosophy, politics and*

society, ed. P. Laslett and W. G. Runciman, pp. 134–56. 3d ser. Oxford: Basil Blackwell.

1972   *Emile Durkheim: His life and work: A historical and critical study.* New York: Harper and Row.

Mamoria, C. B.
1959   *Population and family planning in India.* Bombay: Kitab Mahl, Allahabad.

Maris, R. W.
1969   *Social forces in urban suicide.* Homewood, Ill.: Dorsey Press.

Marks, S. R.
1974   Durkheim's theory of anomie. *Am. J. Soc.* 80: 329–63.

Martin, F., ed.
1872   *The statesman's year-book: Statistical and historical annual of the states of the civilised world. Handbook for politicians and merchants for the year 1872.* London: Macmillan and Co.

1879   *The statesman's year-book: Statistical and historical annual of the states of the civilised world for the year 1879.* London: Macmillan and Co.

1880   *The statesman's year-book: Statistical and historical annual of the states of the civilised world for the year 1880.* London: Macmillan and Co.

Martin, W. T.
1968   Theories of variation in the suicide rate. In *Suicide,* ed. J. P. Gibbs, pp. 74–96. New York: Harper and Row.

Merton, R. K.
1967   *On theoretical sociology: Five essays, old and new.* New York: Free Press.

Miesmaa, J., ed.
1952   *Facts about Finland.* Translated by P. Sjöblom. Helsinki: Otava Publishing Co.

Morselli, E.
1879   *Il suicidio: Saggio di statistica morale comparata.* Milan: Fratelli Dumolard.

1882   *Suicide: An essay on comparative moral statistics.* New York: D. Appleton and Co.

Mulhall, M. G.
1892   *The dictionary of statistics.* London: George Rout-
              ledge and Sons.

Nagel, E.
1961   *The structure of science: Problems in the logic of
              scientific explanation.* New York: Harcourt, Brace
              and World.

Nisbet, R. A.
1966   *The sociological tradition.* New York: Basic Books.
1970   *The social bond: An introduction to the study of
              society.* New York: Alfred A. Knopf.
1974   *The sociology of Emile Durkheim.* New York: Oxford
              University Press.

Parsons, T.
1949   *The structure of social action: A study in social
              theory with special reference to a group of recent
              European writers.* Glencoe: Free Press.
1961   *Theories of society: Foundations of modern socio-
              logical theory,* 1:30–79. New York: Free Press.
1975   Comment on "Parsons' interpretation of Durkheim"
              and on "Moral freedom through understanding in
              Durkheim." *Am. Soc. Rev.* 40:106–11.

Pipping, H. E., and Bärlund, R.
1965   *Finlands näringsliv.* Helsinki: Söderström and Co.

Poggi, G.
1972   *Images of society: Essays on the sociological theories
              of Tocqueville, Marx and Durkheim.* Stanford: Stan-
              ford University Press.

Pope, W.
1975a   Durkheim as a functionalist. *Soc. Quart.* 16:361–79.
1975b   Parsons on Durkheim, revisited. *Am. Soc. Rev.* 40:
              111–15.

Popper, K. R.
1961   *The logic of scientific discovery.* New York: Science
              Editions.

Riley, M. W.
1963   *Sociological research: I. A case approach.* New York:
              Harcourt, Brace and World.

Robinson, W. S.
1950   Ecological correlations and the behavior of individ-
              uals. *Am. Soc. Rev.* 15:351–57.

Rosenberg, M.
1968   *The logic of survey analysis.* New York: Basic Books.

Sainsbury, P.
1955   *Suicide in London: An ecological study.* London: Chapman and Hall.

Sainsbury, P., and Barraclough, B.
1968   Differences between suicide rates. *Nature* 220:1252.

Selvin, H. C.
1965   Durkheim's *Suicide*: Further thoughts on a methodological classic. In *Emile Durkheim*, ed. R. A. Nisbet, pp. 113–36. Englewood Cliffs, N. J.: Prentice-Hall.

Shils, E.
1972   Tradition, ecology, and institution in the history of sociology. In *The twentieth-century sciences: Studies in the biography of ideas*, ed. G. Holton, pp. 33–98. New York: W. W. Norton.

Smelser, N. J.
1971   *Sociological theory: A contemporary view.* New York: General Learning Press.

Sorokin, P.
1928   *Contemporary sociological theories.* New York: Harper and Row.

Stinchcombe, A. L.
1968   *Constructing social theories.* New York: Harcourt, Brace, and World.

Tiryakian, E. A.
1962   *Sociologism and existentialism: Two perspectives on the individual and society.* Englewood Cliffs, N.J.: Prentice-Hall.

Tracy, M.
1964   *Agriculture in western Europe: Crisis and adaptation since 1880.* London: Jonathan Cape.

Wagner, H. R.
1964   Displacement of scope: A problem of the relationship between small-scale and large-scale sociological theories. *Am. J. Soc.* 69:571–84.

Wallwork, E.
1972   *Durkheim: Morality and milieu.* Cambridge, Mass.: Harvard University Press.

Webb, A. D.
1911   *The new dictionary of statistics: A complement to the fourth edition of Mulhall's "Dictionary of statistics."* London: George Routledge and Sons.

Weber, M.
1958   *The Protestant ethic and the spirit of capitalism.* Translated by Talcott Parsons. New York: Charles Scribner's Sons.

Wolin, S. S.
1960   *Politics and vision: Continuity and innovation in western political thought.* Boston: Little, Brown and Co.

Zeitlin, I. M.
1968   *Ideology and the development of sociological theory.* Englewood Cliffs, N.J.: Prentice-Hall.

INDEX

Age: as control variable, 81-85, 87, 89, 91-92, 207-9; and heredity, 174-75; and insanity, 160-61; and marital or familial status, 81-85, 89, 91-92, 206; and suicide, 142-43, 145-47

Alcoholism: consumption, 162-64, 214; indicators of, 157, 161-65, 190; and insanity, 128, 162-63; prosecutions for, 162-63

Alpert, H., 30, 155

Altruism, 12-14, 49, 51, 57-60, 63, 205-6; in military society, 21, 46-47, 101-6, 114-15, 208, 210; in primitive society, 19-21, 36-38, 46-47, 110-13; synthesis with egoism, 22-24, 29

Altruistic suicide, 10-13; and integration, 23, 34, 37-38; in military society, 36, 103-15; in primitive society, 19-21, 33, 36, 101-3, 212

Anomic suicide, 11-13, 31-33, 37, 116-41, 197-98

Anomie, 12-14, 25-34, 41-60, 63, 77, 146; acute, 28-29, 52-53, 57, 100, 152; acute domestic, 27-28, 125-26, 128-29, 135-37, 139-41; acute economic, 25-26, 44, 116-23, 143; chronic domestic, 27, 52-53, 55, 126-41, 147; chronic economic, 25, 27, 42, 72, 123-24, 143; controlling for, 66; domestic, 80, 86-91, 116, 124-25, 141, 174, 211-12; economic, 116-24; falsifiability of theory of, 55-56; synthesis with egoism, 42-44, 49-51, 206

Aron, R., 30

Austria, 144; collective activity in, 180; economic crises in, 116-17; labor force composition in, 151; military society in, 113-15; political society in, 95;

races in, 166-69, 173; religious society in, 64-65, 69-72

Baden, 66, 95, 128, 133-34

Banks, A. S., 69, 206

Bärlund, R., 68, 69

Barraclough, B., 205

Bavaria, 66, 70-73, 93, 96, 98, 118

Belgium, 64-65, 69, 114, 164

Beliefs and behavior, relationship between, 14-16, 101-2

Benoit-Smullyan, E., 155

Bierstedt, R., 2

Biological reductionism, 52, 150, 161, 174-75

Booth, C., 68-69, 151

Broca, 170-71

Carr-Saunders, A., 208

Catholicism. See Jewish-Catholic comparisons; Protestant-Catholic comparisons; Protestant-Catholic-Jewish comparisons

Children, 77, 145; and anomic suicide, 139-41; as control variable, 104-5, 125; and egoistic suicide, 79, 81-92, 207. See also Family size

China, 103

Cities, 73-75, 144, 161, 180, 182-83. See also Urbanization

Civilians. See Military-civilian comparisons

Civilization, 145, 159, 161, 171; as a cause of suicide, 66, 70, 141, 155, 157, 167; as control variable, 66-72, 141, 155

Clark, C., 69, 151

Clark, T. N., 202